S0-ADJ-652

THEIR FUTURE IS NOW

THE MACMILLAN COMPANY
NEW YORK · BOSTON · CHICAGO
DALLAS · ATLANTA · SAN FRANCISCO

MACMILLAN AND CO., LIMITED
LONDON · BOMBAY · CALCUTTA
MADRAS · MELBOURNE

THE MACMILLAN COMPANY
OF CANADA, LIMITED
TORONTO

THEIR FUTURE IS NOW

THE GROWTH AND DEVELOPMENT OF CHRISTIAN PERSONALITY

BY

ERNEST M. LIGON, B.D., Ph.D.

Associate Professor of Psychology
Union College, Schenectady, New York

1947

THE MACMILLAN COMPANY · NEW YORK

Set up and printed.

Reprinted July, 1940

Reprinted February, 1942

Reprinted July, 1944

Reprinted November, 1945

Reprinted January, 1947

Reprinted December, 1947

PRINTED IN THE UNITED STATES OF AMERICA

TO

KENNETH B. WELLES

PREFACE

THIS is a book on character education written especially for parents and teachers, and to meet the needs of students in character education. Many ministers and church workers should find it of considerable value in their work. The problem is approached developmentally; that is, from age level to age level. It is a more complete treatment than books on child psychology [illegible] specific problems [illegible] successive periods of development. The [illegible] this book was made necessary [illegible] strong emphasis throughout the book on the total personality.

The book has some distinctive features which make it of [illegible] significance and practical value.

In the first place, it presents definite goals for character development. Eight traits are proposed, which are based on the [illegible] and developed in the light of modern psychology. These eight traits are in turn subdivided into a great many constituent attitudes. These are presented at appropriate age levels throughout the book [illegible] development. It is hoped that this will make for less vagueness in character education and [illegible] parents and teachers [illegible]. To be able to know specifically what steps can be taken at every age level toward the development of personality, and to be able to see what the ultimate outcome of these efforts [illegible], should contribute much to the confidence and [illegible] of character education in general.

The second feature is the emphasis on individual differences. The value of [illegible] is not new. But the importance of individual [illegible] achievement is not [illegible] of common ways of [illegible]. A comprehensive personality [illegible] methods for the [illegible] of the various traits

PREFACE

THIS IS A BOOK on character education written especially for parents and teachers and to meet the needs of students of character education. Many ministers and church workers should find it of practical value in their work. The problem is discussed developmentally; that is, from age level to age level. It is a more common procedure for books on child guidance to discuss specific problems rather than successive periods of development. The method chosen for this book was made necessary by the strong emphasis throughout the book on the total personality.

The book has four distinctive features, on which must rest its significance and practical value.

In the first place, it sets forth definite goals for character development. Eight traits are proposed, which are based on the teachings of Jesus and developed in the light of modern psychology. These eight traits are in turn subdivided into a great many constituent attitudes. These are presented at appropriate age levels with methods for their development. It is hoped that this will make for less vagueness in character education, and eliminate much of the blind trial and error which parents and teachers have been forced by necessity to use. To be able to know specifically what steps can be taken at every age level toward the development of personality, and to be able to see what the ultimate outcome of one's efforts are, should contribute much to the confidence and purposiveness of character education in general.

The second feature is the emphasis on individual differences. The value of child-centered education is not new. But the knowledge of individual endowments necessary to its achievement is not an item of common sense or intuition. A comprehensive personality profile is presented, with approximate methods for the measurement of its various traits, and a brief interpretation of their significance. It is a fundamental principle of this book that no two children are alike and that character traits have no real meaning except in terms of the personalities possessing them. It is the firm conviction of the author that because of this fact, character education cannot hope to be successful without accurate knowledge of the individuals with whom it is concerned.

The third feature is the effort to measure progress in character education. Hundreds of scales exist for measuring mental disease, but very few for measuring strength of personality. At the end of the discussion of each age level is a questionnaire. It is proposed that these questionnaires be used when the child arrives at each level, in order to see specifically what aspects of his personality can most profitably be strengthened during that period. They should be applied again at the end of each age level to get a measure of the extent of his progress. These are not instruments for detecting mental disease symptoms. They are designed for use with normal, healthy children. They do not give rise to fears in parents of possible mental breakdowns in their children, but set forth possibilities through which the strength and happiness of their children can be increased.

The fourth feature is the presentation of a new method in character education to be called drama-type education. It consists of the development of curricular units in which each child is placed according to his own abilities and needs. It departs radically from the traditional method of regimentation in education, in which all members of a class are treated as if they were exactly alike. At the same time it is shown that quite as much standardization is possible using this approach as in the traditional one. Furthermore it involves neither the economic and practical difficulties of progressive education nor the social maladjustments arising from it. This type of curricular unit will also give intensive and skilled training in social integration.

Briefly then, this book attempts to give parents and teachers definite goals toward which to strive in the development of the personalities of their children; methods for applying their efforts to the specific nature of the individual child; ways of measuring progress, so that they can give more intelligent direction to their efforts and determine the success of their work; and a principle of education which allows full scope for the particular abilities and needs of each child, in projects which give not only individual development but training in social integration.

Such an ambitious statement of purpose needs to be accompanied by a recognition of the difficulties involved and a frank indication of the more probable sources of error. In many aspects, the book is venturing into relatively new territory. It is inevitable that future research will reveal weaknesses and indicate many revisions and refinements. The author entertains no delusions of infallibility or finality and looks forward himself to the discovery of many of these errors.

In order that psychologists may more adequately estimate and evaluate this book, it seems desirable to set forth a brief statement of the psychological convictions of the author which underlie the basic theories set forth in it.

In the first place, the author acknowledges a belief in the existence of generalized traits. Such generalized traits are undoubtedly made up of specific attitudes, but they are not simply those. Transfer does occur. We learn through the medium of these specific attitudes, but general ideas are thus developed which have unity and carry over to new situations. The author is not insensitive to the baffling problems involved in trait theory. He is aware of the absurdity and actual harm in proposing trait theories on superficial though well-sounding trait names. Whatever objections may be raised to these, it should at least be known that they were chosen and developed after much research and with full awareness of the many problems relating to trait theory.

In the second place, the profile is an attempt to represent graphically the total personality. The selection of variables to be included certainly has no claims to finality. This form constitutes the third revision of this profile in six years. It may be that the method of factor analysis will reveal a more final set of variables by which to describe human nature. Until that is achieved, any division must be tentative. No significance whatsoever is attached to the shape of the line connecting the various points on the profile. It is used purely for the purpose of making the profile easier to read. When this has been said, however, the author does believe that the science of mental measurements has now progressed far enough so that psychology ought to perform many investigations which include an attempt to measure the total personality. The time has about passed for giving complete attention to small aspects of our mental life, with no effort to discover their significance in the total picture. In the Union College Laboratory, the use of this profile makes it possible for us to relate even the most isolated details of behavior to every aspect of the total personality. A study of the dark adaptation curve can relate this curve to personality traits of every kind.

In the next place, the author is quite aware of the deficiencies in the questionnaires proposed in this book for measuring character development. It may be claimed, however, that some progress has been made through them toward making character development more objectively definite. The methods and processes of item analysis need to be applied before adequate standardization of these scales is possible. The effort to prepare scales of a purely positive nature had to be made without very much past research on which to build. Advances in personality measurement have been overwhelmingly on the clinical side. There is real need in psychology, however, for scales to measure man's potentialities. In intelligence testing, it happened that when we could detect low intelligence, we could automatically test high intelligence. This is not true in the case of emotional and social maturity. It is not true that if one has no morbid symptoms, he has all of the possible healthy traits, any more than it is true that if one has no physical disease symptoms, he is a great athlete.

On the religious side, this must be pointed out: the author is not quite as well acquainted with the latest literature of religious education as he would like to be. Undoubtedly, there are in that field some contributions, reference to which would have enhanced the value of this book. The only explanation which can be offered is that the author is a professional psychologist and finds the task of keeping abreast of the advances in that field much too great to permit exhaustive reading in the religious field.

Many psychologists have been accustomed to overlooking the significance of religion in personality. Such an oversight seems to the author comparable to overlooking the phenomena of electricity in physics. No one can deny that a great deal of superstition has accompanied the history of religion, as it has people's attitude toward such natural phenomena as thunder and lightning. But the fact remains that religion has wrought great changes in personality, and whatever a psychologist's religious convictions, he must recognize and study all the sources of power in personality. Among the influences which motivate men, religion has been and will always be one of the most powerful. And if men are to be lifted to their highest possibilities, religion must play the leading rôle.

When the question of acknowledging obligations is faced, the task seems impossible. Almost every member of the Westminster Presbyterian Church, including the children of its church school, have contributed to the growth of this character research project. The church school staff and the parents have played important parts. To the young men who have participated in the testing program at Union College must be given a great deal of credit for their splendid work. Of these, two names merit personal mention, Fred Feldman and Richard Trumbull. To my colleagues in the department, Dr. John L. March and Professor Franklin C. Chillrud, I am indebted for many valuable suggestions and much encouragement. To my secretary, Miss Celia A. Larned, for her painstaking efforts both in the project and with this manuscript I am indebted. The very small number of references in the book in no way indicates the broad variety of sources to which it is indebted. It has seemed desirable to confine mention of sources to those directly quoted and those which might be useful to parents and teachers. To all of my former teachers and to psychological writers in great number, I am obligated for the basic facts on which these principles have been built. Three names stand out to whom I owe my deepest obligations and without whom the project would have been impossible, Rev. Dr. Kenneth B. Welles, pastor of the Westminster Church, Miss Dorothy B. Fritz, the director of religious education, and my wife, Lois Wood Ligon, for her invaluable and rigorous work in giving final form to the manuscript.

ERNEST M. LIGON

Union College
Schenectady, N. Y.
September, 1939

HISTORICAL INTRODUCTION

PARENTS LOOK UPON THEIR CHILDREN and dream of their future. What they so often fail to realize is that their future is now. Parents and teachers determine the future of a child to whatever extent they influence his development from year to year, for the adult personality is largely a function of his development.

The value of a character development program is best judged by its sources. Most of us hesitate to use untried theories even in business or politics, and when it comes to dealing with our children we want to be sure that we have available the best posssible sources of advice. It seems wise, therefore, to begin with a brief history of the Union-Westminster Character Research Project, because it is out of this project that this volume has grown.

It becomes obvious immediately that such research in child development must draw heavily on the written and unwritten experience of men and women through the whole history of mankind. A psychologist knows, too, how many hundreds of investigations have been made which underlie every part of his store of knowledge. It would have been impossible to carry on such an investigation scientifically twenty-five years ago, for almost the entire history of scientific child psychology has taken place since that time. Very few phases of science have developed so rapidly or so fruitfully as the study of child development during the last few decades. That it has many problems yet to solve goes without saying, but it has laid a foundation on which solid structures of this nature can be built.

Another indispensable source on which this project has been based is the development of mental measurements. Testing has been one of the chief phases of the growth of scientific psychology during the last fifty years. Now almost every aspect of the personality can be measured with some degree of accuracy. This is a prerequisite to any character research project which could hope to produce permanent results.

Finally, from the field of religion and religious education have come many years of scholarly achievement which have made it possible for religion itself to be efficiently applied to the problem of character development.

While still an undergraduate the author became interested in this problem: Would an individual be mentally healthy or unhealthy if he obeyed implicitly the teachings of Jesus? The attempt to make a contribution on this question occupied some fourteen years, including graduate work in theological seminary and in psychology. In the spring of 1933 he was invited to make a series of lectures in the Westminster Presbyterian Church of Albany, New York, and gave as the content of those lectures the results of this study. At the end of the series, the officers of that church proposed that the principles of character development which had been presented in the series of lectures should be made the foundation for their character education program in the church. The six and a half years which have elapsed since that time have been years of the most intense effort and experimentation.

With funds partly contributed by the church and partly by the college, the Laboratory of Psychology of Union College at Schenectady, New York, was equipped for the necessary task of mental measurements. It is now one of the most completely equipped laboratories of its kind in existence. The children of the Westminster Church School are brought to this laboratory annually or biennially to be tested. Following the testing, a personality profile of each child is prepared. The profile form used will be found opposite page 38. Parent interviews are also held following the testing, during which the adjustment problems of the child under consideration are discussed. In the case of high school students, an additional interview is held with each of them for the discussion of his own profile. The laboratory work has never been in any sense clinical. On those rare occasions when psychiatric cases are brought to us, they are referred immediately to psychiatrists. Our work has regularly been with normal, healthy children.

The character education program itself has been built on eight traits of personality based on the teachings of Jesus in the Beatitudes. The curriculum is centered around these traits and guided by the results of the testing. Efforts have been made to have the church school teachers study the personality profiles of their children and deal with each child according to his individual capacities and needs. This is an ideal which has been approached gradually and even yet is far from complete realization. Efforts have also been made to measure the effectiveness of our character education. These measurements are rapidly attaining standardized form, and will be used even more completely in the future.

It is on the evidence gathered from all these sources, both outside and inside this particular character research project, that the contents of this book are based. That our work is at the beginning rather than at the end we realize, but we are also aware that the results of it have been remarkable and far-reaching, and this book represents a major effort to share these benefits with other character building institutions. Our emphasis has always been that character education is a seven-day-a-week process. Therefore, we have spent almost as much time in parent education as in child education. A project of this sort can never hope to be successful unless it is being actively engaged in by parents as well as religious educators. It is for both of these groups, therefore, that this book is written.

TABLE OF CONTENTS

THEIR FUTURE IS NOW

I

The Nature of Character and Personality

THE PROBLEM OF CHARACTER and personality development has always been and always will be a difficult one. There are no simple, easy panaceas or miraculous short cuts to it, in spite of many popular recommendations to the contrary. The task of studying all the various features and countless activities of the growing personality and molding them into an integrated happy being is a challenge to the best our parents and teachers have to give in love, patience, and ingenuity. However, a majority of the early volumes on child development were so morbid, and so full of warnings about the many dangers attending their efforts to bring up their children, that parents who took them seriously were filled with fears and, as a result, so were the lives of their children. In examining our own characters and the social institutions we have created we cannot avoid the realization that human personality has not made the best of its potential powers. It certainly has not attained the goal set forth by Jesus Christ when he said, "Be ye therefore perfect," and gave us a philosophy of life by which to reach this goal. His method did not follow the easy way of simple panaceas, neither did it warp and distort personality with morbid fears. Modern psychology also endeavors to show the way to perfect personality, by the scientific method. Thus, using this scientific method of modern psychology and applying it to the goals set forth by Jesus in the Beatitudes, this book endeavors to present a method of approach to our problems of character development in the training of children.

The Method of Science

Not everything is science which goes by that name. A real need for the layman today is a scientific definition of science.

A thing is not scientific simply because it can be weighed in a test tube or given a Latin-Greek name. Science is a method. It is a fairly elaborate one. Its requirements are rigid and precise. One can deal with electrons unscientifically or religion scientifically. It is quite beyond the scope of this volume to discuss in detail the scientific method.[1] For our purposes, only one aspect of it needs to be pointed out; namely, exact measurement.

Science progresses in proportion to the accuracy of its measurements. It is only because of the tremendous progress made during the past few decades in the field of mental measurements that a scientific approach to the problem of character is at all possible. No one can deny that some of these measurements still have far to go to reach the refinements desirable. One of the most important of our aims, therefore, should be precisely this, the development of more accurate methods of measurement. An institution, for example, which could find a way to measure leadership ability more accurately would make a real contribution to the problem of leadership itself. The search for laws of character involves the statistical analysis of the traits of character, which in turn presupposes that these traits can be measured. This is the chief emphasis of the method of science used in this book.

The first step toward this goal is accurate description. We must define so broad a term as character in aspects less broad, and these aspects, in turn, in still smaller parts. Let us be willing to learn more and more about less and less, for the history of science has shown that only thus we learn more and more about more and more. Again and again throughout this book emphasis will be put on this point. Parents and teachers will be urged to be sure that they always know exactly what they are doing. This is not an easy task, but a necessary one. Perhaps it will help if, in the very beginning, we point out some of the factors which arise in the problem

[1] Among the many volumes devoted to this subject, a good one is Whitney, F. L., *Elements of Research* (Prentice-Hall, 1937).

of character development and which must be measured accurately if we are to succeed.

First and foremost there is the child himself. He is the most important item in the personal equation. Until we have measured accurately all of the important aspects of his personality, we are not ready even to begin the task of character development. For it is not likely that we shall solve any equation if we are in ignorance concerning most of its terms. The fact is, however, that we do make estimates of our children's abilities, and psychological tests are the best available methods for making those estimates.

In the next place we must know precisely what character is. We must see, step by step, what happens from the time the individual faces his environment until he makes his adjustment to it. It is almost a daily experience for a child psychologist to be asked, "What should one do with a child who steals, or one who lies, or is disobedient, or fights?" Such a question is impossible to answer. One must know what the situation was, the nature of the child, and what the child expected to accomplish by his behavior. The problem will not be solved until some other way is found for the child to accomplish the same result with more acceptable behavior. This solution can be found only with a thorough understanding of all the steps in the process.

Then we must know what the end results are which we are trying to bring about. Many parents and teachers seem to use as their method of character education that of dealing with each specific situation as it arises by whatever methods are at hand at the moment. A recent popular writer suggested that by the laws of chance a group of monkeys poking at random on typewriter keys would eventually write all the books in the British Museum. The possibility of creating strong personality in our children by similar hit-or-miss methods has just about an equal chance of occurring. If character education is to be effective, we must have a very clear idea as to the traits we are hoping to develop. In addition we must know just what step we are trying to take at any particular age level with any particular child. We must also know at the end whether or not we have accomplished what we set out to accomplish. To make this point clearer, let us apply this principle in preparing a curricular unit for a church school class. It is necessary to know first what character or personality traits we are trying to develop by means of this unit. The curricular materials used must be chosen because of their adaptability to this purpose. We must make a careful study of just what steps in the growth of these traits can be taken at the age level concerned, and how the materials can be presented to that end. Then, each individual in the group must be studied carefully in order to discover just what development he needs in these particular traits, and how the material can be applied to bring about this development. These individual studies can then be wrought into a curricular unit. Finally, some sort of examination of the group should be made at the beginning and again at the end of the unit, to see what results have been brought about. This may sound like a very exacting method for church school education. Perhaps it is, but only when such methods are applied shall we make much progress toward our goal of building strong personalities.

The Nature of Character

Character consists of the characteristic forms of reaction of the personality. That is not as simple as it sounds. It can best be described in terms of a single experience of a personality. What we see is an objective situation, the individual, and his response to that situation. But why he responds in that way is not always or even often so clear. As a matter of fact, he does not see the same objective situation as we do, or at least it does not seem the same to him and to us. Obviously, the factors missing in our understanding of this behavior are the factors of the personal equation. A diagram will help us in seeing the problem more clearly.

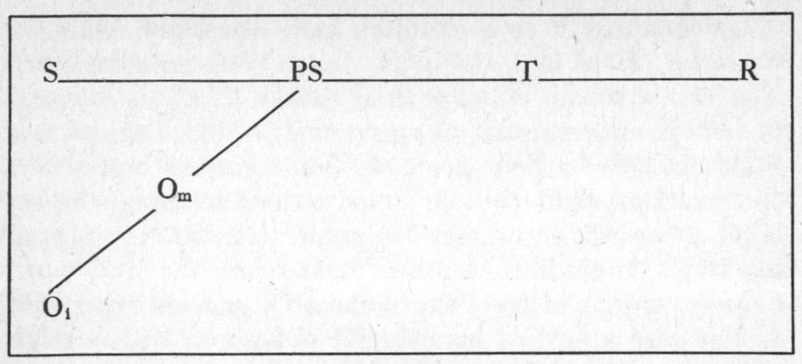

FIGURE I

S may be thought of as the external situation in some objective physical reality. PS is the perceived situation; that is, the way our subject sees it. Now how does he see it? O_i is the innate structure of the individual. It includes his sensory efficiency, his appetites, his aptitudes, and the other factors in his native organism. But through his experience and training various modifications have come about in his structure. O_m is this modified organism. When this meets the external situation it determines how he shall see it. This perception sets up some tension in him, T. We may think of these tensions as consisting of desires for achievement, social approval, and satisfaction of appetites. It is these tensions which bring about the behavior, or response, R, which he makes to reduce the tensions. Now, no one ever responds to a situation! He responds in order to reduce tensions. Let us take a simple illustration. Here is an Italian who, seeing a plate of spaghetti, eats it. How shall we diagram it? S is the spaghetti. O_i is his innate hunger appetite. O_m is his acquired appetite for spaghetti. PS is his perception of the plate of spaghetti as being especially desirable to eat. T is his desire for the satisfaction of this appetite. R is eating, with the purpose of reducing this tension.[2] A little practice will make this diagram seem very simple.

[2] This is obviously an over-simplified picture of the problem of adjustment. For a much more detailed description refer to Shaffer, L. F., *The Psychology of Adjustment* (Houghton Mifflin, 1936).

Let us apply it to a situation more obviously related to character. Here is a boy who steals. Why does he steal? The S is the money which is there to take. The R is the stealing. But to understand it we must know the rest of the picture. S also includes a poor home, favored brothers and sisters, and social unpopularity. O_i includes these features: the boy is fat, awkward, and rather low in mentality. O_m contains all his biases, prejudices, sense of values and the like, which have grown out of the factors under O_i and his experience. In this case a part of his effective philosophy of life might read, "Stealing is daring and will win admiration from my fellows. The money will buy sweets. I can give presents to my fellows to win friends." With this system of thinking, it is easy to see how he would perceive this situation, PS, in which money, possible to steal, is involved. Seeing such an opportunity, a number of tensions, T, would arise, and stealing would be the most natural method of satisfying them. Now, how shall we remedy a situation like this? It is clear that some changes in the environment itself would greatly alleviate the difficulties. But the most important thing is changing the O_m. And here is a point which represents a wide departure from traditional methods. Shall we preach to him about the evil of stealing, or threaten him with punishment? No wholesome results can be expected from either of these approaches. We must find out what desires are being satisfied by his behavior, and at the same time help him discover better ways of satisfying the same desires. In this case it is obvious that stealing satisfies desires for achievement, desires for social approval, and desires for the satisfaction of the hunger appetite. We shall not have solved his problem until we find some other behavior which accomplishes just as much or more. By the use of tests, abilities were discovered which he had not known he possessed. Forms of achievement were gained by the use of them. They also gained social approval. A mechanical ability made it possible for him to produce far the best model airplanes in his neighborhood. He now began to gain the social approval which he could not hope to hold unless his conduct was socially acceptable. Finally, this led to a modest income by which his craving for sweets could be satisfied within reason. Medical advice made this craving less strong and the ambition for a better physique a counter-motivation.

It may be stated as a major principle of character education that you will produce a real effect in the child's personality only if and to the extent that you find for him better methods for securing achievement, social approval, and satisfaction of appetites. Because this simple diagram of behavior is so fundamental to effective character education, it seems desirable to devote a paragraph to each part of it. It is important that it be clearly understood if it is to be used efficiently.

S is the objective situation to which the individual must adjust. Serious errors are involved, however, if one thinks of this as being the world of the physicist. None of us has to adjust to all of the physicist's world, for we cannot perceive it all. Thus, I am somewhat color blind. These colors, then, which I cannot see are not a part of the S in my case, for I do not have to adjust to them. A friend of mine is totally blind. He does not have to adjust to color, light or darkness, for he is aware of none of them. S, then, includes only those features of the external world about us to which we can adjust. It is obvious that this differs from individual to individual. Here is a boy, for example, for whom punishment by whipping did no good. Examination revealed that his pain sense was very dull. He, therefore, did not have to adjust to pain. It is quite important to know what constitutes the external world for any individual if we are to understand his behavior. It consists of those phenomena in the external world which he has the sense organs to perceive.

PS is even more difficult to grasp clearly. For example, probably most of us think of our eyes as little windows through which we look at the external world as it really is. Such is far from being true. What actually is the case is that we interpret the world. It is entirely possible for a dozen people to look at the same thing objectively and for each to perceive it differently. How do we make this interpretation?

The simplest way to think about it is that we interpret things in terms of use. Ask a young child to define words. A chair is a thing to sit on. A horse is a thing to ride. A doll is a thing to play with. This is perception in its basic and elementary form. One person sees an orange as something desirable to eat. Another hardly notices it at all. Two people looking at houses see different aspects of them, and correspondingly classify them as more or less desirable. A lover sees beauty in his beloved which others find much less conspicuous. A paranoid interprets the actions of his fellows as being those of deadly enemies, whereas a normal individual looks on the same behavior as friendly. So different, then, is this PS from the external world that unless we know what it is, we are helpless to understand behavior at all. The PS is the actual environment to which the individual is adjusting.

What determines how we interpret this world of ours? Now we must look to the organism itself. First there is the O_1. This consists of our inherited nature. It includes all our aptitudes and native abilities. The special aptitudes, such as musical, artistic, and mechanical abilities, are inherited, and are a part of O_1. Furthermore, since each ability in human nature has a tendency to express itself, it constitutes a drive. From a personality point of view, this dynamic quality of the factors of the O_1 is the most important, for through it behavior is affected. In addition to our abilities and aptitudes, our drives include the physical appetites and our innate social tendencies. There are enormous individual differences in all of them, and the sum of our endowments in them constitutes the limits of our personality power. We are not too certain of the exact nature of man's social tendencies. But we do know that they are there, and that there are individual differences in them as in all of the traits of personality. Even the physical appetites differ so enormously that for one man the physical basis for living to eat is far greater than for another. For our purposes, then, let us think of the factors in the O_1 as being drives. These drives include, first, our intelligence, motor coördination, capacity for learning, and special aptitudes. They give rise to our desires for achievement. Then, secondly, there are the physical appetites. They give rise to our desires for satisfaction of appetites. Finally, there are the factors of our inherited social nature. They give rise to our desires for social approval.

All men are not born equal, but even if they were they would not behave alike. These native drives find many forms of expression. The forms of expression they take are the result of experience and training. One man likes to eat garlic and spaghetti, another hot tamales and chili, another strudel and Wiener schnitzel. All have the same basic appetite, but experience varies its form of expression. One man likes classical music, another swing; one man chooses the old masters in art and another modernistic creations. These are the same endowments in the O_i but different forms of expression. One man likes one type of friends; another chooses entirely different ones. Both are equally social. One man gets a sense of achievement from moral behavior and another from antisocial conduct, with the same capacity for achievement in their natures. One man feels that social adjustment is to be found through suspicion and greed; another chooses to have faith in his fellow men. They both have the same inheritance socially. When drives are so modified they are called motives. This is purely an artificial distinction, but one very desirable to keep in mind. Drives as such seldom, if ever, bring about behavior. It is these drives, modified by experience into motives, which result in the type of action carried out. These motives constitute the O_m. They constitute a man's effective philosophy of life. It matters little what he says he believes. It matters immensely what his motives are.

When these come into contact with the S, then we have the PS. It is in terms of these motives that we interpret the external world. It is quite as important to know the motives of men as to know the external world itself. Indeed, for understanding their behavior and predicting what they will do, it is far more important. It is in the O_m that changes in character are brought about. Character education consists essentially in the formation of motives. How this is to be done will be clearer as the book progresses.

As a result of perceiving a situation, some tension, T, is set up. It may be called desire. It always has to do with achievement, social approval, and satisfaction of appetites. It, too, grows out of the nature and present condition of the O_m. But it is these desires or tensions which bring about our activity. We think about behavior most accurately when we consider that all activity takes place to reduce these tensions. However, these tensions often conflict with each other, and a person is torn between two courses of action. These conflicts have more to do with weak personality than any other single factor. If it could be brought about that there was never any conflict of tensions in an individual, he would have the strongest personality of which he was capable. To avoid conflicts, or, to put it positively, to bring about integration takes us back again to the O_m. If the right effective philosophy of life is formed, that is, the right motives, conflict can be avoided. This is character education.

Finally, R is our behavior, or the responses the individual makes to reduce his tensions. In early childhood various types of response are tried, pretty much by trial and error. Then those which work are adopted for permanent use. If temper tantrums get attention and perhaps even secure what the child demands, they are adopted permanently to reduce corresponding tensions. If coöperation gets better results than obstinacy or negativism, then it is accepted. Whether fighting or running, crying or laughing, studying or idling, working or playing, the characteristic behavior of the child depends on which actions reduce more tensions. But whether they work or not depends on the tensions themselves, and they in turn upon the O_m.

The Process of Character Education

Now we have the basis for seeing more clearly the nature of character and personality. We understand each step in the process of behavior. We can see now how one goes about the task of molding or changing personality. By way of summary, let us picture the form which effective character education should take.

Traditional notions of character education were simple enough in the old days. The Sunday school teacher needed only her quarterly, and parents only a rod and common sense. Now we find it necessary to introduce methods which require ten times the preparation and many times the care and effort. The fact is that the older methods were almost as useless as they were simple. Researches have been made to measure the effectiveness of such character education, and there is no evidence that it had very much value.

What must the modern church school teacher do? In the first place, he or she must know the members of the class. This means that profiles of each child must be constructed and studied carefully. A knowledge of their abilities, both physical and mental, and of their special aptitudes is the minimum basis on which to proceed. Then, their effective philosophy of life must be known. A clear picture of what portions need changing or forming is the blueprint for purposive character education. The modern church school teacher, in other words, must know very precisely just what is to be accomplished with each and every member of the class, and just how the lesson material can be made to achieve this purpose. Lesson materials are a means to an end, and not an end in themselves. Finally, he must find out whether or not his objectives have been reached. It was much more comfortable under the old regime, when the only criterion of success was the use of the entire lesson period without rebellion. But the thrill that comes with success is one of the greatest that life provides.

What of the parents? Do they play a part in this picture? If they do not the whole picture is hopeless. The home must always remain the center of character education. The church school, at best, can only hope to guide character and contribute to its social integration. The great bulk of the work has to be done in the home. Parents, then, must also know all of these data. They must be very clear about what the teacher is trying to accomplish and back up this purpose with careful and purposive education at home. This central position of the home will become more and more apparent in the chapters dealing with the growth of the eight traits at the various age levels. The public school, too, must contribute its share. The modern public school teacher is rapidly outgrowing the idea that all she needs to teach is arithmetic. She knows that character and personality are even more important. One of the most hopeful signs of the times is the great interest shown by school teachers in genuine efforts at character education.

II

Dynamics of Character

DOES WHAT A MAN BELIEVES have anything to do with the strength of his personality? If we limit this question to those beliefs which are the basis for his actions, the answer is that they make the difference between weak and strong personality, between mental health and mental disease. It would not matter much if he held doubts as to whether Columbus discovered America in 1492; but his concept of the value and dignity of his job is of tremendous importance. To be sure, his aptitudes, abilities and appetites are largely a function of his inheritance and cannot be very much increased or decreased by education or experience. But each one of them may express itself in many different forms. Hunger may range from cannibalism to a taste for caviar. The desire for achievement may take the form of piracy and gangsterdom or willingness to endure crucifixion for a high ideal. Love may express itself as lust and jealousy or as self-sacrifice and devotion. One man's life is filled with fear, anger, hatred, suspicion. These are the symptoms of mental disease. Another man, with the same inheritance, has courage, magnanimity, and faith in his fellow man.

It would be possible to defend the hypothesis that the only sources of mental disease are fear and anger. If, then, one can replace them with faith and magnanimity, mental health is the reward. Some try to bring this about by controlling the environment. They endeavor to protect the child against poverty, disease, danger and the many social cruelties which men inflict upon one another. There is nothing wrong in this in itself. But even if it were possible to carry out completely, what a weak personality would result. On the other hand, there is no environment so cruel that some men have not found ways of transcending it. They face danger with courage, and injustice with forgiveness. What is the difference?

It is in what a man believes. The dynamics of character are deep-lying attitudes which govern the way in which a man's inherited sources of power express themselves, and determine whether he faces his environment with fear and anger or with courage and magnanimity. These attitudes are what we call traits. The problem of traits is one of the most difficult in psychology, and some would solve it by denying their existence. No one well acquainted with the human mind can doubt that many of the traditional traits of character taught our children do produce conflict, repression, fear and weakness. And, in our churches where ethical traits are emphasized, we do find people who are good, but not good for anything. The fact remains that our civilization has been built on the foundations of honor, devotion to duty, moral ideals, loyalty, self-sacrifice, vision and indomitable courage. The solution does not lie in simply discarding them. It lies in rebuilding our concepts of character traits to include traits which will retain all of the values of these traditional ones; and at the same time result in mental health and strong personality. The choice of the eight traits which are proposed in this book is an effort in that direction.

There can be no doubt that one of the most important reasons, perhaps the chief reason, why our efforts at character development have been so ineffective is our lack of purpose. It is little wonder that we do not get anywhere when we do not know either where we want to go or where we are, at any time, on the journey. One of the most persistent superstitions of men is that they inherit a conscience which tells them the difference between right and wrong. Actually this theory was effectively denied a long time ago by the writer of the book of Judges when, again and again, he said that every man did that which was "right in his own eyes";[1] but it was evil in the sight of Jehovah. As parents and teachers, ask yourselves these questions about your efforts to develop character in your children: Just what is it I am trying to accomplish? Just what am I trying to do now with this particular child to produce what end result? And how do I

[1] Judges 17:6.

know that it will produce this end result, or if it does, that this end result is worth producing? It is the central aim of this book to describe these dynamics of character which we call traits, and to show how they are to be developed at the various age levels from infancy to maturity. Purposive character education is the only sort that can hope to succeed. Aimless character education, based on vague generalities and meaningless platitudes, must of necessity result in purely accidental personalities. There may be a few great personalities, as there have been through the ages. But the casualties will outnumber the successes a hundred to one, as they have in the past. A successful character development program initiated by the church and carried out in the home would result in more human happiness and social stability than have all the advances of the physical sciences. It would constitute the greatest contribution of the church in its entire history.

Criteria of Selection

The selection of a group of traits or goals is a very difficult problem. Traits, chosen haphazard, however high sounding and socially desirable they may seem, are almost certain to result in conflict and weakness. The selection and description of a proposed group of eight traits as the goals of character education is one of the chief contributions of this book. The eight chosen are based on the Beatitudes as interpreted in *The Psychology of Christian Personality*.[2] There are many criteria which a trait theory must satisfy if it is to be valid. In order that the reader may better evaluate these eight, the most important of these criteria will be described.[3]

The first requirement for traits, if they are to be a part of Christian character education, is that they must be Chris-

[2] Ligon, E. M., *The Psychology of Christian Personality* (Macmillan, 1935).

[3] Those who may wish to study this problem more completely should consult the excellent volume published as a yearbook of the Department of Superintendence. Department of Superintendence, *Tenth Yearbook, Character Education*. National Education Association, Washington, 1932.

tian. It is obvious that not everything which has been taught in the name of Christianity or religion is mentally healthy. So much fear and anger have been taught in the name of Jesus that the results of it will be found in all our mental hospitals, and deeply written in the annals of our social and political tragedies. There are even those who seriously question whether the Christian religion is mentally healthy or not. Some parents keep their children out of church schools because of what they think they learn there. Fear and anger are harmful to personality whether they are taught in the name of religion, patriotism, or tyranny. Are they a part of Jesus' own concept of personality? The basic teachings of Jesus from this point of view have been set forth in *The Psychology of Christian Personality*. It is my belief that the eight traits chosen here represent accurately the concepts of human personality held by Jesus, and that they are productive of strong character and wholesome personality. It was Jesus himself, however, who advised us to judge our theories by their fruits. And he would be the first to urge us to try them, refine them, and develop them until we find the methods for producing the type of personality which he envisioned. But why turn to religion at all? Can character not be developed without religion? The answer which this book will defend is that religion is an essential factor in personality, and one's maximum personality cannot be developed without it.

The second requirement has already been implied several times; namely, that our traits must be mentally wholesome. This is the point at which most of our traditional codes break down. As the Department of Superintendence Yearbook puts it, "The proposed traits, virtues, and ideals do not have any integral and coherent existence in the makeup of human beings." [4] The common assertion that human nature cannot be changed is one of those half truths which have been so often the excuse for doing whatever one wants to do. The true half, however, is the essence of this point. Our fundamental nature, which is born in us, cannot be changed.

[4] *Ibid.*, p. 44.

All of the functions of this nature must be expressed in one way or another. None of them can be eliminated. It has been a very common fault of negative ethics systems of morality to insist that they must be eliminated. This can result only in disaster. Then there are other theories of character which have tried to call forth in men types of activity for which there is no fundamental basis in human nature. This is equally impossible. Any character traits chosen must be based on human nature and must utilize all of it to its fullest extent. The whole theory of asceticism, with its emphasis on the total neglect or denial of our bodily appetites, inevitably failed because of this fact. At the other extreme, demanding of a child achievement requiring more intelligence than he possesses, or more athletic ability than he has, must lead to mental maladjustment. Any theory of character development, then, must be built on the actual structure of human nature.

But there is another side to this statement that human nature cannot be changed. It is true that these innate drives of human nature cannot be changed in amount, but the form which they take in motives for action is one of the most variable and changeable things in the world. The range of possible expressions of hunger, desire for achievement, and love has been pointed out. There is hardly a drive in human nature for which there are not hundreds of methods of expression. There is probably not a single form of human behavior which could not be modified. The innate basis remains the same, but the form of expression is different. Is war a part of human nature which cannot be changed? To be sure it is an expression of certain factors in human nature. They cannot be changed, but they can be turned into other forms of expression. As far as human nature is concerned, war can be eliminated. If man is to attain his highest possibilities in strong personality, it must be.

Each of these innate drives in human nature is a source of power. In order to reach his maximum strength a person must be able to utilize all these natural resources. There are two common ways in which men fail to do this. The first has already been indicated: namely, repressing some of these drives, calling them evil in themselves, often refusing to admit that they even exist. Each of them subtracted from the personality results in weakness. They must all be utilized. A second way of losing the strength of these drives is even more common, and that is through conflict. Inasmuch as any of these drives may take many different forms, it often happens that we choose forms of expression which conflict with one another. Let us choose an example from war. A man is taught to be brave and patriotic, willing to lay down his life for his country. Then he is taught to have faith in his fellow men, to admire them and coöperate with them in building a finer social order. Suddenly, in the name of the former he is asked to deny the latter and start killing. No man can kill his fellow men and remain entirely sane. Whoever makes soldiers of a nation destroys an important part of the personalities of its people. The end result can only be degeneration.

Here is another example of conflict. A boy is taught that he must use his God-given endowment to the fullest extent, but also that salary is both the source of happiness and the only form of personal security. His abilities suggest a vocation in which financial rewards are relatively meager. What shall he do? Whichever way he goes, he must have the feeling of an unsatisfied tension regarding the other. An ideal character education program would not put him in this dilemma. The ideal set of traits, then, would result in integration of one's drives and the elimination of conflict. This is another reason why haphazard decisions on what is right or wrong at the moment are so dangerous. Every such decision should be made in terms of all the other parts of one's social code, to make sure that there are no conflicts. Some of the most well-known character traits, the power of which must never be lost to civilization, are nevertheless subject to this criticism. Honesty is the best example. It is necessary to civilization, but impossible in human nature. These eight traits, then, must satisfy this criterion, if they are to result in the most dynamic personality possible.

Why do men "lose their heads"? Why do they become so terrified in the face of danger that they behave in cowardly fashion? Why do so many people have temper tantrums during which they do and say things which cause them deep mortification as soon as they are sane again? Why can a nation be swept off its feet by war propaganda? The answer again is disintegration. This time, however, it is not so much conflict as simply lack of being completely integrated. Any one impulse may gain complete control of the personality without regard to the rest of it. Thus, many football players are afraid, but they do not run from the field. They throw the energy created by this fear into a better game. Most speakers are nervous when they face an audience, but they do not faint nor sit down speechless. They make even better speeches because of this tension. It is only when an impulse runs amuck and cannot be integrated into the total personality that people "lose their heads". Infants are entirely ruled by the impulse of the moment. A part of the process of growing up is learning to consider impulses in terms of the total situation. Whenever an adult mind is capable of being violently moved by any one impulse, that mind is to that extent weak. And forces which stimulate men to violent emotional action are disintegrative forces whether they are in the form of evangelism, patriotism, or political propaganda. The integrated personality responds to propaganda objectively and is not moved by its emotionalism. Therefore, when one chooses character traits, they must be traits which result in integration not in disintegration.

Training children in character traits of whatever nature is more easily said than done. Any parent will vouch for that. Character traits, if they are of value, must be capable of being taught. And what is not so obvious is that they must be of such a nature that their foundations can be laid even in infancy. No quality of personality has much solidity unless its roots are found throughout the whole developmental life of the individual. Of course, no adult concept, as such, can be taught a young child. We have tried to do exactly this in the past. But teaching the child of four to repeat the

Lord's Prayer or the Beatitudes is not equivalent to his understanding them. As a matter of fact, not one of the concepts involved in these two classic passages can be understood earlier than the teen age. Parents and teachers who exhort young children on these subjects are wasting their time. Yet the fact remains that if these concepts are to become a part of the adult personality, foundations for them must be laid even at the earliest age levels. Character traits acquired in the later years of development are inevitably weak and superficial. This is why the sudden conversion so often cools off with the passing of time. It has no foundations. When conversions last, it means that the conversion experience was only the final consummation of a long period of growth and change. One of the most difficult tasks in evolving this program was finding ways of developing these eight traits at the various age levels. The chart [5] shows the results of this study schematically.

Finally, there is the criterion, already implied, that the traits must be socially acceptable. Ideals chosen solely on the basis of their value to society are very often impossible to teach in personality without the destruction of potential power. But the fact remains that we must live together in social organizations. No system of character training would be of value which did not take this fact into account. Perhaps in no part of our social life has this point been so clearly brought to the fore as in our sex adjustments. All through the ages men have tried to find a solution to this problem which would utilize the power of the sex drive in personality and at the same time not result in social chaos. That our present concepts of sex morality are inadequate is obvious to anyone who considers the numerous conflicts which result. Repression, perversion, unhappy marriages, mental disease—these are some of the fruits of our failure to adequately solve the sex problem. A man would be rash who attempted to state a final solution. One way to test the validity of these eight traits would be to consider the sex

[5] The chart is included in the back of this book and should be used for reference throughout.

morality of an individual possessing them. Would it be wholesome or not? In this world of chaos, this criterion is one of the most important, for it must be solved if civilization is to persist.

Perhaps no one will now imagine that the choice of a theory of character education is easy. At the same time no one can deny that it is necessary. Whatever method we use for developing character in our children, we must assume some theory of character. It may be loosely defined or not even defined at all. It may be haphazard and inspired by the necessities of the moment. But the fact remains that we must do something, and what we do is our theory of character. The following theory of character is offered with humility. Every effort has been made both by study and actual experiment to construct it in the light of all these criteria and many others not mentioned here. Only time and further research will reveal its strengths and weaknesses and make possible refinements and changes which may eventually lead to a better understanding of the universal laws of personality which seem to have been recognized by Jesus.

The Goals of Christian Character Education

We are now prepared to set forth the eight traits which have been selected as the trait goals for the Union-Westminster Character Research Project. They constitute, on the one hand, legitimate interpretations of the teachings of Jesus and, on the other, they have been developed both experimentally and logically in an effort to make them psychologically valid and mentally healthy. It is hoped that they are practical educationally and, if learned, will result in the type of personality on which our intricate social structure can safely be built.

If one looks at the various phenomena of mental disease, one is impressed with the important place occupied by fear and anger. In fact it is possible to classify all of the mental diseases of the functional variety in terms of the fear and anger habits which constitute their major symptoms. On the other hand, if one reads with care the teachings of Jesus, he is equally impressed with the central position of faith and love. It is no accident that these stand in opposition to the two former traits. Jesus' insight into the nature of human personality was of most remarkable clearness. Unfortunately the history of Christianity has shown a wide variety of interpretations of both these words, faith and love. Sometimes each of them has received a connotation which is far from being characteristic of mental health. At any mental hospital will be found a number of patients whose religion would seem to characterize a part of the causation which put them there. It is exceedingly important, then, if we are to approach our problem of character education either accurately or wholesomely, to define specifically what we mean by faith and love. In the Beatitudes, which are placed at the beginning of the so-called Sermon on the Mount, are collected what were probably the most important of Jesus' ideals for personality. There are eight of them, and they can be readily divided into two groups—the first group is descriptive of the sort of *faith* that Jesus taught and the second group his concept of Christian *love*.

Experimental Faith

Let us turn first to the characteristics of Christian faith.[6] The sort of faith Jesus taught might be called an experimental faith. He himself had a faith in the fatherliness of the universe which made him optimistic in the face of whatever disappointments and hardships came to him. He did not seem to have a strict type of creed which remained unchangeable, but rather a dynamic experimental faith which was constantly changing and being refined. When asked how to distinguish between true and false prophets, he did not make dogmatic assertions but rather suggested the eternal

[6] These as well as the other portions of the Sermon on the Mount have been dealt with in some detail in Ligon, E. M., *The Psychology of Christian Personality* (Macmillan, 1935). Chapter II is entitled "An Experimental Faith."

principle, "By their fruits ye shall know them." [7] When we have examined the four traits which constitute the first group it will be clear just what sort of faith this is.

1. *Vision*

Happy are the poor in spirit: for theirs is the kingdom of heaven.—*Matthew 5:3*.

Adjusting to one's environment is not synonymous with being satisfied with it. A scientist loves his field of research, but devotes his whole life to changing it. No progress is made except where the need of progress is felt. To the young child, happiness seems to consist in the satisfaction of whatever appetite or urge happens to be dominant at the moment. He lives in the present, and if his immediate desires are being satisfied, all is right with the world. If the child has wise parents and teachers, he is taught to look forward to greater rewards, and even to sacrifice something if necessary to secure them. Poverty of spirit is the faith, that however great a man's achievements are, there are greater things to be accomplished in the future. It does not imply that one should not rejoice in what he has done, but that he should make each achievement a challenge to a greater one. Many a scientist has demonstrated this spirit by his life. As a lad in high school he imagines that his high school diploma will represent almost the acme of human knowledge. He eagerly works for it. Having obtained it, instead of being satisfied, he looks forward now to his college degree, certain that this will be the mark of an educated man. When that goal has been reached, graduate degrees beckon to him. They, too, give way to successive dreams of greater achievements. There is no end to the process for these men.[8]

When this trait, which can be called vision, is studied in terms of the developmental steps in its growth, one finds a large number of smaller, more specific attitudes which form the body of this major trait. A list of these specific attitudes, which should be given to the child in his growth toward maturity in this trait, will help define it more carefully. In the

[7] Matthew 7:20.
[8] *The Psychology of Christian Personality*, pp. 28-40.

discussion of the various psychogenic steps in the development of Christian personality, all of these specific attitudes will be mentioned. A few of the more important ones with respect to this trait are these: constructive imagination, a wholesome desire for self-improvement, enthusiasm for life's possibilities, being subject to the inspiration of the lives of great men, having a high vision for one's vocation however humble, having an optimistic desire for a better social order, and the ambition always to do things better.

2. *Love of Righteousness and Truth*

Happy are they who hunger and thirst after righteousness: for they shall be filled.—*Matthew 5:6.*

An important mark of physical well-being is a good, healthy appetite. Jesus believed that this is also true of spiritual well-being. If one has acquired an appetite for good food, he eats with zest, and health is his compensation. If, however, the time of his eating is irregular, and if the foods he eats are overrich or unnourishing, he soon finds his appetite reduced to a minimum, and his health at a low ebb. The body may crave indigestible foods, if it has acquired a taste for them. One can learn to crave almost anything. He will be healthy, only if he is taught to enjoy wholesome foods. If one stops eating, his body ceases to be hungry. After about three days of fasting, he no longer experiences any craving for food. These facts which apply to physical hunger are equally applicable to other phases of human behavior. It is obvious that one will not hunger and thirst for anything unless he feels a lack of it. But, while hungering and thirsting presupposes being poor in spirit, it does not necessarily follow it. Even if students are sincerely "poor in spirit" with respect to their knowledge, no instructor can help them much unless they also hunger and thirst for knowledge. Tube feeding is not very healthy in either physical or mental nourishment. To Jesus, righteousness consisted of the laws which govern the spiritual and social universe. It is difficult to imagine being hungry and thirsty for learning the things one should not do. Indeed, it is safe to say, that when people do seem to have such an appetite very strongly, there is something unhealthy in their personality. This attitude must be learned in early childhood, and can be taught the child by using his natural tendencies. One of the natural tendencies of any intelligent child is to ask questions. On the basis of this natural tendency to ask questions can be built a true hunger and thirst for knowledge, which will become a life habit.[9]

A few of the specific habits which need to be inculcated into the development of this trait are these: a genuine interest in the things about you, a genuine interest in one's school work, a desire always to know the truth, a tendency to think out problems that arise, accurate judgments instead of all-or-none statements, logical and coherent thinking, a genuine reverence for and interest in the finer values of life, willingness to change one's mind in the face of new evidence, a tendency to consider all sides of a thing before reaching a decision, a tendency to experiment and reach conclusions by objective means, moral integrity without prudishness, keeping one's promises, having a wholesome attitude toward religion, the habit of periods of thoughtful meditation, and willingness to admit one's mistakes.

3. *Faith in the Friendliness of the Universe*

Happy are the meek: for they shall inherit the earth.—*Matthew 5:5.*

This trait, which may be called faith in the friendliness of the universe, is the central trait in Christian faith.

Some people have imagined that meekness is a spineless, groveling attitude. This notion of meekness is far from the attitude of mind described in Jesus' teaching. As he prayed in the Garden of Gethsemane, he gave a magnificent demonstration of meekness. This willingness to subordinate his will to the will of God was meekness. Moses has frequently been described as the meekest of men. The people whom he led out of Egypt, still slaves at heart, would be a trial to any man. Yet, with the exception of one instance, Moses was patient with them, never losing his faith that they were worth saving. His contributions to spiritual progress grew from this meekness. Meekness can be defined as the unshakable faith that the universe is lawful. Christian meekness is

[9] *Ibid.*, pp. 40-44.

the faith that the universe is fatherly. When trouble, sorrow, and suffering befall the meek man, he is certain that it is the working of a fatherly universe. He does not always understand why such things happen, but he does believe that if men knew all of the spiritual laws, they would not only understand but be able to prevent these tragedies. Whoever accepts the universe and tries to discover its nature will be much better adjusted than he who tries to fight it. Meekness has come to be the normal attitude toward nature. Scientists have complete faith that the universe is lawful. They stand before the most bewildering chaos with the certainty that what seems to be chaotic will prove to be orderly, when they have discovered the laws governing its behavior.[10]

Some of the specific attitudes which describe the developmental steps in this trait of faith in the friendliness of the universe are these: physical courage, learning to respond wholesomely to failure, eagerness to try out new things, willingness to try things alone without fear, no tendency toward discouragement, lack of stubbornness, an objective attitude toward failure, faith in a Father-God, ability to recover quickly from a lost contest, ability to recover quickly from disappointments, a tendency to evaluate one's ability objectively, being enthusiastic about one's abilities even if they are not popular, a sense of well-being, confidence that however often one has failed there is a place in the world for him, faith that everything, however hard, can be worked out for good, lack of objective fears, self-reliance, and coolness in the face of danger.

4. *Dominating Purpose*

Happy are the pure in heart: for they shall see God.—*Matthew 5:8.*

This describes a trait which we have called a dominating purpose in the service of mankind.

Purity of heart signifies singleness of purpose. The more enthusiastic one is about his purpose, the more valuable its effect on his personality will be. A dominating purpose is one which is

[10] *Ibid.*, pp. 44-52.

constantly in the focus of his attention, is the strongest motive in his behavior, and is the source of his greatest pleasure. Insight into the problems of nature frequently have come in a flash. Everyone can cite famous instances of it. A falling apple brought the insight of gravitation to Newton. Observe carefully the causes of these insights. It was not an accident that the millions of others who had observed falling objects failed to discover the laws of gravitation. Only Newton had the background for such a discovery. Only those who have made it the dominating purpose of their lives to search for such insights, have them. Jesus said that only the pure in heart really see God. As one observes the brilliant insights of Jesus into the spiritual problems of his day, he sees the very incarnation of this Beatitude. Great discoveries remain to be made both in science and in the spiritual realm. Only the pure in heart will make them.[11]

Some of the many steps that need to be taken in helping the growing child to develop the type of purposefulness so important in wholesome personality are these: learning to use all one's abilities, perseverance through activity, initiative and aggressiveness, tendency to constructiveness, ability to work under pressure, getting satisfaction from doing things well, the ability to persist in disagreeable, boring tasks, working with confidence and pleasure, a tendency to finish what one starts, the ability to work with concentration, the ability to work wholeheartedly at second-choice occupations, the ability to work at the optimum level of energy, a dominating vocational purpose, choosing one's vocation in line with abilities, choosing life work on a service motive, the courage to carry out one's purpose even in the face of poverty, having many hobbies, and being dependable.

Here, then, are four traits which characterize the Christian faith. Perhaps they do not seem to include most of the traditional creeds and items of faith which have constituted so large a portion of the dogma of the Church. They do, however, adequately describe what Jesus meant by faith, and they will produce the powerful type of personality so badly needed in our modern social chaos.

[11] *Ibid.*, pp. 52-65.

Fatherly Love

When one turns to the word love, he finds an even less definite notion of its meaning than was true in the case of faith. The Christian Church has taught through the centuries that brotherly love was the central motivation of Jesus' teaching. Yet when one looks at some of the statements that Jesus made about our duty to our fellow man, he finds that they seem very difficult to inculcate in human nature. Loving our enemies is simple enough in theory but extremely difficult in practice. Turning the other cheek is often thought of as an act of cowardice. Returning good for evil certainly does not seem to be the best way to deal with injustice. Interestingly enough, when one examines the various drives in human nature, he finds one type of love in which these high ideals are not only possible but common. This type of love is parental love. Turning the other cheek is so common a type of behavior for parents that only the most abnormal father or mother would expect it to be otherwise. When one keeps in mind this aspect of human personality and then reads the teachings of Jesus with care, he becomes convinced that this was precisely the type of love Jesus taught. Fatherly love is a much better description than brotherly love. Then, when it is realized that this parental instinct can be elicited in a child as early as eighteen months of age, and finds abundant expressions in all age levels, through dolls, pets, and care of younger children, he realizes that this type of love can be the central motivation for a very dynamic type of personality.

Perhaps it may occur to some that fatherly love on the part of everyone toward everyone else might not be too possible. Not everybody would like us to go about trying to be a father to them. Such an objection, however, is due to the inclusion in the term fatherliness of some of its least important aspects. Bossiness, the pretension of infallible knowledge and the like are not the major characteristics of parental love. Let us turn now to the four Beatitudes which best describe this aspect of Jesus' teaching. I think it will be granted that all of them are desirable for wholesome and universal application.

5. *Being Sensitive to the Needs of Others*

Happy are they that mourn: for they shall be comforted. —*Matthew 5:4.*

Common sense would never have suggested to men that happiness could come from mourning. Only when we interpret correctly the meaning of the word mourning do we grasp fully its significance as the first characteristic of fatherly love. Let us turn to parenthood to find its meaning. Long before a child is born he becomes a source of worry to his parents. That worry is likely to continue as long as the child and the parents both live. They are anxious to bring him up to be a fine, happy, worthwhile man. They mourn when any obstacle gets in the way of that goal. Here, then, is the first characteristic of fatherly love. If a man is sensitive to the sorrows and failures not only of his own children but of all men, he has this personality trait with which we are dealing. It is not any longer common for us to let men starve. The religion of Jesus has thoroughly engrained that idea into society. It is, however, very common to commit worse crimes. Consider the young men in any community who become criminals or worthless parasites on society. In almost every case one of the causal factors is a lack of sympathetic and understanding friendship among his elders. This trait, too, can be built on a natural drive in human behavior. Psychology has far to go before it can speak very definitely about man's inherited social nature, but it is perfectly certain that man is by nature a social animal. Furthermore, he is by nature sympathetic. Why, then, are there so many unsympathetic people in any social group? The answer is, repression. Actually no one who is not sympathetic with other men gains a perspective which makes him able to see his own troubles in their true light. One who is not sensitive to the needs of others would be astonished at the amount of suffering that is going on all about him, often in his closest friends. Quite apart from any sense of duty or ethical standards, this attitude of being sensitive to the needs of others is essential to mental health. Much mental disease is fundamentally self-centeredness.[12]

[12] *Ibid.*, pp. 65-72.

As we look for the many small habits which we may teach the growing child in the hope of developing in him this quality in its fullest and dynamic form, these are a few of the more specific traits: unselfish social contacts, the tendency to like people in general, the capacity for being moved by the sufferings of others, being considerate of others, having many friends of both sexes, trying to know and understand others, sensitiveness to social good taste, being interested in what others are doing, having faith in people in general, tendency to see the best in others, and making oneself congenial with others.

6. *Forgiveness*

Happy are the merciful: for they shall obtain mercy.—*Matthew 5:7.*

There are some people who are sensitive to suffering but do nothing about it. Mercy is not a passive process, but one that expresses itself in action. Its simplest definition would be the prevention of suffering in others, whether physical or spiritual. Parents try to predict the hard knocks their children may meet, save them from as many as possible, and give them the strength to meet the others. When we consider this type of mercy we can understand how loving one's enemies is possible. Consider how frequently we are deeply offended at some injustice done to us. We usually find it difficult to forgive even when amends are made. A parent, however, would have no difficulty forgiving a child any number of such offenses. For the merciful, then, forgiveness, even of enemies, is a natural part of their personalities. It is not always easy to know how to be merciful. Parents spend many sleepless nights searching for wisdom to keep their children from rushing into sorrow and unhappiness. Mercy does not always express itself by withholding punishment. Often, punishing a child may be more merciful than spoiling him. We are merciful only if we bring it about that righteous behavior is the natural expression of personalities. The same methods used to instill the attitude of mourning apply in teaching the child to be merciful. The impulse to help those who are suffering is instinctive. It simply needs to be intelligently developed. Let the young child have opportunities to express this impulse toward animals and younger children.[13]

[13] *Ibid.*, pp. 72-75.

Forgiveness has been so commonly tied up with forgetting that we have forgotten that originally it always implied regeneration. Perhaps a good way of describing the attitude implied in this trait would be to say that it is the determination to give every man his chance at happiness and success. Forgiveness has no meaning of value apart from this more dynamic attitude. A few of the more specific personality habits which form the basis and are a part of this attitude are these: willingness to assume social responsibilities, insistence on a democracy of contacts, kindness to animals and children, parent-like desire to give everyone his chance, the ability to apologize, to be good-natured, hard to irritate, to make new friends easily, to share community responsibility, to take responsibility for younger children, sense of fair play, generosity, social coöperation, and the habit of seeing that others have a good time at social events.

7. *Magnanimity*

Happy are the peacemakers: for they shall be called the sons of God.—*Matthew 5:9.*

Man is instinctively a social animal. He does not, however, inherit, ready-made, the social structure by which he can live with others without friction. Thus, men often seem to be unable to live either with one another or without one another. The man who can resolve these conflicts and make men able to coöperate with one another to form a society of genuine good will, must be of almost superhuman qualities. There are three kinds of conflict which challenge the peacemaker. The first is the struggle between the various forces within the individual. The second is the conflict which arises between the individual and his society. The third consists of those forms of economic and political warfare which constitute the most serious of our social problems. All three of them are essentially one, however—inner conflict. These inner conflicts can be classified in three groups: lusts, fears, and anger. Everyone knows them as the great sources of unhappiness. A man who has lain awake nights in terror of possible calamities in the future does not have to be told the mental fear of torture. When one is constantly losing his temper in violent anger he is indeed unhappy. The man who can help us gain control of our appetites, give us courage to meet our dangers, and teach us magnanimity with which to replace our angers, is a real peacemaker. Since peacemaking consists in dispelling fear, anger, and greed from the world, two factors are necessary in the development of this trait in a child: his own personality must be free from these elements, and he must be capable of influencing others to get rid of them. In respect to ridding his own personality of them, the best plan is prevention rather than cure. Never permit the child to form them in the first place. A child can learn to be characteristically courageous, magnanimous and unselfish as easily as to show fear, anger and greed. The best sort of training for preventing the conflicts between a child and his social environment is the development of sportsmanship.[14]

If we were to seek a single phrase to describe this trait it would be, the determination to resolve the conflicts within men and between and among them—magnanimity. Sportsmanship is one of its central features. A few of the specific attitudes which go to make it up are as follows: coöperation with authority, respect for property rights, the willingness to play what others want to play even against one's own wishes, aggressive social contacts, the ability to work with others, the ability to do one's best against a vastly superior opponent in a game or contest, the tendency to assume the friendliness of others, an objective attitude rather than fear as the basis for choosing one's leadership, the ability to profit by negative criticism, the ability to be optimistic when others about you are depressed, the objective attitude in a crowd instead of the mob spirit, the feeling of self-possession in social situations, tolerance of other people's points of view, the ability to remain cool in the face of hate and injustice, wholesome reaction to failure due to frustration by others, capacity to inspire confidence, and keeping cool in face of social hysteria.

8. *Christian Courage*

Happy are they which are persecuted for righteousness' sake: for theirs is the kingdom of heaven. Happy are ye,

[14] *Ibid.*, pp. 75-83.

when men shall revile you, and persecute you, and shall say all manner of evil against you falsely, for my sake. Rejoice, and be exceeding glad: for great is your reward in heaven: for so persecuted they the prophets which were before you. —*Matthew 5:10-12.*

The prophets of the world, of whatever time or creed, have regularly met persecution and just as universally been happy in spite of it. We may be sure that Jesus was not preaching asceticism. He does not say a man who is persecuted for righteousness will be happy, because by that token he will know that he is righteous. It is obvious, that if this Beatitude is to be descriptive of wholesome personalities, we must find a natural basis for it in normal people. We do not have to look far to find numerous illustrations of those who rejoice even in suffering. The boy who risks his life for his beloved gets joy from that very risk. The football player, filled not only with a love of the game but with a loyalty for his college, rejoices in the injuries received while playing for the honor of his school. But highest of all, a mother, whose love for her child more closely approaches divinity than anything else on earth, will gladly sacrifice her life for that of her son. It should be clear, then, that being happy even when persecuted has much basis in normal human behavior, especially in parental love. It is clear that real courage is always necessary if one is to espouse an unpopular but just cause. The crowd generally opposes progress. This attitude in all probability is one of the easiest of all to teach children. It can be built on some of the strongest natural drives in human nature. The same natural impulses which have led to courage on the battlefield can be utilized in developing this attitude. Human nature responds to the challenge of courage. Vanity, rivalry, self-assertion, fighting, and exhibitionism are all forms of reaction to the same instinctive drive on which this attitude can be built. If one would teach a child a wholesome courage, let the motivation, then, be not fear or anger or selfishness, but love. Here is a boy of ten who is afraid of water and refuses to learn to swim. He is, however, very fond of his mother. When it was suggested to him that his ability to swim might some day save his mother's life, he gritted his teeth, overcame his fear of water, and soon learned to swim. This is courage stimulated by love.[15]

[15] *Ibid.*, pp. 83-88.

We may describe this last of the eight traits as being determined to serve men, whether they want to be served or not. One can see that it is closely tied up with dominating purpose and that, if one has a genuine purpose in the service of mankind, there will be many times when this eighth trait will be called to the test. It is the trait which through all the centuries has been most characteristic of the men who have been responsible for progress. There is nothing morbid or unhealthy about it. On the contrary, it is the very essence of courage and power. When we think of the many steps that must be taken in developing this trait in the growing child, here are a few of the preliminary attitudes: training in leadership, ability to endure pain without stopping one's work, being able to do one's best regardless of what the audience expects, acting because of the value of the activity itself and not for praise, willingness to perform minor and menial details in serving the group, willingness to take a chance alone in a situation of doubtful outcome, having a religion which is a stimulation to meet life courageously, getting one's satisfaction in achievement rather than in social approval, the determination to be worth more than you are paid, being dependable as a friend in need, healthy normal self-control, ability to see the best in an enemy, the courage to carry out one's purpose even in the face of poverty, the determination to achieve one's purpose even in the face of hate and injustice, and the determination to carry out the dictates of one's conscience no matter what the cost may be.

These last four traits: sensitiveness to the needs of others, the determination to give every man his chance at happiness and success, the tendency to endeavor to resolve the conflicts in human nature, and the determination to serve men whether they want to be served or not, all of these are the everyday normal type of behavior of parents toward their children. They can be taught to children as the characteristic forms of reaction to their social structure. This is the sort of love, then, which Jesus taught. Together with the four characteristics of Christian faith it constitutes the type of Christian personality which he challenged us to develop. In the succeeding chapters we shall see how each of these eight traits gradually grows to its consummation in the adult Christian personality.

III

The Personal Equation

Know thyself! This has been recognized as an important prerequisite of human happiness for a great many centuries. But only within the last two decades has it been possible. The science of mental measurements has made great progress during the last quarter century. And today, making full allowances for its inadequacies and need of further development, it is possible to measure with a reasonable degree of accuracy almost every important phase of human personality. This science has come of age so recently that its possibilities have hardly been realized, but there is evidence to believe that it will prove to be the greatest contribution to human happiness yet made by the scientific method.

A boy was brought to a psychological laboratory because he had been stealing. It was assumed by his parents that his case was psychiatric, inasmuch as the boy had grown up in a Christian home and under the constant guidance of a Christian church. In the laboratory the factors of his personality were measured. With the aid of the personality profile thus obtained, the problem was easily analyzed, the solution was obvious, and adjustment was made with remarkable quickness. How was this mysterious transformation brought about? Let us look at the profile. In the first place, the boy tested low in intelligence. His mother wanted him to be a doctor and had always severely criticized his low school marks. He also felt his intellectual inferiority. Secondly, he was short of stature, and also tested low in motor coördination. His father wanted him to be a football player, and the boy was taunted by his fellows for his lack of athletic prowess. However, he tested very high in music and was above average in art. No one had discovered this, so he had had no opportunity to get training or a sense of achievement in these fields in which lay his real abilities.

All his efforts had been made in fields in which he could not possibly compete successfully. The only thing in which he had found a sense of prowess had been in his daring to steal. Most of the other boys his age would not do that. When his vocational aims were revised, and his school curriculum changed to conform to his abilities, his moral problems disappeared like magic.

A girl, aged nine, and in the third grade, had not learned to read or write. She refused to pay attention to her teacher, and was constantly poking and kicking the other children in her room. Her parents were called to the school concerning her disciplinary problems nearly every week. Finally, she was brought to the laboratory. Her intelligence tested quite normal. But when the various factors which enter into reading ability were analyzed, the source of her difficulty was discovered and remedied. Her progress in reading became remarkable and swift. As soon as this was accomplished, her social difficulties disappeared.

A young man, college sophomore, came to college as an engineer. Only a few weeks were necessary for him to discover that his choice of a vocation had been a very unwise one. Where should he turn next? He came to the laboratory. He was found to be of modest ability in mechanical aptitude, but tested very low in mathematics. A good rote memory accounted for his apparent previous success in mathematics. But his art ability tested high, as did his aptitude for language and also his creative imagination. Analysis of his interests suggested advertising, especially on the artistic side. A shifting of his courses toward this end resulted in a good college adjustment, enthusiasm for his new vocational aim, and confidence in his ability to reach that aim.

A boy of five was finding kindergarten very distasteful, and expressed his feelings about it by unruly conduct which threatened to destroy the morale in the entire kindergarten. Tests revealed that his highest ability, in addition to activeness, strength, and coördination, was drawing. Opportunity was provided for him to draw, especially airplanes, which were his greatest enthusiasm. He soon realized his drawing superiority, and, in the unofficial capacity of assistant drawing instructor in this kindergarten, he lost his troublesome ways and entered with energy and enthusiasm into this new form of achievement.

I have not found a single instance in four years of using personality profiles in which a problem could be adequately solved until the testing was completed and a profile prepared. In almost every instance the preparation of such a profile has revealed to the parents or the individual himself some native assets of which he had been unaware, and which formed the basis for planning his activities much more intelligently. How is one to know what his abilities and aptitudes are unless they are measured? True, if one is at the genius level in music or art, it is likely to become obvious at an early age. But barring these exceptional cases, few people have any very accurate idea of their abilities and disabilities. No one who has ever used such a profile can doubt its value. It seems unlikely that the problems of personality can be satisfactorily solved without it. The application of this principle of the personal equation seems likely to become universally used in both school and church.

The Factors of Personality

What are the factors in the personal equation? Are there ten or a thousand? How well can they be measured? And having measured them, what is their significance in the problem of character development? It is obvious that all four of these questions must be answered tentatively. Many contributions to our knowledge of mental measurements are made every year. The profile used in our Union-Westminster project is already in its third edition, and it is certain to need still further revisions as the science of mental measurements progresses.

Into how many parts may a line be divided? Obviously the answer is that the number may range from two to infinity. But whether we use millionths of a millimeter, inches, or miles as units depends on the nature of the problem at hand.

If one is solving a problem in electron theory, the minutest measures are necessary. If one is planning a trip across the continent, miles are accurate enough. Into how many parts may personality be divided? The number should be based on the needs of the problem at hand, in this case the development of character. In actual experience we sometimes find the need for some divisions not included in our personality profile, but the effort has been made to construct the profile short enough to be practical and not confusing, and at the same time detailed enough to give a complete picture of the personality. The exact number of human traits is certainly not a closed book in psychology. A recent development in the field, which is referred to as factor analysis, may eventually result in a more scientifically determined grouping.[1] But until further research has been done the criteria of selection must be practical in their nature. An examination of Figure II will reveal that we have selected a four-fold division dealing with physical development, intellectual development, the special aptitudes, and character and personality traits.

There are those who will say, "This is all very nice for those who have access to the large laboratory and professional consultants, but what of the great majority of parents and teachers to whom no such advantages are available?" The fact is that there are simple and non-technical methods of measurement for all of the traits on the profile. That these methods are not as satisfactory as the more scientific ones, no one can deny. They are, however, far better than none at all. A complete discussion of methods of measurement is to be published in a companion volume to this one.[2] In it will be found methods for measuring all of the traits included on this personality profile. In each case some measures will be described which are simple enough to be used by those to whom laboratory equipment and professional assistance are not available. Also the more elaborate and tech-

[1] A thorough but very technical discussion of this method will be found in *Vectors of Mind* by L. L. Thurstone (University of Chicago Press, 1935).

[2] Ligon, E. M., *The Personal Equation*, to be published.

nical methods of the well-equipped laboratory will be included. This volume should bring the method of personality measurement within the reach of everyone.

Physical Development

Does a child's height or weight, or motor coördination, or sensory efficiency have anything to do with the development of his character and personality? The place of athletic achievement in social approval, the importance of good vision and hearing in school success, the emphasis placed on height and weight along with other factors of physical attractiveness in the minds of adolescents—these are only a few illustrations demonstrating the significance of physical development in the problem of adjustment.

Physical development, on the profile, is subdivided into four parts. The first one deals with growth. Height, vital capacity and weight are the traits included under it. Height in itself is largely a function of inheritance. There is not much we can do about it except to adjust to whatever height we have. However, this is more easily said than done. There is hardly a condition of height in which both boys and girls do not experience some adjustment problems. Among the more obvious of these are the difficulties of adjustment experienced by tall girls and short boys. Especially during adolescence is this an important problem. Each feels that he or she is much handicapped in the game of life, especially in the race for popularity. The short boy or man often tries to compensate by being pugnacious. Anger is found to be much more often a dominant characteristic of short men than of tall ones. Girls who are over-tall often stoop, are sensitive, self-conscious and ill at ease. They bemoan the fact that they are not short and "cute". Actually, of course, there is no point in the scale of height which does not have its advantages. Many a fine tall girl has learned to be proud of her stature, and many a short boy finds that life provides as great opportunities for achievement as if he could add cubits to his height.

PERSONALITY PROFILE

NAME JAMES W— NO. X 125

DATE OF BIRTH 7 5 25 (MONTH DAY YEAR) SCHOOL GRADE 9 SEX MALE

AGE IN YEARS 15 (ON LAST BIRTHDAY) DEPARTMENT SENIOR DATE OF TEST 9 10 40 (MONTH DAY YEAR)

AGE IN MONTHS 182 NUMBER OF TIMES TESTED 2 ND

THE TOTAL PERSONALITY

PHYSICAL DEVELOPMENT				INTELLECTUAL DEVELOPMENT						SPECIAL APTITUDES				PERSONALITY	
Physically unusually well developed	Very high athletic ability	Excellent visual acuity	Excellent auditory acuity	Excellent use of language	Excellent rote memory	Unusual range of information	Unusual ability for solving practical problems	Very well adjusted learning attitudes	Very high general intelligence	Unusually fine imagination	Very highly gifted in artistic ability	Very highly gifted in musical ability	Unusually high mechanical aptitude	Splendid emotional maturity	Socially unusually well adjusted
Good physical development	Good athletic ability	Good vision	Good hearing	Above aver. in use of language	Good rote memory	Good Range of information	Solves practical problems efficiently	Good learning attitudes	Above average intelligence	Good imagination	Good artistic ability	Above average musical ability	Good mechanical aptitude	Emotionally well adjusted	Good social adjustment
Slightly deficient physical development	Below average in athletic ability	Poor vision	Poor hearing	Below aver. in use of language	Below aver. in rote memory	Limited Range of Information	Has difficulty in solving practical problems	Some poor attitudes toward learning	Slightly below aver. in intelligence	Below average in constructive imagination	Below average in artistic ability	Below average in musical ability	Below average in mechanical aptitude	Emotional adjustment not entirely satisfactory	Social adjustment not entirely satisfactory
Physically very poorly developed	Very awkward and unathletic	Very poor vision or blindness	Very poor hearing or deafness	Very deficient in speech and use of language	Very deficient in rote memory	Very Poor Range of information	Very little ability to solve practical problems	Very badly adjusted toward learning	Marked deficiency in general intelligence	Very poor or distorted imagination	Very little artistic ability	Very little musical ability	Very little mechanical aptitude	Emotionally immature and maladjusted	Very poor social adjustment shut-in personality
1,2,3,7,12,13	4-6	8,9	10,11	14,15,16,17	20	22	21,23	24-27	28,29	30,31	32-35	36-39	40-43	44-51	52-59

ANALYSIS OF PERSONALITY

I PHYSICAL DEVELOPMENT

PHYSICAL GROWTH			BODILY COORDINATION			APPETITES	SENSORY EFFICIENCY						
Very tall for age	Very high vital Capacity or stamina	Excellent proportion weight to height	Excellent physical coördination	Very much right handed	Unusually active and vigorous	Unusually strong healthy physical appetites	Unusually high visual acuity	Unusual ability for visual perception	Excellent auditory acuity	Unusually good auditory perception	Not at all sensitive to pain or touch	Not at all sensitive to warmth or cold	100 – 93 – 84
Above average in height	Good vital capacity	A little heavy or light	Good physical coördination	Right handed	Above average in activeness	Good normal physical appetites	Fair visual acuity	Normal visual perception	Fair hearing	Normal auditory perception	Not very sensitive to pain or touch	Not very sensitive to warmth or cold	70 – 50
Below average in height	Somewhat deficient in stamina	Definitely over or under weight	Below aver. in physical coördination	Left handed	Tendency to be somewhat inactive	Tendency for physical appetites to be weak	Deficient in visual acuity	Has some difficulty in visual recognition	Poor hearing	Has difficulties in recognizing sounds	Sensitive to pain or touch	Sensitive to warmth or cold	30 – 16
[illegible]	[illegible]	[illegible]	[illegible]	Very much [illegible]	Very low [illegible]	Very weak physical appetites	Very deficient in visual acuity or blindness	Very low ability in visual interpretation	Very poor hearing or deafness	Very deficient in interpreting sounds	Very sensitive to pain or touch	Very sensitive to warmth or cold	7 – 0

13

FIGURE II (reduced to one-half of the original size of chart)

CAPACITY FOR LEARNING										LEARNING ATTITUDES				INTELLIGENCE		
ability	articulation	fine vocabulary	reading and spelling ability	Advanced in school more than one year	In highest quarter of school grade	Excellent rote memory	Unusual ability for solving practical problems	Unusual range of information	Very high mathematics proficiency	Unusual ability to concentrate	Very keen interest in school work	Very efficient study habits	Very strong healthy curiosity	Very high I.Q. on language tests	Very high I.Q. on performance tests	100 / 93
Language ability satisfactory	Good articulation	Good vocabulary	Above aver. in reading and spelling	Advanced in school one year	In second quarter of school grade	Good rote memory	Solves practical problems satisfactorily	Good range of information	Mathematics ability satisfactory	Concentrates fairly well	Well adjusted to school work	Satisfactory study habits	Curiosity above average	Above aver. I.Q. on language tests	Above aver. I.Q. on performance tests	84 / 70
Not very good language ability	Slight stuttering or stammering	Vocabulary below average	Has difficulty in reading and spelling	Retarded in school one year	In third quarter of school grade	Rote memory below average	Has difficulty with practical problems	Limited Range of Information	Has some difficulty with mathematics	Has difficulty in concentrating on work	Rather indifferent or antagonistic to school	Inefficient study habits	Curiosity below average	Below aver. I.Q. on language tests	Below aver. I.Q. on performance tests	50 / 30
Very poor language ability	Very poor ability to speak distinctly	Very deficient vocabulary	Marked deficiency in reading + spelling	Retarded in school more than one year	In lowest quarter of school grade	Very poor rote memory	Has great difficulty with practical problems	Very Poor Range of information	Has great difficulty with mathematics	Very distractible almost impossible to concentrate	Very badly adjusted to school work	Very bad study habits	Almost complete lack of curiosity	Very low I.Q. on language tests	Very low I.Q. on performance tests	16 / 7 / 0
14	15	16	17	18	19	20	21	22	23	24	25	26	27	28	29	

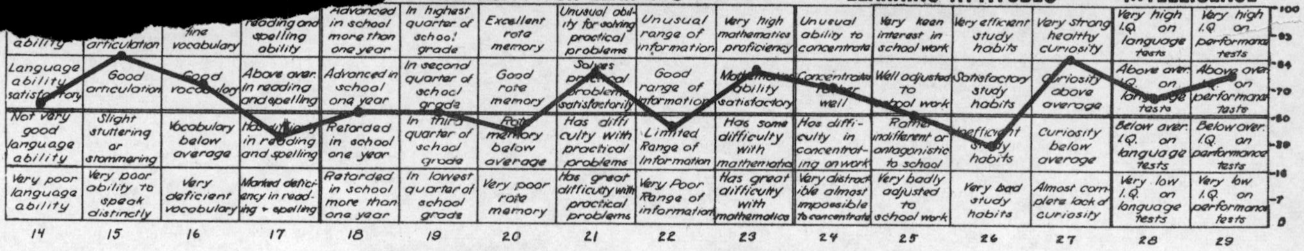

III SPECIAL APTITUDES

IMAGINATION		ARTISTIC ABILITY				MUSICAL ABILITY				MECHANICAL ABILITY				
Strong Vivid imagination creative	Very high constructive imagination	Unusual ability for perception of forms	Unusual ability for discrimination of colors	Unusually high drawing ability	Very high capacity for appreciation of art	Very keen tonal discrimination	Excellent tonal memory	Very fine sense of rhythm	Unusual musical performance	Unusually high mechanical imagination	Unusually high mechanical information	Unusually high mechanical performance	Unusually high mechanical analysis	100 / 93
Vivid but somewhat unrealistic imagination	Good constructive imagination	Good form perception	Good color perception	Good drawing ability	Above aver capacity for appreciation of art	Good tonal discrimination	Good tonal memory	Good sense of rhythm	Above aver musical perform	Good mechanical imagination	Good mechanical information	Good mechanical performance	Good mechanical analysis	84 / 70
Excessive day dreaming	Poor imagination	Below aver. in form perception	Color weakness	Below aver. in drawing ability	No very much aptitude for art appreciation	Little tonal discrimination	tonal memory below average	Inefficient sense of rhythm	Below aver success with musical perform.	Below average in mechanical imagination	Below average in mechanical information	Below average in mechanical performance	Below average in mechanical analysis	50 / 30
Strong tendency to abnormal fantasy	Little or no imagination	Very poor in form perception	Marked color blindness	Very poor drawing ability	Very little or no aptitude for appreciation of art	Very little tonal discrimination	Very poor tonal memory	Very bad sense of rhythm	Very little success with musical perform.	Very little mechanical imagination	Very little mechanical information	Very little mechanical performance	Very little mechanical analysis	16 / 7 / 0
30	31	32	33	34	35	36	37	38	39	[illegible]	41	42	43	

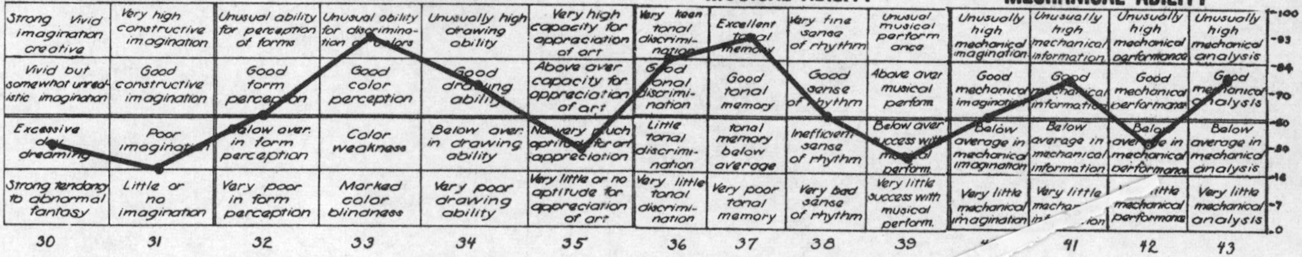

IV CHARACTER AND PERSONALITY TRAITS

EMOTIONAL MATURITY								SOCIAL ADJUSTMENT								
Very high degree of ambition	Very high degree of social and moral maturity	Mature and emotionally stable	Has very few fears cool in face of danger	Very high degree of initiative and aggressiveness	Has wide variety of hobbies + play interests	Very dependable	Very high degree of purposiveness in [illegible]	Very [illegible] with others	Very popular with others	Very high degree of social vision	Wholesome coöperative reaction to authority	Unusually even tempered and good natured	Very marked capacity for leadership	Very high degree of social selfconfidence	Highly developed philosophy of life for age	100 / 93
Above average in ambition	Above aver. in social and moral maturity	Very enthusiastic	Not often afraid faces danger with courage	Some initiative and aggressiveness	Has several hobbies and play interests	Reasonably dependable	[illegible] purpose	Has many friends	Has many friends	Above ave. in social vision	Some tendency to argue	Does not lose temper often	Occasionally acts as a leader	Above ave. in social selfconfidence	Rational outlook on life	84 / 70
Tendency to indifference	Below aver. in social and moral maturity	Over emotional	Has several fears and tries to avoid difficult situations	A little too submissive	Rather few hobbies [illegible]	[illegible]ble	No very definite purpose in activity	Makes relatively few friends	Makes relatively few friends	Below ave in social vision	Tendency to be obstinate	Loses temper rather frequently	Tendency to shyness and self-consciousness	Below ave. in social selfconfidence	Somewhat irrational attitude toward life	50 / 30
Complete surrender + lack of initiative	Socially and morally very immature or perverted	Emotional instability	Unusually fearful becomes frantic in the face of danger	Ver[illegible]	[illegible]	[illegible] at all dependable	Very marked lack of purposiveness	Very unpopular same sex	Very unpopular opposite sex	Total lack of social vision	Very negativistic	Constantly losing temper very irritable	Very shy and submissive	Total lack of social selfconfidence	Total lack of philosophy of life	16 / 7 / 0
44	45	46	[illegible]	[illegible]	[illegible]	50	51	52	53	54	55	56	57	58	59	

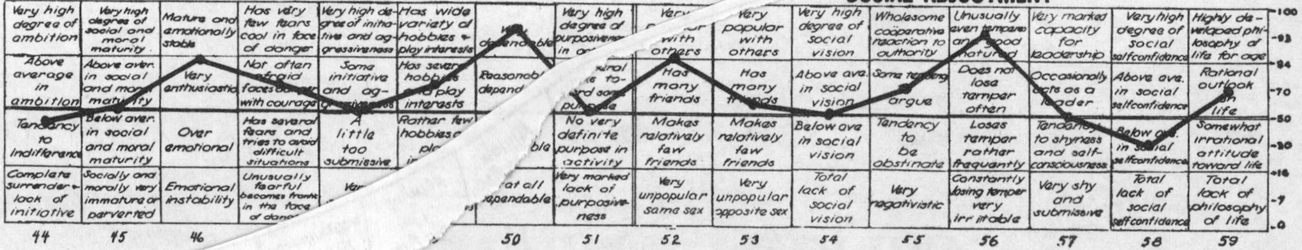

Vital capacity, which means stamina or endurance, becomes an important factor in many adjustment problems. To what extent it is a function of inheritance cannot be said with certainty. It is probable, however, that the innate factor is large. What athletic sports one can choose, or what tests of endurance he may undertake, are decided in part by the measurement of this trait. It is not uncommon to find children who, because of purely emotional factors, fatigue easily, whereas their endowment in this trait shows that they could undergo much more severe strain. Other children will go on until they drop, driven by a nervous energy, when their constitutional stamina indicates that this is too much to expect of them. Having strong physical endurance is not an indispensable quality of strong personality, but one's capacity for it needs to be accurately ascertained in choosing his activities.

Weight is usually more a function of one's endocrine glands than a result of one's diet. Dieting can sometimes become the source of serious loss of health. Usually, it can be controlled within reason by intelligent care and exercise, but when it cannot, the fact remains that social success is quite as possible for those above average in weight as for those below. It is certain that girls and for that matter boys will adjust best and happiest by accepting with enthusiasm their native endowment in this as well as in other traits. High school and college girls need to learn that the young men with whom they can be happiest in life will prefer health and cheerfulness to slimness. This same philosophy, of course, goes with the other variations of weight. Is it obvious then that even such simple factors as weight and height play vital rôles in the problem of adjustment?

The cruelties which children inflict upon one another are nowhere so apparent, during some age levels, as in relation to coördination. During the junior and senior high school periods, boys usually place the highest evaluation on athletic ability. The boy who cannot hit a ball or catch a pass has his troubles in winning the respect of his fellows. The girl who does not dance well will have her sad moments when the world looks very dark. The fact is that this coördination is largely a function of inheritance. It can be measured early in life and is an important part of the personal equation. Fathers who begin to impress upon their four- and five-year-old sons the importance of football letters will do well to discover first whether their boys have any chance of achieving this goal. A basic principle for solving the problem of adjustment is to discover by measurement what are the greatest capacities in the child's inheritance, and then give him visions of achievement in the fields which utilize these abilities. Every child has some abilities in which his endowment is higher than in others. Most children have outstanding endowment in at least one thing. There are forms of competition for every type of inherited superiority. To guide the child along this line is to give him a much greater chance of happiness. The boy or girl who has athletic ability will gain and should gain great pleasure and profit from achievement of this sort. But it is not necessary or even desirable for the whole population to become athletes. Those whose endowment is modest in this regard should look elsewhere for achievement.

Some of the most interesting problems in psychology today center around the question of handedness. How handedness originates is still a problem for research. Its significance in adjustment is greater than is commonly supposed. Speech, reading, writing, spelling, athletic performance and probably other factors are strongly influenced by handedness. It is not easy to measure. The ratio of superiority of the preferred hand varies from activity to activity. The same individual may test right-handed in some activities and left-handed in others. Very few test entirely either one way or the other. In our own laboratory a number of different activities are measured in which handedness appears, and some of the findings are of great interest. Former tendencies of parents and teachers to try to teach the left-handed child to be right-handed have about disappeared. Nevertheless it often happens that children show greater ability with the non-preferred hand than with the preferred hand.

It is common to associate appetite with food, or else to use the word figuratively to apply to every persistent wish. The fact is, there are six important physical appetites: hunger, thirst, sex, elimination, comfort, and rest. While, of course, it is difficult to measure them quantitatively, it is possible through the medium of parent questionnaires to estimate the relative strength of each of them. The important part played in personality by these physical appetites is obvious. What men do of both good and evil for food and drink is an item of common knowledge. The part played in civilization by sex is so great as to need no enlargement here. Parents who have worried about their children's difficulties with bowel control and bed wetting will not doubt their importance in development. Inferiority feelings and temper tantrums, as well as food restrictions, influence and are influenced by the efficiency of elimination. Few of us deliberately seek pain, and most of us at times are tempted from the path of duty because of our desire for comfort. As for rest, not a few converts have been moved most by the promises, "Come unto me . . . and I will give you rest." [3] Some people show themselves to be quite intemperate in this appetite. The problem of appetites is not by any means entirely a moral one. Native appetites differ in strength among individuals quite as much as any other functions of the personality. It requires more self-control for one person to master the appetites than for another. Furthermore, they must be thought of as driving forces which constitute important resources in one's potential personality power. All of that power needs to be conserved for the total personality. However admirable temperance may be in any of these appetites, this power is not conserved by mere self-denial. This is simply accepting loss without compensation.

"I know what I see with my own eyes." "Seeing is believing." It is probable that most people consider sight their most valuable and trustworthy possession. Whether this is wise or not is open to debate. Many people have lived splendid lives without it. But the fact remains that few parts of

[3] Matthew 11:28.

the human body play as important rôles in adjustment as the eyes do. Most of the functions performed by the eyes are known to everybody. But there are factors in visual efficiency which require technical methods to measure, and which have effects in adjustment so indirect as to be detected only after professional examination. Reading and spelling difficulties often find their beginnings in poor vision. Likewise, outstanding performances in these fields are due in part to outstanding endowment in visual acuity. Social adjustment is at times greatly handicapped by poor eyesight. Many emotional maladjustments find their origins in visual difficulties. It is not enough simply to measure visual acuity and the common refractory errors, but the capacity for visual perception, which includes the ability to visualize in one's imagination, is also significant.

The effective functioning of the ears may be even more important than that of the eyes. Language is the most important of man's social institutions. A great majority of his language experiences are oral. When his capacity for such experiences is lowered or even eliminated, serious adjustment difficulties may result. These difficulties are not confined simply to the ability to understand what is said. They range from reading and spelling difficulties to general school failure, from suspicion of one's fellows to the deepest sort of depression and introversion. In the case of those problems which also involve sight as well as hearing, it is important to know which one is the dominant factor. Poor spelling ability which results from difficulties in hearing differs from that involving poor vision. Furthermore, finely sensitive ears constitute a basic requirement for the appreciation of music, and are probably fundamental in the production and appreciation of beauty in the quality and style of speech itself. On the personality side, it is difficult for those who do not hear to avoid developing delusions of reference; that is, imagining that people are talking about them. Yet it is also true that wholesome personality can be developed whatever the sensory endowment.

Do you have a sixth sense? Actually there are more than

a score of sense fields which contribute to human experience. Each of these sense fields plays its own rôle and no one dares say that it is not an important one. In the last two columns of the profile, in the section devoted to sensory efficiency, are grouped all these other senses. Whether taste, smell, sense of balance, touch, cold, warmth, pain, and the various internal senses are unusually acute or dull is of significance in adjustment problems of many varieties. Some of them can be measured with considerable accuracy. The others can only be approximated by subjective estimates. It makes quite a difference, for instance, whether excessive sensitivity to pain is due to an organic condition of the sense organs, or whether it is entirely an emotional reaction. The latter is far more common, but the former occurs frequently enough for a recognition of it to be necessary. High sensitivity carries the possibility for a rich and varied experience denied those not thus gifted, and at the same time it presents problems of adjustment which require skill and patience in solving. To recognize all the senses as a portion of the child's endowment and to capitalize their advantages for fine personality is a challenge worthy of the best efforts of any parent or teacher.

Intellectual Development

At the present period in the world's history few things are as much desired by parents for their children as a high I.Q. Parents swear by it, especially if their children test high in it. However, if the test results are less favorable—well, they never did believe in intelligence tests anyway. The fact is that the I.Q. represents only one of a number of mental abilities. Furthermore, having an unusually high I.Q. often produces more problems of adjustment than if one is more modestly endowed. The time has come for more intelligence to be applied by parents and teachers, as well as by psychologists, to the use and evaluation of the intelligence quotient. We shall be better prepared to do this if we get a fairly clear picture of the whole intellectual development of the child. The second section of the profile is devoted to this development in all its various aspects.

In the first place, the use of language is a vitally important factor in adjustment. One who is adept in it can often compensate for a considerable lack in intelligence itself. Excellence in public speaking and in literary style were once much more in popular favor than they are today. Debating and oratorical societies are far less conspicuous than they were a few decades ago. Contests involving writing of compositions go begging for contestants. But the fact remains that language is still the only efficient means of social integration. The man who can express himself clearly and forcefully in speech or writing has an asset of real value. That the use of language is a special aptitude can hardly be doubted. Training can give to any person of average intelligence the capacity for expressing himself clearly, but only to those who are highly endowed in this special aptitude can the use of language become a real art. An attractive style in writing is as much dependent upon native ability as is outstanding excellence in athletics.

Like most of the special aptitudes this language ability is not a unit, but consists of several smaller contributing traits. One of these is oral speech. It ranges all the way from bad stuttering to the fine diction of our best speakers, when it becomes a treasure to be highly valued. Good public speakers can lack style and even high intelligence and still carry conviction to their audiences. Poor speech is a handicap which has reduced the efficiency of many a man or woman who had much to give to society. Most stuttering can be cured, and training will improve the effective quality of any person's voice.

A word is the symbol of an idea. The extent of a man's vocabulary is a good index to the breadth and accuracy of his ideas. Vocabulary tests are amazingly accurate and constitute one of the most reliable criteria for measuring language ability. Word studies are as valuable for increasing clear thinking as in acquiring a wider vocabulary.

The capacity for effective fast reading is rapidly becoming one of the most indispensable abilities to possess. A considerable number of college and high school students fail in some of their courses every year, not because of low intelligence or poor preparation, but because of their inability to read efficiently. Reading habits are subject to coaching. Most slow reading can be improved with training with an improvement of from fifty to two hundred percent in speed and retention. One of the most interesting phases of the measurement program in the Union-Westminster Character Research Project has been the testing work done with slow readers. The results in many cases have been very striking. The effect of increased reading efficiency on the whole personality of these children is apparent to those who know them. It is not surprising that disciplinary problems and feelings of inferiority accompany a deficiency in this indispensable ability of our modern life. Ability to read is vitally important to character development.

The second major aspect of intellectual development is the capacity for learning. This again is not a simple ability, nor is it synonymous with intelligence, although intelligence is perhaps the most important factor running through it. Rote memory is of genuine value for school success. Of all the learning capacities it is the least intimately related to intelligence. Some feeble-minded children have remarkable memories. A few of them are famous for their feats of memory. On the other hand, some very famous scholars have been characterized by a marked lack of ability to remember. Not infrequently a good rote memory is an actual handicap to higher learning, especially in a subject like mathematics. The reason is that the child is strongly tempted to substitute memory for understanding in the earlier years, and thus gets into difficulty when the more abstract phases of the subject are reached. Rote memory is nevertheless an asset when properly used, and is of special value when abstract intelligence does not test high.

School progress and class standing are measures of the child's actual ability to adjust to his educational environment. But every educationalist knows how many problems arise in regard to them. Retardation in school may often give rise to problems of social adjustment far more important than the mere question of class performance. Skipping grades is likely to produce much the same social difficulties. An important principle to observe in questions of this sort is that the child should be able to make an adequate social adjustment to the group with which he works in school. A child who is in advance of his age both physically and intellectually may be advanced a grade without difficulty. But a child who thus enters a group of children who are much larger physically than himself may find the going more difficult. Then, too, the question of marks is not as mechanical as commonly supposed. Some children are inspired to greater efforts by high or low marks. Others are depressed and discouraged if their marks are in the lower ranks of the class. Dividing classes into faster and slower groups has its disadvantages, because of this problem, as well as its advantages in recognizing individual differences of performance. Aptitudes for science and mathematics are in part special abilities which fit some individuals for good work in those fields, and the lack of them predestines others to failure in the same work. When it is remembered that a sense of achievement plays one of the most important rôles in character development, it is easy to see why such factors as these are quite as important in character education as in the child's more formal learning.

Then, there are the learning habits and attitudes. Interest in school work is both a cause and a result of success there. Nothing in human nature is more pleasant and stimulating than a sense of achievement. If the child is successful in his early school years, he likes it, and this helps him to further success. But often the reverse cycle sets in, and a vicious one it is. When a child shows an intense dislike for school and is subject to disciplinary problems there, the place to look for the answer is in his school success. His ability to concentrate should be measured in the things he likes to do, not in the things he dislikes. If he works for hours with model airplanes and cannot stick to algebra for five minutes, the difficulty is not in his ability to concentrate, but in his lack of success in algebra. Good study habits are also subject to training. Extensive research has been done in this field by educational psychologists during the last quarter of a century, and there are many methods of greater economy and efficiency in studying which can be taught.

Curiosity is probably largely an innate trait. The individual differences in this trait are revealed by the behavior of both children and adults in their response to it. Some seem entirely content with their immediate environment and condition. Others seem to possess an insatiable appetite for travel and learning. That a high endowment in curiosity is a source of personality power goes without saying.

Last, but of course not least, is intelligence itself. It is beside the point here to enter the many technical problems which interest the professional psychologist concerning it. Let us define it as the fundamental capacity to succeed in school and vocation, quite apart from the special aptitudes. The I.Q., Intelligence Quotient, is its most common measure. Average intelligence is 100 I.Q. by definition. The average intelligence for students in our major colleges is between 120 and 125. Not many large changes occur in the I.Q. from year to year. When children are tested in the pre-school years, later tests sometimes do differ widely from the earlier results obtained. This probably does not mean that the I.Q. has actually changed, but rather that pre-school tests are not as reliable as tests appropriate to the later age levels. This is, however, a debated question in psychology at the present time, which must be left for final judgment when the evidence is clearer. On the profile, a distinction is made between language tests and performance tests. Professional psychologists will recognize this distinction at once. For the layman, it is sufficient to think of the former as dealing with abstract intelligence and the latter with practical intelligence. This distinction is probably not entirely valid, but it will do for practical purposes. The place of intelligence in any sort of education, character or otherwise, can hardly be questioned. It is remarkable that we have neglected measuring it for so many years.

The Special Aptitudes

The third section of the profile deals with the special aptitudes. Four of them are described there: imagination, artistic ability, musical aptitude, and mechanical ability. Technically speaking, a special aptitude is defined as an innate ability which shows individual differences and does not depend directly on any other ability. Thus the common belief that artistic and musical ability are found more often together than either of them with mechanical ability is not correct. Imagination, as it expresses itself in behavior, is unquestionably limited by intelligence, but is certainly not synonymous with it. There is no basic reason why athletic ability, language ability, rote memory, number ability, curiosity and leadership capacity should not be spoken of as special aptitudes. Placing them in different sections of the profile was done for practical, not for theoretical reasons. All of them need to be considered in dealing intelligently with the individual.

Imagination is especially important in connection with developing the trait of vision. Like all of the other abilities it differs widely from individual to individual. However, even in its most limited endowments, it is not inconsiderable. Everyone has some imagination. Whether it becomes creative or fantastic is a matter of experience. Whether the adult retreats from a dull reality into a world of pleasant daydreams, or utilizes this aptitude in planning new achievements in reality, is also a matter of habit. In common vocational guidance procedure, imagination is seldom thought of as one of the more important aptitudes, but in character education there are few which are more so. A large portion of one's philosophy of life is a function of this aptitude. It may not seem necessary to use it to distinguish the difference between right and wrong. But if one's ethics are to consist of convictions about which he is enthusiastic and determined, they must be the outgrowth of a real comprehension of their importance in society. This is impossible without imagination. The great reformers and prophets of all times have been men of vision, and their greatness has been due in no small measure to their high native endowment in imagination.

Artistic ability is very much a special aptitude. If our own tests are characteristic of society as a whole, artistic ability appears in considerable amounts more often than does musical ability. This is all the more interesting, when we think that so little emphasis has been put on it in our American educational system. It seems probable that almost every child desires to create something beautiful in some medium. Painting, drawing, modelling, cutting out colored paper with scissors, wood carving and so on are, in one form or another, of interest to every child. It seems probable that the child ought to be given a great deal of freedom in choosing his own medium and some guidance in using it. However, since we distinguish in our tests between sensitivity to proportion and balance, color sensitivity, and drawing ability, we can often see which of these mediums best fit the child's natural bent. Some forms of expression require mechanical ability also, and even good physical coördination. Whether the child has artistic ability in large or small amounts, he ought to be given ample opportunity for developing it, and training where such training is warranted.

Musical ability, in large or small endowments, plays an important part in the life of many children. Girls are often forced to learn to play the piano simply because girls ought to do such things. Boys often refuse to do so because they think of it as being a girl's activity. There is no justification for this in nature at all. Girls do not seem to excel boys in musical ability. There are many girls who have so little of it that it is sheer cruelty to force upon them the drudgery of doing something they cannot do well, while many boys would find immense satisfaction and a splendid form of achievement in this field because of their large native endowment. Fortunately this feeling against music on the part of boys is rapidly disappearing, and many of those who can are entering the field with enthusiasm. On the basis of the four different phases of musical ability listed on the profile, a great deal can be done to guide the child into the right medium of expression.

Mechanical ability, from the point of view of vocational guidance, is the most important of the special aptitudes. It enters into more different forms of vocation than any other. In our modern machine age it is especially emphasized. The boy with marked mechanical ability is pretty certain to find employment all his life. The boy without it will by the same token find many fields closed to him. Contrary to popular opinion, there is little or no evidence that boys have it in any greater abundance than girls. Only social custom has suggested that this might be so. In sewing and cooking, mechanical ability is just as important as in fixing the car and mending the radio. In all of our activity programs in character education, rôles for mechanical ability are numerous.

One of the basic principles in this program of character education is expressed in the attempt to construct curricular projects in which each child plays a rôle which fits his abilities. The value of this in teaching social coöperation is obvious. The necessity to measure the abilities of our children is clearly a prerequisite to such programs.

Character and Personality Traits

Under this heading Hildreth[4] lists 514 different tests which have been constructed to measure some aspects of character and personality. To include all of the traits measured by these tests, even when the duplicates are eliminated, is manifestly an impossibility. The fourth section of the profile, which is devoted to this aspect of the personal equa-

[4] Hildreth, G. H., *A Bibliography of Mental Tests and Rating Scales*, Second Edition, pp. 190-223 (The Psychological Corporation, New York, 1939).

tion, is limited to sixteen traits. This division has been somewhat arbitrary and entirely based on practical needs. It is as widely different from the first revision of the profile as that one was from the original form. The traits chosen conform rather loosely to the eight traits chosen as goals for our character education program. Some of them have been included because of the availability of excellent measuring scales. Others are added because dealing with the practical problems of adjustment which have arisen in the years of this project has shown that they are important ones in personality development. Dependability is a good example of this. It is a rather difficult trait to define or to measure. Yet, because it plays such an important part in personality development during adolescence, it seemed impossible to omit it. The first eight traits are included under the heading, Emotional Maturity, and the second eight under the heading, Social Adjustment. These correspond somewhat loosely with the traits of Experimental Faith and those of Fatherly Love. A table (p. 54) showing the relation between these sixteen traits and the eight traits which form our character education goals will make this relationship clearer.

Two of the eight traits have corresponding profile traits in other sections of the profile. Profile traits 30 and 31 are intimately related to Vision, and traits 25, 26, and 27 are important in the measurement of Love of Righteousness and Truth. This relationship is of great importance in using the profile to the best advantage in our character education program. In the questionnaires, included at the end of each chapter on the developmental stages, are methods for measuring each of the eight traits. The study of these questionnaires will show clearly what the status of the child is at the time and what the possibilities of development are.

Emotional maturity can be thought of as the attainment of stability in adult behavior as compared with the complete emotional instability of infancy and early childhood. Thus, the infant acts entirely on the impulse of the moment. The adult considers the future consequences of a situation in judging its significance. He can as a result face

CHARACTER AND PERSONALITY TRAITS

EXPERIMENTAL FAITH—EMOTIONAL MATURITY	FATHERLY LOVE—SOCIAL ADJUSTMENT
I. Vision	V. Sensitive to Needs of Others
44 Vision	52 Friends of same sex 53 Friends of opposite sex
II. Love of Righteousness and Truth	VI. Forgiveness and Mercy
45 Moral maturity	54 Social vision, sportsmanship
III. Faith in the Friendliness of the Universe	VII. Magnanimity
46 Self-reliance, fear 47 Inferiority feelings 48 Emotional stability	55 Reaction to authority 56 Anger
IV. Dominating Purpose	VIII. Christian Courage
49 Hobbies and play interests 50 Dependability 51 Purposiveness	57 Leadership 58 Social self-confidence 59 Philosophy of life

Showing the relationship between the eight traits of Christian personality and the traits of character and personality used on the Personality Profile.

FIGURE III

with courage a situation from which the child would flee. Then again, the child reacts with emotional violence. He cries as lustily over a slight irritation as over a more important calamity. The adult learns to react with emotions which are in some proportion to the seriousness of the situation. It is obvious, however, that some people never outgrow the tendency to overestimate the importance of the present, nor to control their emotional outbursts in due proportion.

The eight traits subsumed under this heading, emotional maturity, are for the most part self-explanatory for our purposes here. Methods for measuring them must be left to the companion volume, *The Personal Equation.* Vision is to be understood as the habit of mind fully described as the first of the eight traits. In view of what has been said in the last paragraph, it is easy to see how important this trait is in the development of emotional maturity. Seeing things in their wider perspective is best attained by learning this trait of vision.

Moral maturity is not easy to describe. It does not refer entirely to ethical factors. It, too, is closely related to emotional impulsiveness. The psychopathic personality steals, lies, commits sex crimes, and so on, simply because he has never learned the self-discipline which makes the inhibition of some impulses desirable. His motto is like that of the infant, "I want what I want when I want it." He never learns the moral principles which prohibit the thoughtless satisfaction of each appetite as it appears. When the appetites are integrated into a larger purpose, then they are governed accordingly. This is moral maturity. The college student who cannot inhibit the desire to go to the theatre even in view of his vocational ambitions is to that extent immature. The inability to study for an examination until the day or so before it takes place is a similar example. A little thought will show that such behavior is much more a matter of emotional integration and maturity than of ethical concepts.

Self-reliance may well be the chief contribution of Americanism to its youth. Those who have travelled in Europe are impressed with the greater degree of self-reliance displayed by American boys and girls over that of European youth. Americans of thirteen undertake expeditions alone which would not be thought possible by the average European youth of seventeen. This trait is closely related to fear. The infant is not intelligent in his fears. But maturity gives greater judgment in the evaluation of what things are worthy of fear. Fear is not synonymous with caution. Caution may be thought of as fear grown up. The intelligent foresight of caution is a far different thing from the disintegrative nature of fear. Inferiority probably does not play as important a rôle in human society as Adler thought it did, but no one will deny that it does play an important one. A sense of inferiority is due as much or more to ignorance of one's abilities and consequent fear of failure as to real inferiority. Measurements which give a fairly accurate estimate of just what one's endowments are do much to eliminate this fear. The many forms in which the inferiority complex expresses itself, such as conceit, undue sensitiveness, pugnacity and so on, show how valuable to human happiness the elimination of inferiority feelings would be. Emotional stability is not mutually exclusive of all these others. It refers specifically to one's capacity for continuing on an even emotional keel. The individual who is up today and down tomorrow is emotionally unstable. Nervous breakdowns are, fundamentally, forms of emotional instability. The indifferent, completely shiftless individual demonstrates an entirely different form. There are different inherited emotional natures. The rather calm, phlegmatic type, when stable, is quite as desirable as the enthusiastic type. The difference is a function of inheritance and not of maturity.

Purposiveness is at the very center of personality integration. Hobbies and play interests have an important rôle in its development, especially at the early ages. During a large part of childhood, it is probable that one's play life is a more important part of his growth than his formal education. In the training of abilities, as well as in social integration, play is the chief source of development. Dependability may seem to some a very much more ethical trait in its nature. Experience with young people of high school and college age shows that it is not only rare, but is one of the most important of all traits for one's future success and happiness. Numerous lacks in native endowment can be compensated for by a thorough grounding in this personality habit. It is related to emotional maturity, for lapses in dependability are seldom intentional. They are usually explained as forgetfulness. But this is largely a matter of the emotional evaluation of things. One does not forget the important things. When trivial things interfere, they are simply being over-evaluated.

Social adjustment is probably quite as emotional in its nature as the traits we have just described. But the distinction is a valid one from a practical point of view, whatever its theoretical fallacies. The ability to live together is a learned ability and a necessary one. We do inherit social tendencies and capacities, but the art of using them is acquired with difficulty. Only a few of the more important social traits are included in the profile. The art of friendship is one of man's most valued assets. When boys and girls fail to make friends either among their own or the opposite sex, they need help badly. This type of social adjustment is entirely necessary for wholesome personality, and however difficult it may be to any child, it must be learned. Often it is learned only by way of much suffering and persecution, but learned it must be. Having friends of the opposite sex is as important to personality development as any other social trait in adolescence. If a young man or woman says that he or she does not care anything about the other sex, the thing one can be sure of is that he or she has not found the secret of this type of social success. It can be learned and successfully achieved by any young man or woman, and needs to be if life is to be lived at its best.

A sense of fair play or sportsmanship is a general habit in life. Our athletic departments would have us believe that it is best and most certainly acquired by participation in athletic sports. Whether this is true or not may well be questioned. Certainly, the will to win, whether by fair means or foul, does not teach it. And even if the coach is the fine true sportsman he ought to be, it is doubtful how much tendency there is for his students to carry over this sportsmanship into the other phases of their lives. The fact remains that it is a habit essential to social stability both in society and in the individual.

How one reacts to authority is an index of his social maturity. Even in early childhood the ability to coöperate with authority is an important part of one's training. The ability to follow is perhaps as important as the ability to lead and probably is prerequisite to it.

Anger is a form of emotion which is indicative of a lack both in mental strength and character. The nature of magnanimity is indicated in the derivation of the word itself and great-minded men are, in part at least, characterized by the capacity to control their tendency to anger.

Leadership is the most needed asset in any social structure. Certainly, most observers agree that its lack in modern society is a conspicuous cause of much of our present social chaos. How much of leadership is due to innate leadership ability and how much to training, is still an unsolved problem. Until there is evidence to the contrary, it will be wise to assume that it can be trained. Certainly there must be as many of its innate characteristics in human nature today as at any other time in history. Whatever lack of it there is, then, must be due to training. Social self-confidence is not synonymous with leadership. Many of the best followers have even more confidence in their position in society than the best leaders. However, society is not always fair or kind to us. It requires courage, therefore, to attain this social self-confidence.

Philosophy of life may seem to some a very questionable trait to include. Since history has brought forth a number of philosophies of life, it may seem presumptuous to decide upon one and try to measure that. Fortunately this is not necessary. By philosophy of life is meant one's outlook on life, whether it be healthy or morbid, optimistic or sad. In early childhood it may be measured by a sense of humor. In adult life it is best judged by the courage of one's convictions. In either case it requires a strong element of social courage.

Conclusion

This, then, is the personal equation. Let us recall that character traits have no meaning except as they are descriptive of individuals. In any individual they have no meaning except as they characterize his particular habits and abilities. Purposefulness is quite absurd aside from using one's abilities and aptitudes. Vision differs widely, depending on one's native endowment. There is not a single character trait which can be understood practically, except in terms of individuals themselves. The personal equation is an indispensable part of successful character education.

A rating scale is included here in order to make possible the use of the profile. Rating scales are not very reliable forms of psychological measurement. However, when two or more persons who know the child well make ratings independently of each other, the average of their judgment increases this reliability. Beside each section of the profile will be found percentile positions for various scores. Corresponding scores are used in the rating scale. If the average ratings are placed in appropriate positions on the profile, a fairly useful personality picture will be available. Measures of greater reliability and validity can be accomplished only with such methods as those described in *The Personal Equation.*

PERSONALITY RATING SCALE

This rating scale is designed to be used in securing tentative estimates for the personality profile now employed in the Union-Westminster Character Research Project. The questions are numbered to conform to the trait numbers on the profile. Where more than one question are related to the same trait, these are designated by the letters a, b, and c, following the trait number.

Following each question is a line with eleven scale units designated: 100, 90, 80, 70, 60, 50, 40, 30, 20, 10, and 0, respectively. These numbers refer to percentiles. In making a rating for the child in any particular trait, a check should be made on the line to indicate your judgment of the position of the child with relation to other children of the same age and sex. Thus if, out of a hundred children of the same age and sex chosen at random, this child in your opinion ranks at the top in this trait, the check should be made at 100. If he exceeds about seventy of them and is below thirty of them, the check should be made at 70. If he is in about the middle of the group, the check should be placed at 50, and so on.

The best rating for any child in any trait is the correct one. Rating a child too high is quite as unfair to him as to rate him too low. Some parents tend to rate their children too high. Others are afraid they will not be modest unless they rate them low. The only worthwhile rating is the most accurate one you are capable of making.

If, due to the age of the child, or due to lack of adequate information, you are unable to make a rating of a trait, that question should be left blank. Only ratings based on some objective and reliable evidence are of value.

The descriptive statements given below the line are to show the direction of the scale and not to determine points.

I. PHYSICAL DEVELOPMENT

1. How tall is this child in reference to other children of the same age and sex?

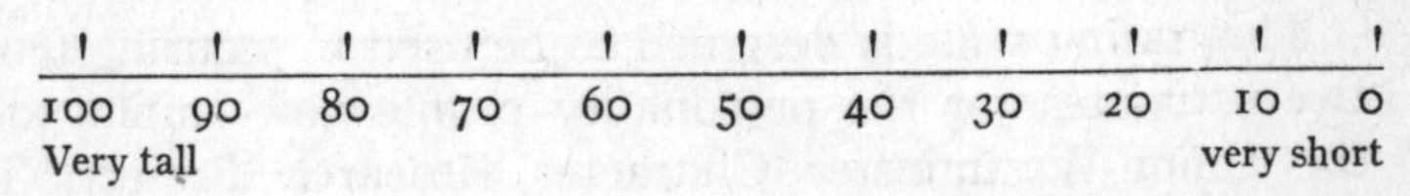

2. How much vital capacity; that is, physical endurance, stamina, and resistance to disease has he (she)?

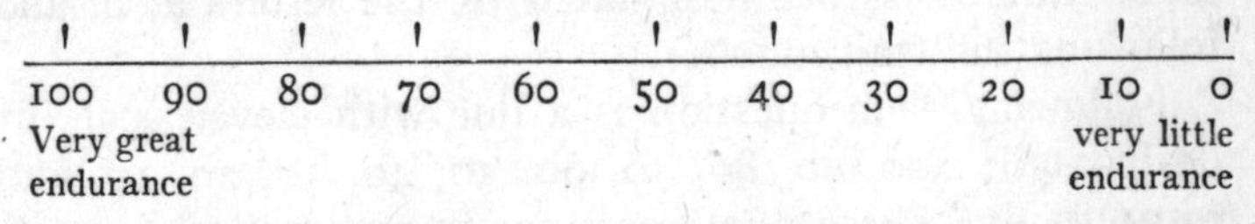

3. How well proportioned is his (her) weight to his (her) height? Scale a. is to be used if the child is heavier than average. Scale b. if he (she) is lighter than average.

a.

100 90 80 70 60 50 40 30 20 10 0

Splendid proportion of weight to height — very heavy

b.

100	90	80	70	60	50	40	30	20	10	0

Splendid proportion of weight to height — very light

4. Has he (she) good physical coördination (natural athletic ability, gracefulness, agility) for his (her) age?

100	90	80	70	60	50	40	30	20	10	0

Splendid coördination — very awkward and badly coördinated

5. Which hand does the child prefer to use in such activities as writing and throwing? In this case the scale goes from extreme right-handedness as 100 to extreme left-handedness as 0.

100	90	80	70	60	50	40	30	20	10	0

Very much right-handed, left hand used very little — very much left-handed, right hand used very little

6. Is he (she) unusually active in physical behavior, or does he (she) tend to be quiet and inactive?

100	90	80	70	60	50	40	30	20	10	0

Very active — very quiet

7a. Does the child eat heartily?

100	90	80	70	60	50	40	30	20	10	0

Enormous appetite — eats very little

7b. Does he (she) require more or less than average to drink?

100	90	80	70	60	50	40	30	20	10	0

Requires a great deal — requires very little

7c. Does he (she) sleep a great deal? How many hours per day? ______

100 90 80 70 60 50 40 30 20 10 0

Sleeps a great deal — sleeps very little

7d. Does he (she) eliminate normally and regularly?

100 90 80 70 60 50 40 30 20 10 0

With perfect regularity — always constipated

7e. Does he (she) seem to have a normal amount of sex drive?

100 90 80 70 60 50 40 30 20 10 0

Very much over-sexed — very little sex drive

8. Does he (she) have good vision, or does he (she) have trouble with his (her) eyes?

100 90 80 70 60 50 40 30 20 10 0

Perfect vision — almost blind

9. Is he (she) a good observer? Can he (she) picture things vividly in his (her) imagination? This is indicated by his (her) ability to describe accurately things he (she) has seen.

100 90 80 70 60 50 40 30 20 10 0

Very vivid visual imagery — very little visual imagery

10. Does he (she) have a keen sense of hearing?

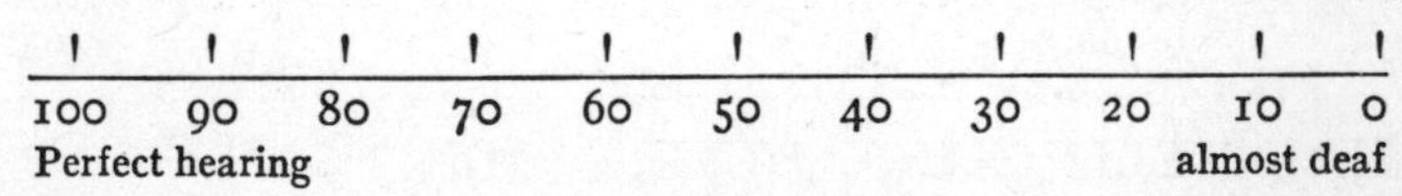

11. Does he (she) have good auditory imagery? That is, can he (she) understand clearly what is said to him (her), or remember in his (her) imagination the melody of a piece of music?

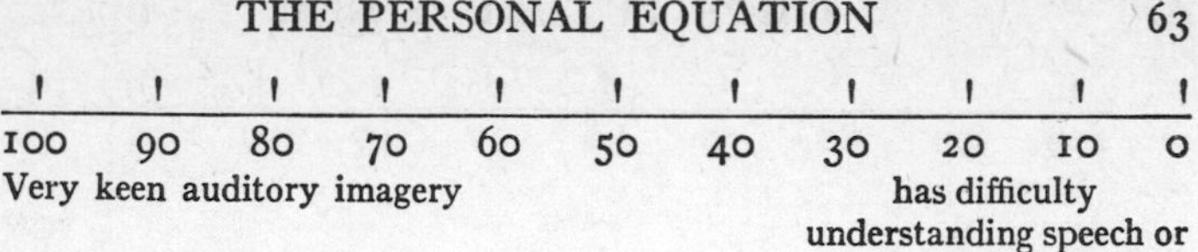

12a. How sensitive is the child to pain? Note the direction of the scale. High sensitivity is rated as 0.

100 90 80 70 60 50 40 30 20 10 0

Not at all sensitive to pain — very sensitive to pain

12b. How keen is his (her) sense of touch? This is best indicated by how easily he (she) picks up very small objects, or in the case of a young child how much he (she) likes to be stroked on the skin. Note the direction of the scale.

100 90 80 70 60 50 40 30 20 10 0

Not at all sensitive to touch — very sensitive to touch

13a. How sensitive is he (she) to heat? Note the direction of the scale.

100 90 80 70 60 50 40 30 20 10 0

Not at all sensitive to heat — very sensitive to heat

13b. How sensitive is he (she) to cold? Note the direction of the scale.

100 90 80 70 60 50 40 30 20 10 0

Not at all sensitive to cold — very sensitive to cold

II. INTELLECTUAL DEVELOPMENT

14. How much natural aptitude does the child show in the use of language; such as, style of speech and writing, use of good vocabulary, or ease in learning a foreign language?

100 90 80 70 60 50 40 30 20 10 0

Unusual aptitude — very little aptitude

15. How clearly does he (she) enunciate his (her) words? Does he (she) use baby talk, slurred speech, mumbling speech, stammering or stuttering?

100 90 80 70 60 50 40 30 20 10 0

Unusually good articulation — stammers and stutters badly

16. How extensive is his (her) vocabulary, for his (her) age?

100 90 80 70 60 50 40 30 20 10 0

Very fine vocabulary — very deficient vocabulary

17a. How rapidly does he (she) read? This refers to actual reading, not to skimming. This can be omitted for pre-school children.

100 90 80 70 60 50 40 30 20 10 0

Reads very rapidly — reads very slowly

17b. How well does he (she) comprehend and remember what he (she) reads? This can be omitted for pre-school children.

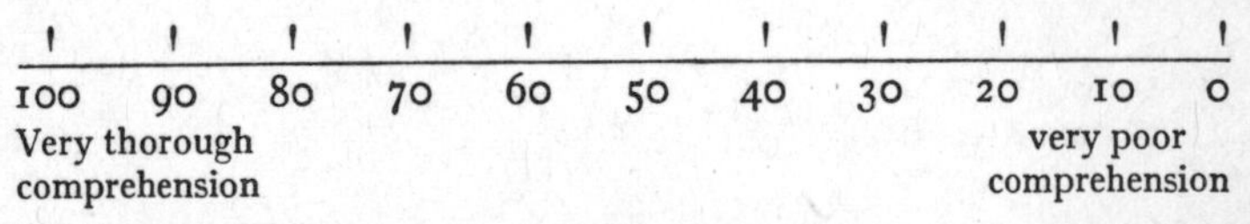

17c. How well does he (she) spell? This can be omitted for pre-school children.

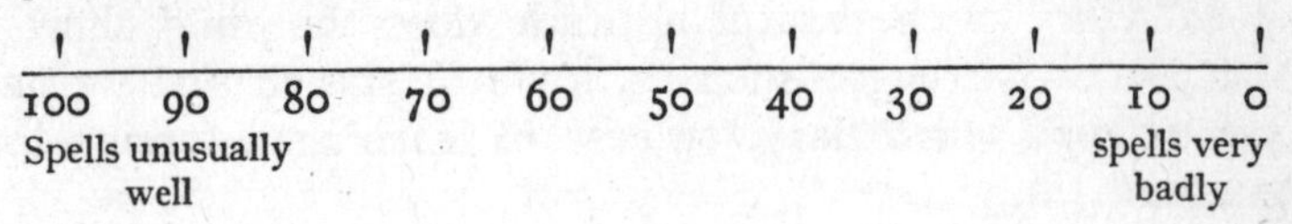

18. How well advanced is he (she) in school grade as compared to his (her) age level? This is omitted with pre-school children.

100	90	80	70	60	50	40	30	20	10	0
Two years ahead of age level					normal grade for age					two years retarded for age

19. How high does he (she) stand in his (her) school classes? This is omitted with pre-school children.

100	90	80	70	60	50	40	30	20	10	0
Leads class										at foot of class

20. How easily and efficiently does he (she) commit things to memory? How good a memory has he (she)?

100	90	80	70	60	50	40	30	20	10	0
Very remarkable memory										very poor memory

21. How much aptitude does he (she) show for solving practical problems? In the upper age levels this may be indicated by his (her) success in science courses; in the lower age levels, by facility with the use of tools and mechanical or construction toys.

100	90	80	70	60	50	40	30	20	10	0
Very marked aptitude										little or no such aptitude

22. How wide is the range of information which he (she) possesses?

100	90	80	70	60	50	40	30	20	10	0
Unusual range of information										decided poverty of information

23. How much facility does he (she) have with mathematics? In the lower age levels, this is indicated by his (her)

natural tendency to comprehend the use of numbers. The ability to recite numbers must not be confused with the ability to count objects.

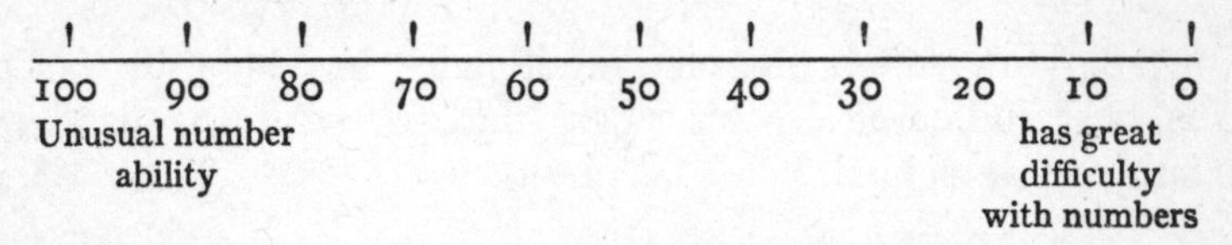

24. How well can he (she) concentrate on his (her) work? This is as much judged by the accuracy of his (her) work as by the amount of time he (she) can spend on it continuously.

100 90 80 70 60 50 40 30 20 10 0

Unusual ability to concentrate — very easily distracted

25. How well adjusted is he (she) to his (her) school work? This is indicated by the interest and enthusiasm he (she) shows for it, as well as the success he (she) has in it. This is not to be used if the child attends no school at all.

100 90 80 70 60 50 40 30 20 10 0

Unusual ability to concentrate — dislikes it intensely

26. How efficiently does he (she) study? This is not to be judged by the amount of time spent in studying, but in the regularity of study habits, the efficiency with which he (she) does his (her) work, the quality of his (her) notebooks, and the like.

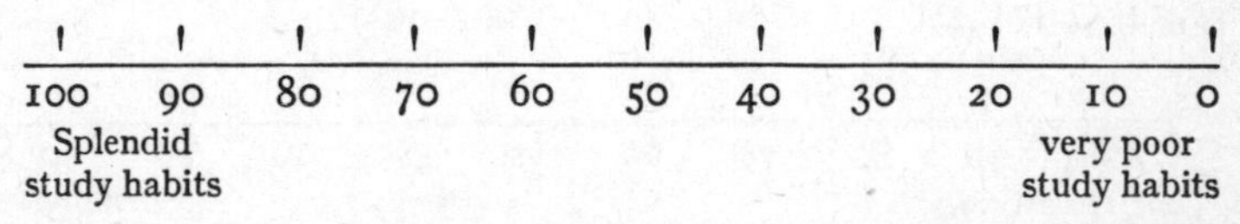

27. How much curiosity has he (she)? In the upper age levels this is indicated by his (her) enthusiasm for taking new courses, wide reading, and travel.

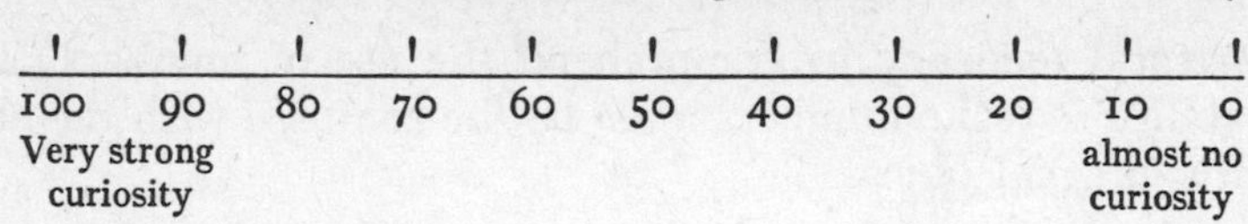

28. How much abstract intelligence has he (she)? This is best indicated by his (her) success with the academic subjects in school.

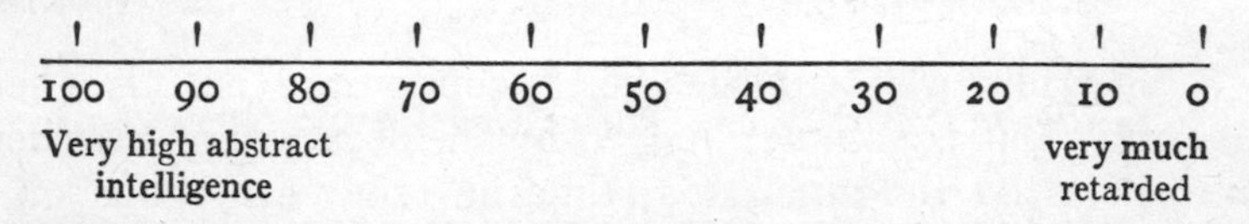

29. How much practical intelligence has he (she)? This is more closely related to what is known as common sense. It is demonstrated by how efficiently he (she) makes the adjustments of his (her) life other than in his (her) school subjects.

100 90 80 70 60 50 40 30 20 10 0

Very high practical intelligence — almost no practical intelligence

III. SPECIAL APTITUDES

30. How normal and healthy is the child's imagination, and how closely related to reality is it?

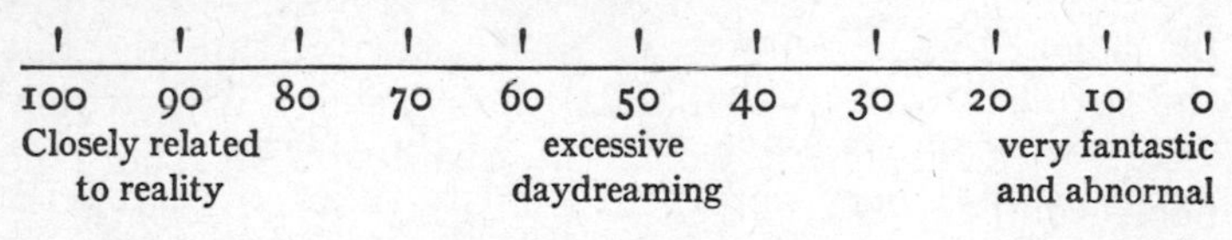

31. How strong is his (her) imagination?

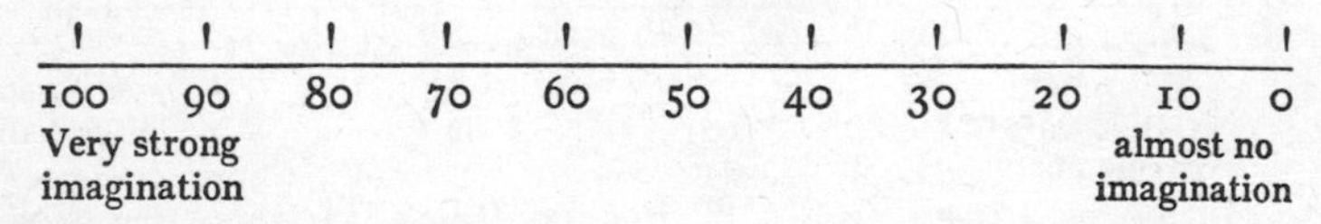

32. How much capacity has he (she) for perception of form? This includes sense of perspective and proportion.

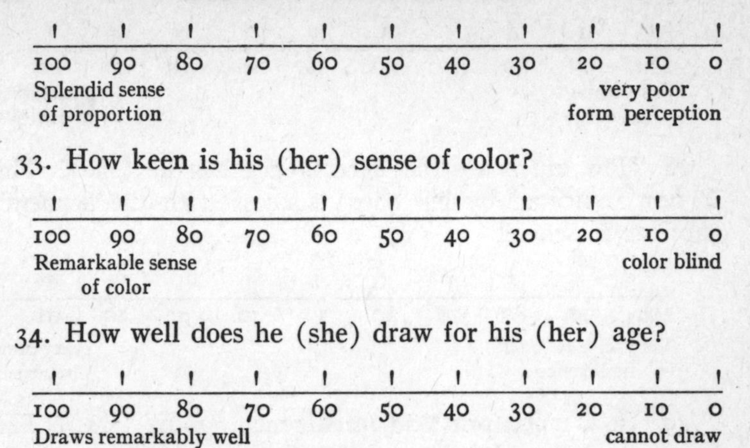

33. How keen is his (her) sense of color?

34. How well does he (she) draw for his (her) age?

35. How much capacity has he (she) for the appreciation of art? In young children this is indicated by interest in picture books.

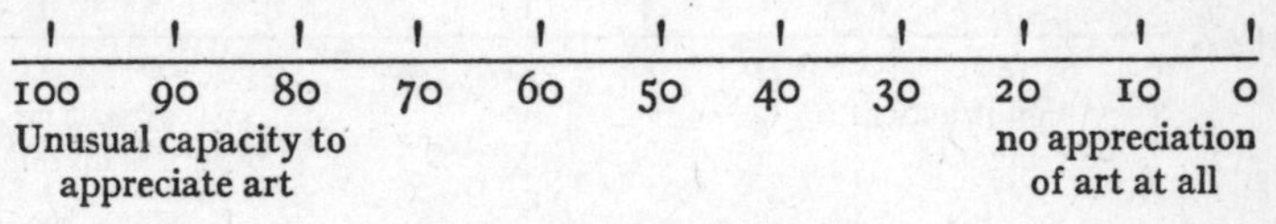

36. How keen a sense of tonal discrimination has he (she)? This is best indicated by pitch and intensity discrimination.

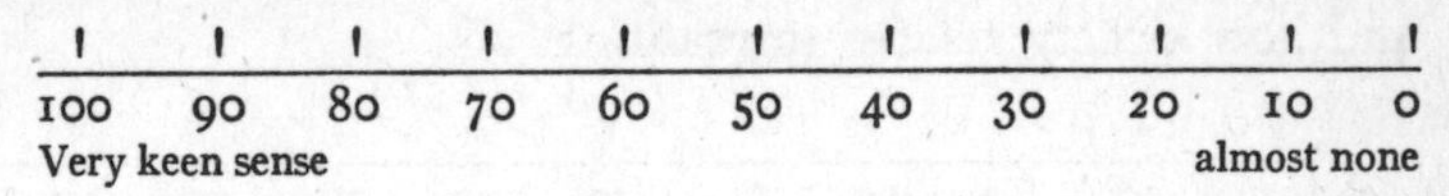

37. How much tonal memory has he (she)? This is indicated by his (her) ability to identify tunes or to reproduce them accurately.

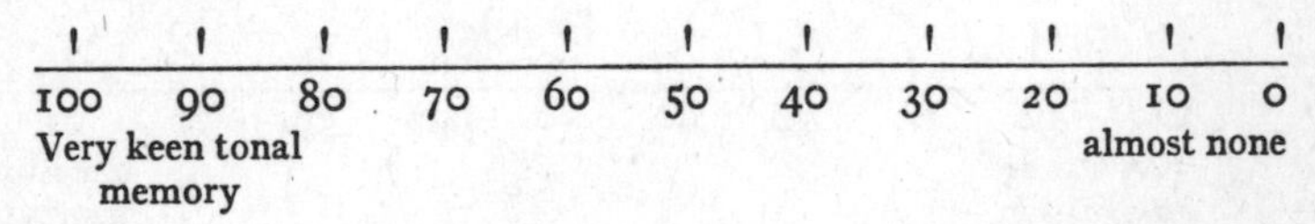

38. How good a sense of rhythm has he (she)? Can he (she) keep time, or dance well?

100 90 80 70 60 50 40 30 20 10 0

Remarkable sense of rhythm — no sense of rhythm at all

39. How much success has he (she) had with his (her) efforts at musical performance in singing or playing an instrument?

100 90 80 70 60 50 40 30 20 10 0

Unusual success — none at all

40. How much mechanical imagination has he (she)? That is, can he (she) plan things he (she) is going to construct, before he (she) builds or even makes drawings of them?

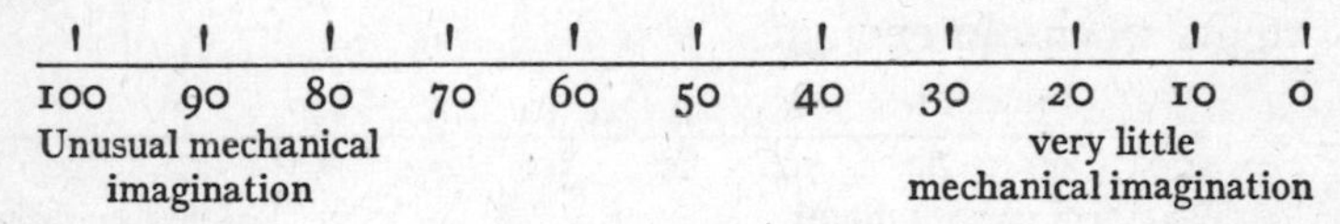

41. How well informed is he (she) in mechanical lines?

100 90 80 70 60 50 40 30 20 10 0

Has an unusual fund of mechanical information — has almost no mechanical information

42. How efficient is he (she) in actual mechanical performance? Does he (she) handle tools well? Does he (she) have the knack of building things nicely? This is related to finger dexterity.

100 90 80 70 60 50 40 30 20 10 0

Unusually high mechanical performance — almost no such ability

43. How much ability has he (she) for mechanical analysis? That is, how well does he (she) comprehend mechanical principles?

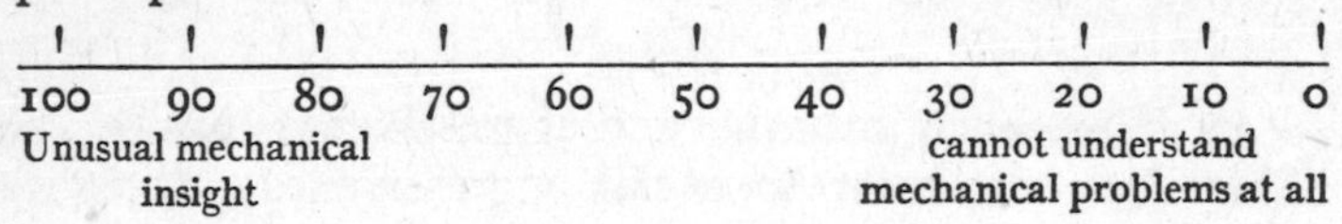

IV. CHARACTER AND PERSONALITY TRAITS

44. How ambitious is the child? This is best indicated by his (her) visions of the future, plus the tendency to do something actively about them now.

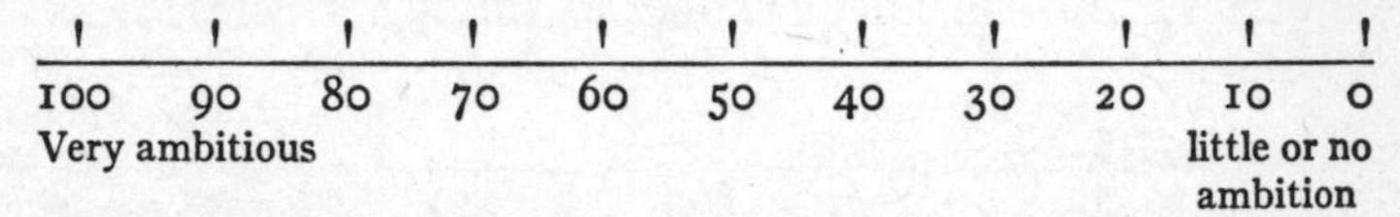

45. How much social and moral maturity has he (she)? This is indicated by how well he (she) conforms to the social and moral requirements of his (her) social group. Refusal to learn to dress himself (herself) when old enough is quite as important in this regard as disregarding property rights when old enough.

100 90 80 70 60 50 40 30 20 10 0

Very high sense of moral and social obligations — almost no social and moral maturity

46. How emotionally stable is he (she)? This is indicated by how much tendency there is for his (her) emotions to be out of proportion to their causes. He (she) may become over-enthusiastic, fly into a rage, or become unduly afraid.

100 90 80 70 60 50 40 30 20 10 0

Emotionally very stable — emotionally very unstable

47. How many objective fears does he (she) have? This should not refer to social fears which are considered in question 58. Fears of objects or natural phenomena, fear of failure, fear of insecurity, fear of death or insanity are included here. Note the direction of the scale.

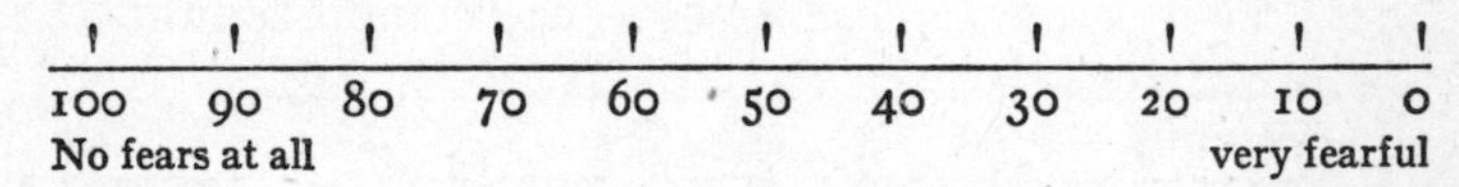

48. How much initiative and aggressiveness has he (she)? This does not refer to social aggressiveness. It is rather

the initiative with which he (she) approaches his (her) academic or vocational problems. Giving up easily when he (she) has difficulty with a school subject would be an illustration of lack of it.

100 90 80 70 60 50 40 30 20 10 0

Very high degree of initiative and aggressiveness — almost none, gives up very easily

49. How wide is the variety of his (her) hobbies and play interests and activities?

100 90 80 70 60 50 40 30 20 10 0

Unusually wide — has very few

50. How dependable is he (she) in carrying out the things he (she) starts or agrees to do?

100 90 80 70 60 50 40 30 20 10 0

Very dependable — not at all dependable

51. How generally purposive is his (her) activity? In the young child this is indicated by the amount of purely random activity he (she) shows. In the older child it is shown by how long he (she) remains at a task, how often he (she) finishes what he (she) starts, and what interest in vocational choice he (she) shows.

100 90 80 70 60 50 40 30 20 10 0

Very purposive — marked lack of purposiveness

52. How many friends has he (she) of the same sex as himself (herself)?

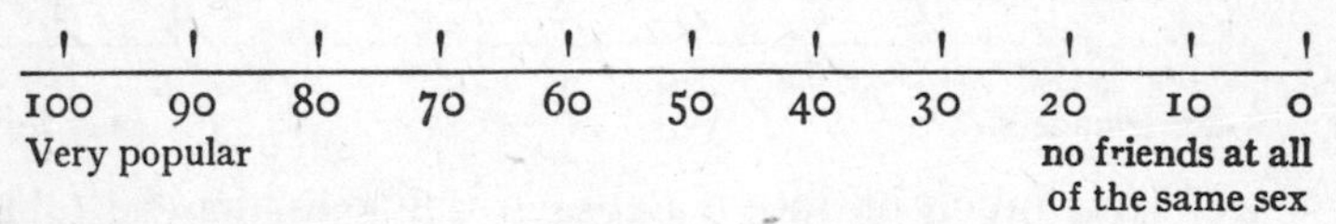

53. How many friends has he (she) of the opposite sex?

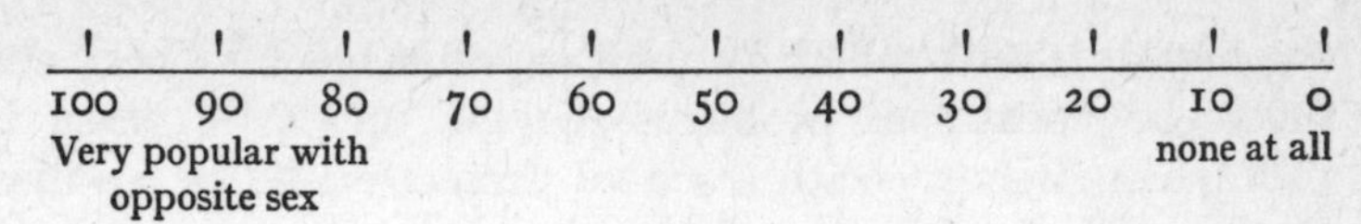

54. How much social vision has he (she)? This is indicated by his (her) ability to contribute to the success of social gatherings, as well as his (her) interest in social and welfare problems.

100 90 80 70 60 50 40 30 20 10 0

Very marked social vision — socially completely self-centered

55. How well does he (she) coöperate with authority?

100 90 80 70 60 50 40 30 20 10 0

Shows splendid spirit of coöperation — very negativistic and obstinate

56. How much tendency has he (she) to outbursts of temper?

100 90 80 70 60 50 40 30 20 10 0

Unusually good-natured and even-tempered — extremely hot-tempered

57. How much capacity has he (she) for leadership? This should relate to the quality of his (her) leadership as well as to the amount of it.

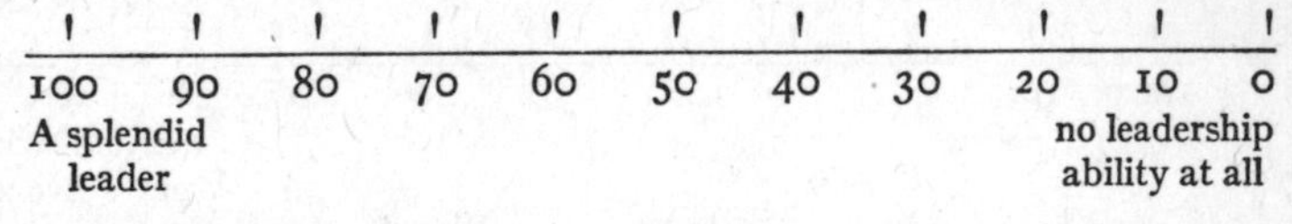

58. How much social self-confidence has he (she)?

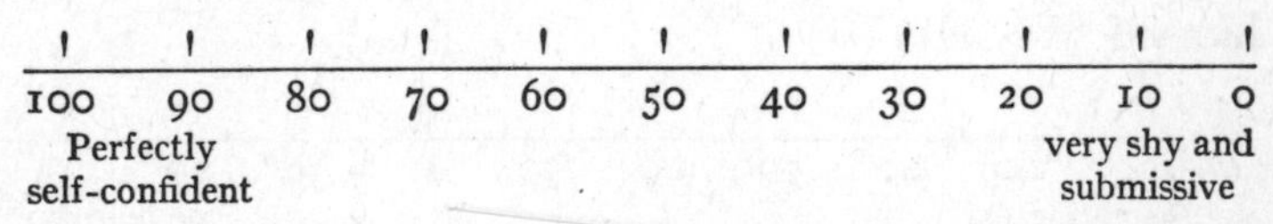

59. How rational and healthy a philosophy of life has he (she)? This should include his (her) sense of humor,

his (her) adaptability, his (her) courage both social and moral, and the wholesomeness of his (her) religion.

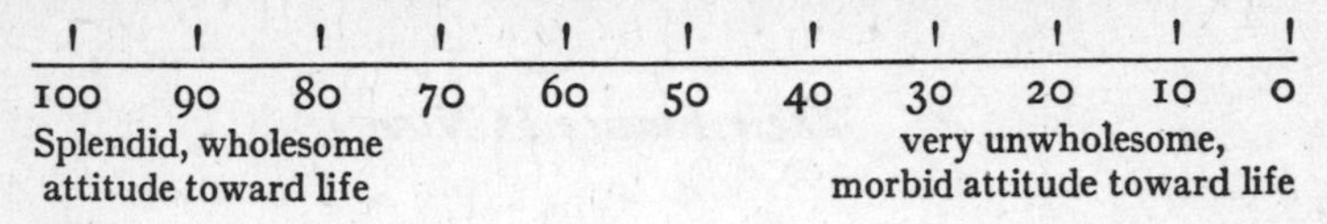

IV

Their Future Is Now

"A CHILD'S CHARACTER is formed before he is three." "Give us a child until he is seven and you can do what you please with him afterwards." "The teen age is the plastic age." These are only a few of the popular theories of when character is formed. But the best answer is, *now!* There is little doubt that some age levels are more important than others. In general the younger the child the more effective are efforts at character development. Nevertheless there are problems peculiar to every age level which can be solved best during and only during that particular period in his life.

In the second chapter, eight traits of Christian character were proposed as goals for character education. At what stages in life is each of them to be taught? The answer again is, *now*. There is not one of them which can reach its full development before maturity, nor a single period from infancy to maturity in which some steps are not possible for every one of the eight. Each of these steps is somewhat prerequisite to those that come after it. Very few of them can be taken in later periods as easily or effectively as during the period in which they normally occur. Much is said about adventurous religion. But, it is difficult to make religious people very adventuresome about their religion unless it is done during those years when adventure is the very essence of life itself. Many a potential Christian of genuine daring and courage is lost to the cause or becomes lukewarm because of the deadly doses of religion fed to him during the period just before the high school years. Helping young people to choose a vocation with a high idealistic vision of its importance to mankind and a faith that it is the will of God in their lives, is one of the greatest contributions the church can make to adolescence. But waste the adolescent period on mere discussion groups and social organizations, and the opportunity passes with very rare instances of its ever coming again. There are decisions and conversions for every age level which can hardly be made at any other.

What are the age levels in human growth? Into how many divisions can the process be divided? The answer is the same as in the case of the number of traits for a profile. Growth is continuous. There are no points at which one stage leaves off and another begins. Any division, then, is an arbitrary one which can be set by the practical requirements of the problem at hand. If the division points were to be determined by the rapidity of growth, of course the divisions would be much shorter in the early years and longer as maturity is approached. For the purposes of character development, two-year divisions seem entirely adequate up to the high school age. Adolescence is discussed as one period, and maturity as one. This is convenient, too, because it conforms to the common ages for entering the nursery, kindergarten, first grade, junior high school and senior high school. If this division is in error, it is in having too few and not too many stages. The range between the extremes in each of the lower age groups is very wide indeed.

Keeping in mind the age levels of growth which we have chosen, it becomes our task to decide what steps toward the development of each of the eight traits can be taken at each level. The outline of this procedure can be seen in the chart at the back of the book.

Unless this procedure is to be simply an item of armchair philosophy, it presupposes two steps. First, a tentative plan must be constructed on the basis of the known facts of child psychology. The second step is frequent revision based on the results of experience and experiment. Such results are the basis for this revision of the chart.

The following chapters, each dealing with one of these age levels, describe first, the most important psychological characteristics of that period, and second, how we can best go about building in the children of that age level another layer in the structure of character. Finally, it was necessary that some method be found for estimating the status and progress of the individuals in the group. This takes the form of a personality examination or questionnaire. Every chapter includes each of these three features.

The ideal of purposive character education, emphasized in this book from the beginning, can be realized only if precise instruments are developed for measuring the character growth of the child. Such instruments would be equally useful in estimating the success of our efforts, by applying them at the beginning and again at the end of any period of development. For this purpose, a questionnaire is found at the end of each chapter. It is not a questionnaire for the child, but for parents and teachers to use in their efforts to know the child more accurately. It ought to be filled out and studied at the beginning of every church school year. When it is completed, the parents will see immediately just what are the steps which can most profitably be taken in the training of the child for the year. The results of this questionnaire study should be made known to the church school and public school teachers. This makes possible coöperation between home, school and church toward the development of the child.

The question may at once be asked as to whether such an estimate by a parent is an accurate one. It is clear that it is not. However, if the two parents answer the questions independently and then discuss the discrepancies, thus preparing a revised rating, the errors are much less significant. If the school and church school teachers also do this, especially if they know the child well, the potential error is reduced still further.[1] This is one of the most significant steps yet taken in our efforts to solve some of the problems of character. To know what the things are which we are trying to accomplish, to be able to discover how successful our ef-

[1] Additional copies of these questionnaires may be secured. Address Ernest M. Ligon, Laboratory of Psychology, Union College, Schenectady, New York. It is obvious to all who have had any experience with mental measurement that the standardization, normalizing, and scoring of such measurements are the work of many years of research. It is hoped that those using these forms will send their results to the Union College Laboratory and thus contribute to this process.

forts are, and on this basis to improve our methods, are the very essence of applying the scientific method to the task.

There is nothing new about the idea of measuring, either in character education or personality development. Methods have been devised and scales constructed which have overcome many of the difficulties of this sort of measurement. The scales proposed in each of these chapters differ from most personality scales in one important respect. They are built on what is technically called the normative norm. That is, they attempt to score the individual in terms of his relationship to the highest attainment possible, instead of his relationship to the average. Again the analogy of the coach is useful. He has no interest in training athletes to do an average performance. He wants them to set records; that is, even better than the best. Most of the children with whom we have to deal in our church schools are normal, healthy-minded youngsters. Our task with them is not to make them average, but to help them discover ways of achieving the best of which they are capable. Of course, statistical norms and weighted scores will be developed as our data accumulate.

Let the first task be then to fill out this questionnaire for the child concerned. Then, with a clear picture of what you can contribute to his personality, study carefully the methods set forth for accomplishing this in the chapter dealing with that age level. A teacher dealing with a group of children should organize their individual needs into integrated curricular units. The methods for accomplishing this will be described and illustrated in Chapter XIV.

With this preview of our task, we may now turn to the first age level in the life of the growing personality; namely, the first two years of life.

V

Before the Nursery

Graduation

GRADUATION IS A MUCH MISUSED WORD which ought to be returned to its true meaning. The word connotes a passing from one step to another progressively. College graduates often seem to think it an end and not simply another step up the scale. In our schools, both secular and religious, graduations nowadays occur at very frequent intervals. Sometimes they mean something; sometimes they represent only the passage of time. In the public school system, a graduation usually represents the completion of a certain unit of work. In church schools, more often than not, it represents a change based, not on the work done there, but on advancement in the public schools. One of the chief reasons for this, of course, is the difficulty of requiring or measuring achievement in the church school. In general, it may be said that church schools at best simply expose children to religion without requiring them either to learn it or to show any evidence of having learned it. But graduation could be made to mean something in character education if we came to use it in its fullest sense.

In the following pages a description of personality growth in infancy is given. Usually children are brought to our church school nurseries at about two years of age. If that department of our church school is to accomplish its purpose, these children must reach a certain stage in their development before entering the nursery. This chapter will bring out the training children should receive during their first two years and the achievements they should be able to accomplish at the end of that time. If it were possible to discuss fully all of the problems of infant behavior, it would be more obvious how much achievement this would really represent. I think it can be said conservatively that a college student in his four years does not make proportionately a fraction of the progress the well-trained infant does in his first two years. And, just as college training is helped or hampered by the efficiency of the preparatory high school training of its students, so is the nursery by the work of these first two years.

It was assumed by everyone not many generations ago, and is believed by most people even today, that the first two years are of no significance in character development and that the problems arising in them are almost entirely physical. In the following pages it will be shown that every one of the eight traits described in Chapter II has its first foundations laid in infancy. It seems highly probable that unless these foundations are laid, the personality of the child will never be quite as strong as it might have been with good character education before the nursery. So even with the infant, his future is now. Let us look first, then, at the general psychological nature of the child during these first two years. Then let us see what steps can be taken toward the formation of the eight traits.

Physical Development

There are so many excellent books available concerning the physical growth of the child that no major purpose would be served by an extended discussion here. A few of the major characteristics of physical development will be sufficient as an introduction to our discussion of character development during this period.

In the first place, it should be emphasized that the rate of physical growth is much greater in infancy than it ever will be in any succeeding period of the same length. The child increases his height one hundred percent during the first year and thirty percent during the second. Weight increases proportionately. Parents have grown accustomed to keeping records of the various physical dimensions of their children and comparing them to the norms available in all of the measurement literature. As a matter of fact, conformity to averages of weight and height should not be considered too important. What is normal for one child may be quite abnormal for another. Resistance to disease and general vigor and health are better criteria than averages for normality in the physical dimensions. The most important thing about the growth of the child is to see that he has every chance of being wholesome and healthy. Adenoids, diseased tonsils, and defects of posture should be dealt with as promptly as the physician advises. Cod liver oil, irradiated milk, and sunshine, plus lots of sleep, are as important to character development now as the most effective spiritual forces can possibly be in later years.

The appearance and development of the various motor abilities constitute one of the most interesting pictures of the growing infant. To the untrained observer, the activities of the infant may seem quite unpredictable and entirely a matter of accident. As a matter of fact, in every phase of the infant's motor activity, fairly definite sequences occur. For example, in gaining control of the various parts of his body, his first success is with the head and neck, then with the chest, followed by the back, the lower trunk, and finally the legs. Progress in locomotion has an entirely different sequence, reaching its high point at about fourteen months when the baby learns to walk alone. After that, learning to run, climb, go up the stairs, stand on one foot, and so on, are later achievements. Hand movements also follow each other in orderly sequence. The simple process of picking things up is done in a characteristic way by the young infant, and the succession of methods employed, until he adopts the adult process, is orderly and can be predicted. Hand preference appears by the end of the first year. The cause of handedness is still an unsolved problem in child behavior. However, aside from the inconvenience of being left-handed in a right-handed world, there are no significant differences in the general characteristics of left- and right-handed individuals. It is certainly true that strenuous efforts to oppose left-handedness often result in mental and emotional difficulties which are far more serious than the inconveniences of left-handedness could ever possibly be.

The various sense organs of the body mature reasonably early. There is reason to believe that the child's visual apparatus is as good by the end of the second year as it will ever be. To be sure, we cannot speak too dogmatically about such factors as color perception, but in all probability the child recognizes at least the differences between bright and dull colors. The other sense organs of hearing, touch, warmth and cold, pain, taste, and smell, all provide sources for the child's becoming acquainted with the world to which he must make an adjustment.

Mental Development

During the last few years a number of mental tests have been developed for the pre-school years. Several of them will be described in *The Personal Equation.* They do not seem to be completely reliable and the few researches that have been made involving repeated measurements leave doubt as to how well they predict mental capacity in later years. Inadequate as they are, however, they are far better instruments for understanding infant development than mere subjective judgments. They do describe accurately the various sequences of development that may be expected and, whatever their predictive value for later years, they are of inestimable value for dealing with the infant at the present. Training of any sort should always follow maturation. The use of these tests gives us a picture of this maturation and makes possible more effective and efficient training.

By far the most interesting behavior which may be thought of as primarily mental is the appearance of language. While the child does not say words in any intelligent sense until he is from fifteen to seventeen months old, he does use vocal expressions which become increasingly differentiated. He begins with mere crying, which is used to indicate every wish. Later he explores with the new sounds which occur in his adventures with his vocal abilities. Then he proceeds to the social contacts made possible through such games as pat-a-cake, peek-a-boo, and waving bye-bye. Still later he engages in word imitation and finally begins to use words and short sentences. In this sequence he has gone through a progress perhaps greater than he will ever make again. There are tremendous individual differences both in the time and extent of talking. Vocabularies at two years of age vary from six words to twelve hundred words. Language is the most important social institution that man possesses and a great deal of the infant's training should center around it. It should be remembered that the child must lead and the adult follow in such training; that is, training must follow maturation.

Social Development

Of course, the child of this age cannot be classified as a social animal. Anyone who has tried to have a birthday party for two-year-olds realizes that a majority of the social graces are still to be acquired. Despite that fact the seeds of social development can be planted during these first two years and thus make later social growth much easier. The first real smile occurs at about two months of age, usually in response to the mother's smile. At birth the child does not even know that his own body is his own, and his first lessons in social adjustment consist in the exploration of that body and the discovery of himself as an individual.

Emotional Development

The new-born baby undoubtedly experiences emotion. Recent research indicates that in all probability it is quite undifferentiated and represents simply a stirred-up state of the organism. Very soon, however, specific patterns of anger and fear begin to appear. Bridges[1] in a very important study has found that during the first two years the emotional life of the child develops somewhat as follows: at birth there is only general excitement; by three months of age this excitement has been differentiated into distress and delight; by six months of age, fear, disgust and anger put in their appearance; and by the end of the first year, elation and affection are shown. This is another example of the genetic patterns found in the growing child. There are tremendous individual differences. For example, according to another investigation, one child had more than one hundred times as many temper tantrums in the same period of time as another.

Character Development: General Principles

At no time in his life can the emotional behavior of a child be more readily modified than in these early years when it is relatively unfixed and unpatterned. Furthermore, the methods used for emotional control during these years are basic ones. When they are understood clearly, the more complex emotional problems of later life can be approached more intelligently. Emotional reactions constitute an important part of the child's repertoire of possible responses with which to meet situations. One can think of development, on the training and guidance side, as being the selection of adjustive reactions. If a child makes an undesirable response, training does not consist so much in paying attention to this response as in helping the child find a more effective one.

It is quite impossible, or at least uneconomical, to teach a child to do things for which his maturity has not adequately prepared him. Parents are often so anxious for their children to be brighter and more precocious than anyone else's children that they produce strain, fatigue, over-

[1] Bridges, K. M. B., "Emotional Development in Early Infancy," *Child Development*, III, p. 340, 1932.

stimulation, and even emotional instability by pushing the child too rapidly. Numerous experiments have shown that, when the proper stage of maturation has been reached, a very short period of training will accomplish far more than training of much longer duration at too early a developmental level. Too much emphasis cannot be placed on this principle. A large share of the child's negative emotions are a result of the difficulties he is called upon to face by his over-ambitious parents.

Let us look now to see what can be done to establish each of the eight traits during these first two years. Some of them are more important for this age level than others. This, of course, is true for every age level. Nevertheless, foundation stones can be laid for each one of the eight traits during infancy.

Experimental Faith

Vision

In order to lay the foundation stones for the trait of vision, it is necessary, from the very beginning, to stimulate a creative use of the imagination. For example, dolls and doll furniture afford opportunities for imaginative play and, because the child tends to project into the doll the characteristics of personality, this provides opportunity for his first dreams of social adjustment. In addition, among his earliest toys should be picture-books which suggest new things to dream about, crayons and pencils with which to make his first artistic creations, and blocks, as large as he can handle, with which to build his first architectural designs.

This makes it possible to illustrate the point that character traits, although they are abstract qualities in themselves, have as prerequisites to their maturity large numbers of more specific habits of thought and action. If, from the beginning, the child develops the habit of making creative use of his imagination, the visions he acquires in later life will be more realistic ones and of greater practical usefulness to society. A very common personality problem which arises in later life lies in the expression of fantastic and unreal forms of imagination. Excessive daydreaming, which sometimes becomes a substitute for instead of a stimulus to action, is a form of this abnormality. Therefore, when the child's imagination is expressed constructively from the very beginning by building things and drawing things and personifying things, important progress is being made toward the development of a dynamic personality.

Love of Righteousness and Truth

Curiosity in varying degrees of intensity is innate in human personality. Children naturally show interest in things about them. There seems little question but that the child with the widest experience is the child of the greatest maturity. The child born in the country where there is a variety of trees, plants, flowers and animals for him to observe is indeed fortunate. However, the mere presentation of a large number of different objects to the child is no guarantee that he recognizes those objects or can differentiate between them. The ability to recognize objects is called perception. Perceptual ability develops with age. It is measured more by the child's ability to see differences than to see similarities.

This ability to differentiate goes along pretty closely with language. We differentiate clearly only those things we can name and, in turn, can name only those things which we can differentiate. Love of truth then, that is, love of finding out about things, is bound up with language development. Effective training in this trait consists of introducing a few new objects at a time and naming them over and over again until the child has quite thoroughly mastered their names. It must be remembered that meaning is not grasped as easily by the infant as by adults. Logical definitions and verbal descriptions are useless to him. His methods of analysis come more effectively through the many sensory experiences he has with objects. To come to know the word "kitty", he must see, hear, touch, and play with the kitty. Even a few scratches make discrimination more complete. Another aid in the child's language development is his love of rhythmical sounds. To sing about an object over and over is a better way to stimulate the child to remember it than by the more common method, "Say apple," "Say dog." At the table, in the bath, during dressing, as each new object is touched or used, the parent can sing an impromptu song about it.

The child also needs equipment for mastering this trait. A sandbox is an essential part of the training school for every infant. Equipment for making mud-pies is more important to his future mental development than the Encyclopedia Britannica. The most important point is to keep his experiences interesting. If his early explorations in the world about him are happy ones he will acquire a love for learning which, unless it be destroyed by some later influence, will be of great value in his developmental career.

Faith in the Friendliness of the Universe

If a child is to grow up believing that the universe is controlled by a Father-God who loves his children, his early contacts with that universe must be happy ones. It is impossible to convince a child of the love of his mother if the mother treats him harshly during his early years. In the first place, his physical condition should be kept as healthy as possible. Low vitality predisposes him to emotional difficulties. Disease makes irritableness and fear more likely to develop. To neglect physical defects during the first year with the idea that the child will grow out of them is bad policy, because the child often does not grow out of them, and also because they lead to unhappiness in this very important early period of life.

Of course the opposite of this trait is fear. To whatever extent fear controls a person's life he does not believe in the friendliness of the universe. Developing faith, then, consists in avoiding fear. But this is not a negative process, it is a thoroughly positive one. In more primitive times nurses were accustomed to scare children into being good by frightening them with stories of bogey-men, policemen, and horrible fates. Such forms of child control are now almost extinct. Older but immature brothers and sisters still sometimes delight in the effect of ghost stories on a young child, but the fear period in child training has just about disappeared. The point is this: there are a number of situations to which the child must adjust. If he has adequate reactions to make to them he will not resort to fear, for fear is a reaction made when no better means are available. He needs lots of toys with which to experiment, large ones which give him a sense of achievement. He should meet animals under the most favorable circumstances, and make his earliest acquaintances with the dark as confidently as possible. A liberal number of bumps and bruises are certain to occur. The important thing is to see to it that they are not so severe that the child cannot meet them successfully. For example, in learning to walk the child needs freedom to practice, praise for success, and a soft place to land when he falls. Bumps and bruises, then, are not especially detrimental unless they are more severe than he can endure with ease. When small accidents happen, the child does not know the appropriate reaction to make, and he often looks to his elders for guidance. Thus, if he falls and gets a little bump on the floor, a fear-stricken look on the face of his mother plus a rush to pick him up will produce tears and fear. On the other hand, laughter on the part of the father and mother is likely to produce laughter on the part of the child.

Finally, it must be recalled that the child is learning the qualities of things as well as the names of things. Consider how we describe an object. The adjectives we use are hot, cold, rough, smooth, soft, hard, heavy, light, dull, and sharp. The child does not have a very wide experience with which to interpret these various qualities. He cannot understand what hot means until he has touched a few hot objects, nor what sharp means until sharpness has made a definite impression on some part of his anatomy. The various experimenting he does, although it sometimes leads to minor disasters, has its value, and if he gradually learns to discriminate between those parts of his environment which he can embrace and those which he must avoid, he is learning lessons of importance in the development of this trait. At this age level, this is one of the most important of the eight traits to emphasize.

Dominating Purpose

It is obvious that we do not expect the child to decide before he is two years of age whether he will be a physician, a lawyer, or a business man. Not infrequently, however, such a decision is made for him, sometimes even before he is born, by a father who speaks with sentiment about his son following in his footsteps. However, despite the fact that vocational choice is still some years off, the foundations of purposiveness can be laid during these first two years. There are a number of important achievements in which he can be trained. Probably the ones which attract the greatest attention from most parents are bladder and bowel control. As a matter of fact, too great emphasis upon these two physiological functions may result in rather serious consequences. In all probability, full control of these two functions should not usually be expected of the child earlier than the middle of the third year. However, a reasonable amount of bowel regularity and control can be accomplished by the eighteenth month. If the child has matured to such an extent that these controls can be gained in part or in whole, they are sources of achievement of major importance, but emphasis must not be laid on their failure. Negative emphasis usually does more harm than good in this respect.

All sorts of activities which have a purpose and lead to some definite end are valuable in the development of purposiveness. A child, pulling off his cap for the first twenty or thirty times the parent puts it on, has a better sense of the development of purpose than the often irritated and impatient parent. Opening and closing boxes, unscrewing jar lids, building towers of blocks, digging and filling up pails from the sandbox, and making mud-pies are only a few of the many forms of activity which develop purposiveness. Sometimes, children as young as two years can even go much further than that. They can help dress themselves. Learning to put the arms and legs through the proper holes in the clothing is a difficult and important achievement. Learning to button or unbutton clothes is another worthwhile achievement toward which to work. Finally, learning to aid oneself is an absorbing task. During the second year the child will become intensely interested in the use of the spoon, and too much help by his mother is likely to stunt his growth more than it saves in spilled food and soiled clothes. Numerous illustrations could be given and will occur of other ways of developing purposiveness. The child does not have perseverance and he will change his interests almost every minute. But even at this age level, he can be taught to get his greatest pleasure from a sense of achievement. Later on, praise becomes an important stimulus and in some individuals the only important stimulus for achievement. The healthy personality, however, is the one in which achievement is in itself the greatest source of a person's pleasure, and this is the age at which this trait can best be learned.

Fatherly Love

Being Sensitive to the Needs of Others

It is not probable that, when the child comes to his second birthday, unselfishness will be his major virtue. Being thoughtful of others is the trait for which there is the least natural basis for development. Nevertheless, a certain amount of social experience paves the way for a fuller development of this trait later on. Games like pat-a-cake and peek-a-boo, after all, do involve consciousness of the presence of another individual. Furthermore, they involve a certain sense of coöperation with that other individual. In the second year, being placed in the presence of other children of his own age level has values, because in this situation he does not have special privileges as he almost always does in dealings with his parents. A too aggressive child learns more about the necessity of social adjustment through the social give and take with other infants than he can possibly learn from his elders.

Forgiveness

The idea of doing anything in infancy about the trait of forgiveness seems quite absurd. As a matter of fact, one situation very frequently arises at this time which sets forth the principle involved in this trait better than any other single example. This has to do with the jealousy which so commonly arises when a new baby comes into the family. Especially if he has been an only child, he has been the center of attention for his whole life. His parents have paid attention to his every wish. Then, suddenly, this attention is not only divided with, but often almost entirely diverted to, another individual. There is little wonder that jealousy arises. How is this jealousy to be avoided? The answer is found in the parental instinct. If, instead of finding himself a competitor, with a younger brother or sister, for his parents' affection, he finds himself, on the other hand, a coöperator with his parents for the protection and care of the newcomer, the whole picture is changed. In the normal child, this protective attitude can be stimulated as early as eighteen months of age. It is the very essence of this trait. Forgiveness implies two changes: first a change on the part of the forgiver by which he no longer holds resentment, and secondly a positive effort on his part to do something for the person forgiven. In the instance cited this is perfectly illustrated. The mental attitude of jealousy has been changed to positive affection with a desire to protect and assist.

Magnanimity

The two chief factors in conflict between men are fear of one another and anger toward one another. When fear and anger and their various kindred reactions, such as jealousy and suspicion, are controlled, this trait reaches its highest maturity. Fear, as has been pointed out, arises largely because of the lack of reaction patterns and the resultant inability to meet many situations. Different types of social fear arise at different age levels. A child is not likely to show fear of strangers earlier than the fifth month. To avoid the development of this fear, it is well to see that the child has plenty of experience with strangers and makes each new contact under the most favorable conditions, preferably in the parent's arms. As he makes his adjustment to each one, this fear, which may seem fairly natural, can be almost entirely eliminated in a short space of time. He will get great pleasure from the stimulation of these new social contacts.

Anger, however, is far more important in connection with this trait. Anger is the child's first aggressive response. It is the first way in which he reacts to that which he does not like, and of which he is not afraid. Anger comes primarily from two sources: the thwarting of a desire and interference with an on-going activity. Perhaps two-thirds of anger situations could be avoided if parents recognized the rights of the child. Undoubtedly, an enormous proportion of these situations are unnecessary and are an unjust demand on the child by the parent. Why should the child cease an activity which he has begun, on parental command? Many of his desires could be acceded to without any loss either to parent or child. Anger reactions in the form of defiance or temper tantrums are used experimentally by the child to see if they get the desired results. If they do not, they are usually discontinued. One of the best ways of dealing with temper tantrums or examples of extreme negativism is to pay as little attention to them as possible, so that the child simply comes to discontinue their use because of their ineffectiveness. To give in to a temper tantrum is to insure its permanency. To punish the child for it may increase its intensity. Parent-child conflicts which arise in eating, sleeping, and bathing are probably largely unnecessary. If the child's rights are taken into consideration and efforts are made to make these three normal experiences pleasant and happy ones, difficulties are much less likely to come up. Finally, being sure that the parents themselves exhibit a minimum of fear and anger is extremely helpful.

A good deal of coöperation with authority can be learned even during this early age. If parents combine the growth of language and the sense of achievement to bring about obedience to requests, the foundation for a wholesome sense of coöperation with authority can be given. It was long thought that temperament was an inherited characteristic. Psychologists cannot pronounce upon this question too dogmatically even yet, for the evidence is not complete. It seems highly probable, however, that fear and anger habits are not inherited, but that they are learned so very early in life as to have given rise to that impression.

Christian Courage

This last trait is perhaps pretty much beyond the child of this age because it presupposes affection of a sacrificial type. The infant does not have such an affection. About all that can be done is to stimulate in the child habits of doing certain things which are not in themselves pleasant but which are socially desirable. A good deal of the process of weaning, both physically and psychologically, consists in the child's learning to endure a certain amount of disagreeable experience. If this weaning is gradual and substitute behavior is provided to replace it, it is much more easily accomplished. The child needs to learn very early that everyone has to do some things he does not want to do and leave undone other things that he does want to do. He learns this partly through discipline, but most effectively when deprivations lead to more desirable rewards later on. This is not so much rational learning as a conditioning process. To whatever extent the child can be given a feeling of pride in the care of younger children, to just that extent can he be stimulated to give up some of his own pleasures and toys to them. It is not wise, however, to push this too far nor to expect too great achievements in connection with it.

Final Examination

In the beginning of this chapter it was suggested that children be admitted to the nursery only if they have reached the developmental levels demanded for effective nursery training. What sort of final examination can be given to the infant for entrance into the nursery? First and foremost he needs physical health. This he cannot gain except through the wise guidance of his parents and the family physician, but it is his right and an asset of the greatest importance to his future development. Secondly he needs to have a working vocabulary. It is very difficult to train children effectively when they cannot understand what is asked of them nor express their own desires in an intelligible fashion. Before bringing children into a nursery, it is desirable to teach them the common words used there, such as the names of the objects with which they will deal and the activities in which they will engage. Then they should also be able to pronounce these words intelligibly. There is no adequate excuse for children speaking with such poor enunciation that they cannot be understood. They have in their repertoire all of the sounds necessary for good speech. In the third place, they should have freedom and confidence in the use of materials such as blocks, crayons, wagons and the like. Furthermore, they should get their pleasure from constructive achievement rather than from the destructive habits which are all too common with first year nursery children. They should know how to respond to authority, so that they can and will obey simple commands. Lastly, they should have learned an element of helpfulness, especially in cleaning up and putting things away.

Conclusion

There are a number of excellent books describing child development somewhat quantitatively, which every parent ought to read.[2] The book by Faegre and Anderson approaches the problems of development as problems. The book by Strang discusses development from age level to age level. Both present in very readable form the results of the great mass of research which has accumulated during the last few years. In addition to these, every parent should own a record book in which to note the child's development. The old-fashioned memoir book is of sentimental value only. Perhaps the best manual for this purpose is the one prepared by Anderson and Goodenough.[3] In addition to adequate spaces for every sort of developmental record, this book includes a discussion of the aspects of personality which may be expected to appear from time to time, and something of their significance in personality development. Such a book, kept from birth to maturity, would be of great value in meeting the adjustmental problems of the child, and of genuine interest to the child in his later life.

The following questionnaire is the first of a series, one for each age level. If parents and teachers fill it out carefully, they will find that the low scores indicate which aspects of the child's personality can best be developed. Most children are normal healthy children, but what can be done to improve on this in bringing about the full realization of all their potential power? The purpose of these questionnaires is to fill this need. They are all prepared in relation

[2] Two which are especially adapted to this purpose are *Child Care and Training* by M. L. Faegre and J. E. Anderson, Fourth Edition (University of Minnesota Press, 1937) and *An Introduction to Child Study* by R. Strang, Revised Edition (The Macmillan Company, 1938).

[3] Anderson, J. E. and Goodenough, F. L., "*Your Child Year by Year.*" *Parents' Magazine*, New York, 1934.

to the eight traits, so that one can see how each new habit is laying a foundation for the mature personality. Too much emphasis should not be put on the quantitative results of these questionnaires. They have not yet been standardized in this respect. At present it is better to use them simply as indicators of possible new adjustments. This is a first step in measuring the progress of our character education methods.

QUESTIONNAIRE FOR INFANCY

In the square preceding each question write a number, 5, 4, 3, 2, or 1. After each question is a series of five possible answers to the question, numbered 5, 4, 3, 2, and 1 respectively. In the square use the number preceding the phrase which most nearly represents your answer.

Psychological Development

☐ 1. Over how much of the body does he (she) have voluntary control?
5 The whole body, 4 all except the legs, 3 the head, neck, and chest, 2 only the head, 1 none of it

☐ 2. How adept is he (she) in locomotion?
5 Can stand on one foot, 4 can climb stairs, 3 can run, 2 can walk, 1 cannot walk

☐ 3. Has he (she) shown hand preference?
R right, X neither, L left

Trait I

☐ 4. How much does he (she) engage in imaginative play, as for example, treating dolls as if they were alive?
5 Very often, 4 frequently, 3 occasionally, 2 seldom, 1 never

☐ 5. Does he (she) enjoy looking at picture books?
5 Does so for hours, 4 very much, 3 often, 2 occasionally, 1 seldom or never

☐ 6. Does he (she) use crayons or pencil to scribble?
5 A favorite activity, 4 often does, 3 sometimes, 2 occasionally, 1 never

☐ 7. Does he (she) like to handle or build with large blocks?
5 A favorite activity, 4 very often does, 3 sometimes, 2 occasionally, 1 never

Trait II

☐ 8. Does the child show curiosity about the parts of his (her) body?
5 Continually, 4 daily, 3 often, 2 sometimes, 1 rarely

☐ 9. Is the child curious about the objects about him (her)?
5 Very much so, 4 more than average, 3 somewhat, 2 a little, 1 not at all

☐ 10. Is the child curious about flowers and animals outdoors?
5 Often, 4 frequently, 3 sometimes, 2 occasionally, 1 never

☐ 11. How many different objects can he (she) identify by name?
5 A hundred, 4 fifty, 3 twenty, 2 ten, 1 five or less

☐ 12. How large is his (her) vocabulary?
5 More than a thousand words, 4 a hundred words, 3 twenty words, 2 ten words, 1 no words

☐ 13. How well does he (she) pronounce his (her) words?
5 Has perfect enunciation, 4 has a few difficult sounds, 3 can be easily understood by a stranger, 2 can be understood only by family, 1 cannot be understood at all

☐ 14. Does he (she) like to play in the sand or make mud pies?
5 A favorite activity, 4 very often does, 3 frequently does, 2 sometimes, 1 never

Trait III

☐ 15. What is the ratio between laughing and crying, happy and unhappy experiences?
5 Almost all happy, 4 laughs more than he (she) cries, 3 about equally divided, 2 cries more than he (she) laughs, 1 almost always unhappy

☐ 16. How healthy is he (she)?
5 The picture of health, 4 above average, 3 average, 2 not very healthy, 1 very sickly

☐ 17. How many fears has the child? e.g., fear of animals, strangers, the dark, thunder and lightning, etc.
5 Two or less, 4 five, 3 seven, 2 ten, 1 twelve or more

☐ 18. What is his (her) reaction to ordinary bumps and bruises?
5 Laughs at them, 4 smiles, 3 indifferent to them, 2 whimpers, 1 cries

☐ 19. How many such qualities as hot, cold, rough, hard, heavy, and sharp does he (she) know well enough to adjust to them?
5 All of them, 4 most of them, 3 some of them, 2 a few of them, 1 none of them

Trait IV

☐ 20. How much bladder and bowel control has the child?
5 Complete when awake, 4 fairly complete, 3 average, 2 not very much, 1 complete lack of control

☐ 21. How persistent is the child in such activities as pulling off his cap (her hat), opening and closing boxes, unscrewing jar lids, building towers of blocks, digging in the sand, and making mud pies?
5 Repeats an activity many times in succession, 4 several times, 3 a few times, 2 two or three times, 1 seldom repeats the same activity twice in succession

☐ 22. How much can he (she) help dress himself (herself)?
5 Puts arms and legs in the proper holes, 4 does this sometimes, 3 submits to being dressed, 2 dislikes being dressed, 1 resists being dressed

Trait V

☐ 23. Does he (she) play such social games as pat-a-cake, peek-a-boo, etc.?
5 Very often, 4 frequently, 3 sometimes, 2 seldom, 1 never

☐ 24. Is he (she) ever left to shift for himself (herself) with other children his (her) age?
5 Very often, 4 frequently, 3 occasionally, 2 seldom, 1 never

Trait VI

☐ 25. Does he (she) react to other babies with jealousy or protectiveness?

5 Almost parental in protectiveness, 4 usually somewhat protective, 3 indifferent, 2 dislikes the other baby, 1 shows marked jealousy

Trait VII

☐ 26. Does the child adjust quickly to strangers?

5 Has complete confidence, 4 adjusts quickly, 3 adjusts slowly, 2 is somewhat afraid of strangers, 1 is very much afraid of strangers

☐ 27. Does he (she) respond with anger to thwarted desires?

5 Seldom or never, 4 occasionally, 3 frequently, 2 usually, 1 always

☐ 28. Does he (she) respond with anger to the interruption of activity?

5 Seldom or never, 4 occasionally, 3 frequently, 2 usually, 1 always

☐ 29. How intense are the anger reactions of the child?

5 Almost none, 4 very mild, 3 average, 2 severe, 1 very intense

☐ 30. How long do his (her) anger reactions last?

5 Over very quickly, 4 do not last long, 3 a few minutes, 2 a half hour, 1 very long

Trait VIII

☐ 31. Does the child willingly put away his (her) toys, go to bed, take a bath, etc.?

5 With glee, 4 gladly, 3 indifferent, 2 holds back, 1 dislikes it very much

☐ 32. Does the child give up his toys to other children?

5 Often gladly, 4 frequently, 3 sometimes, 2 seldom, 1 never willingly

VI

Character Development in the Nursery

THE CHILD IS NOT USUALLY PERMITTED to venture into social groups outside his home before his second birthday. By this time he is really no longer an infant but a child. He can walk and talk now, two indispensable abilities to social life which he lacked at birth. Unless he is retarded, he should now possess both abilities in sufficient amounts to get about, climb, handle materials and convey his wants to others. This first venture into society is vitally important. It will make the more difficult social problems of the future much easier if he has had experience in nursery school.

Physical Development

Compared to infancy, physical growth during the third and fourth years of life (from the second to the fourth birthdays) is, relatively speaking, very much more gradual. Actually, however, there is a very wide jump between the two extremes of this age range. The child grows more than five inches in height and gains on the average about eight pounds in weight. This is in the neighborhood of a twenty-five percent increase in these two major criteria of growth. The most important physical ability which the child has during this age, which he did not have until the end of infancy, is the ability to walk. Usually he walks very readily when he reaches his second birthday and, before his fourth arrives, he can run and climb with fair speed of movement and considerable precision and steadiness of action. Indeed, on the physical side this is his greatest purpose in life. When he gets to the kindergarten, he will be walking to get somewhere and most of his activity will have a purpose apart from the activity itself. In the nursery, however, the purpose of activity is to be active. The nursery child seems, to those who do not understand him, to be restless and constantly on the go during his waking hours. As a matter of fact, that is the way he should be, for he is practicing the art of going and learning how to coördinate his large muscle groups into efficient activity. The amount of time he sleeps becomes less, ranging from twelve to fourteen hours out of the twenty-four. It is important that the child get all the sleep he needs, but equally important that foundations should not be laid for future parent-child conflict by forcing him to sleep more than he needs. It should be kept in mind that there are wide individual differences as to how much sleep an individual needs. This is true at this stage of development as well as in later life.

A point will be made now which will recur so frequently in this book that none of its readers can ever forget it. This point is that there are wide individual differences between children. This would seem to be a matter of common sense, but it is an item of common sense more frequently disregarded than perhaps any other single fact. In our laboratories it is possible to measure the motor and physical development of the child reasonably accurately, and show how it relates to that of other children of the same age. This is important for an intelligent guidance in various problems of adjustment.

Mental Development

Far and away the most important factor in mental development is the rapid growth in the use of language. At this point the child has only recently begun to use words as words, so during these two years his interest in language is pretty much practice in the use of this new medium. When he reaches the kindergarten level, he will be using language as a rather automatic method of communication, but now his major interest is in the language itself. His language development should be guided with this in mind. Efficiency in speech is important. By the end of his nursery school training, the last vestige of baby talk and poor articulation should have disappeared. Clearness of speech all the rest of his life will be influenced by the habits he forms at this early age. There is no reason why perfect articulation should not be possible by the end of the third year. All of the physiological mechanisms are mature by that time and can be put into use if the child is so trained. However, language develops in response to needs. If the child can get what he wants by the use of baby talk and poor articulation, he will do so. If, on the other hand, good speech is the necessary road to the securing of satisfaction for his wishes, he will learn good speech fast enough. His use of sentences varies in length from an average of about two words at the age of two to around five words at four years. At three years of age he will have a vocabulary of about nine hundred words, and at four years of age fifteen hundred. A large proportion of his vocabulary will be the names of things. The discovery that everything has a name is the first innate tendency to stimulate vocabulary development. His attention level increases somewhat during this period, but diversity is more stimulating to him than concentration. It would be good training for him to have a fairly wide group of objects which he can explore and manipulate and of which he can learn the names. Then, add new objects to this group from time to time so that his daily life becomes a continuous process of new discoveries. One should not expect him to pay concentrated attention to one thing very long. His memory span is only about twenty minutes and it is not strange that he should forget in a relatively short period most of the things he is told.

Many tests have been developed for the measurement of mental growth during the nursery school age, but the necessary predominance of motor abilities in these tests makes it somewhat doubtful as to how predictive they are of future mental development as such. They are, however, of great value in the immediate adjustmental problems of the child. During the early school period we should be able to measure intelligence as such, but not during the nursery school age. In mental growth, as in physical, there are wide individual differences, and each child will need to be dealt with in accordance with his own native endowment.

Special Aptitudes

The measurement of imagination, musical ability, artistic ability and mechanical aptitude is not possible in any complete sense during this age level. Rather, what happens is that certain very specific abilities appear in children, sometimes frequently, sometimes very rarely. One of the most common examples of that is the desire of children of this age to drive nails into things. This is so common as to be almost universal. The child does not desire to build anything by this process, as he will at the kindergarten level, but he just likes to drive nails. If a good hammer and nails with a soft piece of timber are provided he will be satisfied, and with less disaster than if he can find no other media than the household furniture. Visual abilities mature very early, and the child can be taught color names by the time he is three years old. He will probably learn them of his own accord before he is five, but will get a lot of pleasure out of acquiring this ability somewhat earlier. Very few children show signs of rhythm during this period. When this ability is present it should of course be developed. There are wide individual differences in the ability to use crayons for drawing and coloring and scissors for cutting paper. All children of this age thoroughly enjoy using blocks, not so much for building something as for simply handling things. The larger the blocks, the better for them, if within the range of their capacity to lift them. Permitting them to carry blocks from one place to another is quite as useful at this period as the building of complex structures will be a couple of years later. Finally, in this regard, they like to explore the various capacities of their sense organs. Something to make a noise with, something to smell, bright things to look at, soft things to touch, things to tear, all are sources of activities through which children train their own sensory discrimination. It is well to remember that the child is getting acquainted with himself and his abilities, and the more opportunity there is for him to do this, the happier for all concerned.

Social Development

The social activity of the nursery school age can be characterized best as being parallel rather than coöperative. Children of this age like to be with other children, but they do not like interference with their own activities. They prefer to play near other children rather than with them. When they play together it is fairly rare for groups of more than two to play successfully. A primitive type of dramatization can be utilized, but it must be constructed on the basis of each child reacting to a central theme in a particular way. The fact that this produces group integration will be the result of careful planning on the part of supervisors and quite accidental to the child himself. That this group experience is valuable cannot be doubted, but that the child has any considerable sense of group consciousness is not to be expected. Children do begin to use their imagination, however, and many of them spontaneously create imaginary playmates during this period. During the second year of this period, the child can be stimulated to do helpful things for younger children. This can be achieved through the stimulation of the parental drive, which is already very strong in the child. To suggest to him the desirability of helping older people take care of a younger child is an extremely effective incentive. Finally, a measure of coöperation with authority can be obtained. Regularity brings about an automatic compliance with routine, and the child's innate desire for achievement makes him respond quickly to the admonition to help his elders.

Emotional Development

The infant's emotional reactions are entirely of the all-or-none character. By the time the child has reached the age of the nursery school, however, a great deal of differentiation in emotional reaction has been learned. During infancy, crying played the central rôle in emotional reaction. By the time the child graduates from the nursery, crying should be reasonably rare. Laughing should be a much more frequent response. Perhaps the most striking emotional development during this period is the growth and decline of negativism. In his repertoire of possible reactions a child has one which he innately tends to try out as a method of getting what he wants. This is the temper tantrum. From two to three years of age is the period during which he experiments with this method. There is nothing remarkable about this fact. Every child instinctively uses all of his possible reactions in an effort to make life worth living. If these reactions do not gain what he wants, he soon abandons them for others. Temper tantrums should have almost completely disappeared by the child's third birthday. One must remember, however, that the force behind the temper tantrum, which expresses itself in obstinate and negativistic behavior, is power. It must not be destroyed, but guided into the right channels. It is the stuff out of which will power and perseverance later come to be developed. Parents who feel that implicit obedience is a major virtue, and insist on breaking the child's negativistic tendencies, destroy in him one of his best sources of energy.

Character Education

Character development during this period consists entirely in the establishing of specific reaction habits. They must be desirable in wholesome personality and social integration and must be ones which are chosen by the child because he likes to do them. Too much of the goodness of past generations has consisted of a code of the things which people should not do. If it seems to a child that everything he wishes to do is naughty, he quickly comes to feel that all that is nice is naughty, and in the minds of some people it really is. How we could ever imagine that people could be taught to hunger and thirst for this sort of righteousness is a little difficult to see. Certainly the whole trend of Jesus' teaching was toward happy personalities. He believed in a righteousness about which people would be eagerly enthusiastic. It is vitally important to realize that the inculcation of good habits in any powerful sense of the word is possible only if those habits are formed with enthusiasm and pleasure by the child. A religion which would not use all one's inherited drives and abilities in a wholesome and powerful fashion would certainly be below the Christian ideal. Three factors influence the formation of every desirable habit: first, the demands of the situation in which the child finds himself; second, his innate nature and ability; third, the influence of his past experience. Emphasis needs to be placed upon the second of these, for it again calls our attention to the principle of individual differences and urges against the regimentation that has characterized too much of our educational method in the past.

Experimental Faith

Vision

Vision, in its mature form, is a well-trained imagination in its finest and most useful expression. To make vision reach its highest efficiency presupposes training the imagination as such and giving it material with which to build. Even the most bizarre type of imagination is limited by past experience. What, then, can we do during the nursery period to lay the foundations for this trait? In the first place we find that the child naturally begins to create imaginary playmates and to use simple forms of dramatization. Good education consists in producing the most favorable situations in which natural tendencies may express themselves wholesomely. Here are two natural types of imaginative behavior which begin to function during the nursery school age. Let us see that they have every opportunity to do so. In addition to these, we can add numerous materials, thus broadening the child's experience and giving him more things to deal with in his imagination. From birth every child sets out to discover the world about him. In the long run, the more of it he discovers the better chance he has of thinking intelligently about it. During infancy his chief discoveries are about himself. During the nursery school age his chief discoveries should concern his environment. Imagination, then, is one of the child's capacities which needs exercise with its resultant strengthening. It is this capacity which in later years becomes the high quality of character which we call vision. But vision is not likely to be either strong or broad unless its early foundations are well laid in the nursery.

Love of Righteousness and Truth

This trait which involves a keen interest in learning and a keen interest in morality in its broadest sense makes large strides during this period. It has been emphasized again and again that the primitive concepts of morality, which consist largely in negative ethics, are contrary to human nature and destructive of wholesome personality. Developing a moral stability in a child, which is, on the one hand, of the highest ethical nature, and on the other, wholesome and attractive, is not easy. It is important that we see clearly the whole basic attitude which is involved in this trait. What relationship has love of learning to morality? If love of learning is only idle curiosity, it has little or none, but if this curiosity can be given a strong purpose its whole nature is transformed. Let that purpose be to know the will of God. If a child comes to think of God as exerting His will in everything about him, and also to think of Him as a father, the doing of whose will leads to happiness and achievement, then his whole educational life can be made a search for the will of God. This may be in knowing the processes of nature, learning the thoughts of the past, or understanding the problems of modern society.

Genetically, this means that the growth of this trait first consists in a genuine interest in things about him. The child should have as broad experiences as possible. He should be keenly aware of his environment and an effort made to see that he learns something new every day. What things he learns are partly determined by the directions which his curiosity takes. Let us mention two habits commonly supposed to be bad. One of them is running away. Distracted mothers spend much time searching for children whose curiosity leads them into wider fields than the family provides. It is not probable that a child of this age runs away from home because he is dissatisfied with his home, nor is it probable that his imagination would lead him very far away. One mother simply let her child go, following him unobserved at a distance to see that he got into no serious difficulties. Every day for a week he explored in almost every direction. Then, he had apparently satisfied his curiosity and decided that home was the happiest place to be. No further difficulties were encountered in connection with running away. Let the child, then, have his exploring experiences. If they are a natural tendency at this age, the tendency should be utilized.

Then, too, this is an age when children begin to ask embarrassing questions. One of the most common ones is, "Where do babies come from?" A collection of the false answers to this question given by parents would fill a book. How can we imagine that a child can be taught to love the truth when his first questions are answered falsely? It is difficult to understand how a child is going to grow up with a splendid, wholesome attitude towards sex and all its related problems if good foundations are not laid. To be sure, technical answers are as bad as false answers, for they go beyond the child's comprehension. A guiding principle about answering such questions, either now or later, is to tell the truth as far as the child is capable of understanding it. Whatever embarrassments may result are far less serious than the problems that so frequently arise from morbid or prudish sex knowledge.

One last source of learning is in the child's progress in the use of language. Accurate knowledge is one of the characteristics of knowing the truth. It will be found that the accuracy of one's knowledge correlates very highly with the extent and accuracy of his vocabulary. Teach the child the correct names of things whether they be parts of the body or objects in his environment. Furthermore, teach him to pronounce them correctly. As has been pointed out, baby talk should have disappeared before the end of this period.

Faith in the Friendliness of the Universe

This trait should develop further, perhaps, than any other of the eight traits during this period. This is the time when most fears are developed. It is possible to develop some fears during infancy, but the child's perceptive abilities are not broad enough to make them very numerous. Now, however, his environment is growing by leaps and bounds. He is meeting new things every day. And he is forming some emotional tone toward each of these new things. It is of the greatest importance that it should not be fear. The child is unfortunate who constantly shrinks from notice, or cries easily when things of fearsome nature appear in his environment, or is easily discouraged by the slightest mishap in his adventures, or who has developed a strong fear of germs instilled by parental over-solicitude. He can quite as easily learn to have confidence in the use of materials and confidence in the use of his abilities. It is not good pedagogy to keep a child off high places because he may fall and get a bump. It is much better to teach him to climb by degrees, first on a low chair, then on a high stool, until he finds by safe trial and error what his capacities are in this respect. Of course, certain dangers in our modern world do beset the child and he must be given a genuine caution against them. However, caution and fear are two separate and distinct things. Caution about automobiles is one of the basic essentials to self-preservation in our modern civilization. A genuine fear of automobiles is probably worse than complete recklessness. If the child does develop some fears, which he almost certainly will, teach him to overcome them by positive achievement methods. For example, if he shows a fear of the dark, play games with him which lead into dark rooms, first in company with someone in whom he has confidence, and finally by himself. Give the dark room a positive characteristic. If possible, teach him how to make it light at his own wish. Almost any child can overcome a fear of the dark by this method.

Then, again, his bumps and bruises now become more serious and numerous than during his first two years. To teach him to take them with a grin; getting from that a sense of achievement is some of the best character development a child can have. It should be recalled that, fundamentally, the desire for achievement and courage is far more intense than fear. To stimulate him positively and gradually to seek achievement and to show courage is putting the emphasis where it belongs. On the other hand, the tendency to cry is natural and fears are common. To attempt to eliminate them with shame simply increases their intensity. Such training defeats its own ends by enlarging the very things it is designed to overcome. By the end of his nursery school period, then, the child should be easily adaptable to new situations and glad to try new things. He should be willing and happy to stay with new persons in whose charge he is left.

Dominating Purpose

The young child does not select a vocation for himself. This does not mean, however, that purposiveness may not come to be a quality of his personality. This, in turn, does not mean that the nursery school child should set forth on a problem and spend a whole day at it. Purpose in this sense is not characteristic of the nursery. It will begin to appear during the kindergarten level. The nursery school child is more interested in behavior as such than in the results of behavior. This is the key to his training with respect to this trait. He may carry blocks from one end of a room to another and back again. He may climb everything in sight that is climbable. He may seem to be simply blowing off steam. If, however, his movements are increasingly efficient, more accurate, if he carries the blocks better and climbs with more agility, that is the end toward which he is working. He is training his muscular abilities. If he can be taught to use these abilities actively, aggressively, and confidently, that is the chief value of this age.

Certain elements of actual achievement, however, do give the beginnings of genuine purposiveness. In the first place, it is during this period that he should gain complete bowel and bladder control. Unless our over-modest parents have destroyed the value of this training by shame and guilt elements, this achievement, which is the greatest of his life so far, can be made the source of a great deal of satisfaction and pride to him. Then, too, he will have discovered that building things such as towers and walls brings praise from his elders and he will start seeking attention through such achievements. This is quite all right, for he is much too young yet to be expected to get pleasure entirely from achievement itself. Some children find destructiveness much more attractive than constructiveness. It is easier, and it does give a sense of accomplishment. It seems like a great achievement to kick down a pile of blocks in a second, a pile which required a considerable period of time to build up. If, however, no attention or praise is forthcoming the child is likely to find that this sort of achievement is not as desirable as it seemed to be on the surface. If, at the same time, opportunities are sought to stimulate him with praise to build things, it will be found easy to substitute constructiveness for this destructive tendency. A wide variety of play objects should be placed before him so that whichever ones are most in accord with his own aptitudes and abilities are present.

Finally, it is during this period that one of the most serious handicaps in human personality has its beginnings. This handicap is fear of failure. Parents, over-concerned that their children shall be unusual and outstanding, are likely to put a good deal more emphasis on criticizing their failures than on praising their successes. When children of this age come to the laboratory, obvious evidence of this fear of failure shows up more frequently during this age than at any other. Negative criticism and scolding are much less wholesome stimuli to achievement than the more positive method of approach. Failure is as inevitable as progress. Unless the child can learn to see its value as a step toward achievement, failure will not contribute to the child's character all that it should. Vaudeville acrobats commonly use a psychological trick for their feature stunt; that is, they fail the first time, to make the audience all the more appreciative of success the second. It is quite as easy to develop in a child at this age the realization that an achievement which follows a number of failures is far more to be admired than one which can be realized at the first attempt. Fear of failure, then, should never be allowed to appear, but instead the increased desire to achieve as a result of failure.

Fatherly Love

Being Sensitive to the Needs of Others

Genuine social coöperation does not appear in any large degree until the kindergarten level. However, during the nursery school period a great many things can be done to pave the way for rapid development in the kindergarten. The first two years of a child's life are likely to be confined largely to association with his parents and momentary views of others who come in to exclaim upon the qualities of so fine a baby. From two to four, however, the child must begin to get acquainted with other children his own age, and to find ways of living in a universe in which they have equal privileges with himself. In developing this fifth trait, it is not so important that the child can actually become sensitive to the needs of others as that he can become sensitive to others and to the necessity of adjusting to them. Teaching him the ability of parallel play, in which toys are at the disposal of other children as well as himself, and in which the area of play has to be shared with others, is valuable training to the child to whom the whole universe has been in obedience up to this time.

Mentioning a few of the most common negative traits found in children when they enter the nursery will point out the progress to be made in this connection during this period. The tendency to destroy other children's possessions and creations is very common. The tendency to live by the slogan, "I want what I want when I want it," is a fairly natural one for an energetic, aggressive child. The tendency to be totally indifferent to the presence of other children, to be fairly self-centered and to play alone even when in a group, are evidences of how unsocial a child can be. If the older children in any nursery school group can be urged to be helpful to the younger children, the best possible beginning for the child's social initiation has been made. This will indeed help the child to make new friends easily. It is perhaps just as well in the beginning not to let new children come into too close contact with each other. Do not force the new child to join the group quickly. Let him sit by and watch for a while. Among the toys and play materials should be many which are socially stimulating; that is, their use is more fun if several participate. When a child has learned to construct something from some of the materials, it is well to devise coöperative enterprises in which he contributes this construction. When he shows too great selfishness in his demands for available toys, see that he gets neither the toy nor too much attention. Gradually he will come to realize that other children also must have some of the play materials.

This may seem to be a far cry from the keen sensitiveness to the needs of their children characteristic of parents, but even this will become apparent during the second year of the nursery. It is quite easy to stimulate the parental urge in a three-year-old child. Therefore, if the second year group in the nursery are stimulated to this sort of parental sympathy while the first year group are learning their more primitive lessons of parallel activity, tremendous strides will be made in the development of this trait.

Forgiveness

Forgiveness, as such, is a concept which the child cannot understand for many years to come. In fact, a fairly considerable number of adults have quite a warped notion about it. However, some of the basic forms of forgiveness can be learned during this period. Jealousy of younger brothers and sisters can easily be transformed into parental protectiveness, and this is forgiveness in its fullest sense. In addition to this very common jealousy, one finds many children during this period whose feelings are very easily hurt, those who are supersensitive, those who are sullen and remain angry for a long time and those who are extremely revengeful. In addition to the principle mentioned for the treatment of jealousy, there are other things of great value in the development of this trait which can be done during the nursery school period. The ability to laugh at one's bumps and bruises has already been discussed. If teasing can be added to the list of troubles at which one laughs, the child has learned a most valuable lesson in social adjustment, and one which is intimately related to forgiveness. Then, too, it is inevitable that the child will find himself being constantly frustrated by the superior strength of older children. This, too, must be put in the same category and responded to in the same way. These two principles, then, on the one hand, replacing negative emotions with protectiveness and, on the other, getting a sense of achievement from ability to laugh at one's misfortunes, both physical and social, will take care of a large share of the situations which are likely to be difficulties in the path of learning this trait.

Magnanimity

The most important word in understanding the full social significance of this trait is anger. When one examines conflicts in society, whether they are between individuals or groups or nations, he finds that they are pretty largely the result of anger and its kindred reactions. If Christianity ever hopes to bring about peace in the world, it can do so only by developing personalities characterized by this trait of magnanimity.

One may think of three stages in the development of traits. The pre-school period is largely one of conditioning, the elementary school period of learning facts, and the high school period of philosophizing and the formation of ideals. But ideals are hollow things indeed if they are not based on fact, and they are not very powerful or dependable unless they have the conditioned temperamental qualities learned during the pre-school period. Every church has had the experience of witnessing numerous conversions resulting from some highly enthusiastic period of inspiration, only to see a vast majority of the most enthusiastic converts lose interest within the next few months. This is because their fundamental lessons were not learned in the pre-school period. Perhaps the highest ideals of Christianity can neither be learned nor understood until more mature years, but they will never be solid without the lessons of the nursery.

Let us look at some of the seemingly minor but actually very important habits or characteristics of the young child, as he comes into the nursery, which we must change before he graduates. Impatient anger in dressing, the attitude of "I don't want to" as a reaction to authority, extreme negativism in resistant behavior, the habit of grabbing toys from other children, the tendency to tease and torment other children, and temper tantrums for unsatisfied wishes are all examples of what we are talking about. It has been pointed out already that every one of these habits is based on a native drive in the child, which makes it pretty natural for him to use these forms of expression. It has also been pointed out that this native drive is a source of power which must not be destroyed but transformed into more desirable traits of character. During this period the child can easily learn to replace temper tantrums with socially more desirable methods of getting his wishes. He can learn a rather elementary sense of property rights. If a wholesome type of coöperation with authority proves to be the best way of getting what he wants, it will become his reaction to the inevitable and constant thwarting which arises in family life. If routine is regular and inevitable and if nothing is gained, not even attention, by rebellion against it, the child is likely to find cheerful compliance the most desirable form of reaction. Again, the two years of the nursery period are somewhat different in their growth in this trait. The first one is likely to be mostly the discovery on the part of the child that negative responses are not productive of happiness. By the end of the first year, he should have pretty much chosen a socially acceptable type of responses. During the second year he can be given a certain amount of social responsibility, especially in respect to individual children or with respect to specific problems, and coöperation with authority can become a very positive thing. He can be stimulated to give some of his own playthings to younger children in the same way, thus developing the type of property rights that is most wholesome.

Christian Courage

That quality of unselfishness and fearless service to mankind so much desired in our social leadership today has its beginnings during this period. When one examines it carefully, he finds that it implies several things: first, of course, social purpose. This aspect of the trait, however, will not be developed very much during the nursery school period, for the child's social vision is limited. But along with social vision goes social courage, the determination to serve even when that service outwardly brings persecution instead of reward. Again, this is too much to expect of the nursery school child. If one looks carefully, however, he can find a number of things which the nursery school child can learn which do become foundations on which to build this larger trait. The child who is afraid to participate in group activities and who is obviously extremely shy is not likely to grow into a man of social courage. Nor is the child whose whole interests are unsocial and self-centered likely to choose a self-sacrificing life of social service.

Methods have already been discussed to show how the elements of social coöperation and social aggressiveness can be begun during this period. Even a certain element of leadership can be stimulated. If a child is excessively shy, find out what his abilities are, and teach him some achievement in which he uses these abilities until he is highly efficient in this achievement. Then bring him into group situations in which this superiority on his part will become evident to him as he watches other children try to do the same thing. Experiments have shown that very submissive children can be tremendously improved in ascendancy by this method. Also, using this as a beginning, the child will become increasingly willing to take social responsibilities. It is natural for a child to enjoy achievement. Therefore the suggestion that he can be helpful to his elders will be responded to with enthusiasm by most nursery children. The gradual development of the ability to play wholeheartedly and, of course, to learn to laugh at bumps and bruises and social difficulties, both lay foundations of great importance for the future development of this trait. The nursery school situation, which by its very nature teaches independence of over-solicitous parental protection, together with its wide variety of opportunities to share things and to be helpful, is of the greatest value in character development.

Conclusion

The nursery was once just a place to leave the children while the parents attended church. Now, some of the most effective character education of the whole church school program takes place in the nursery. In the early years of the Union-Westminster Character Research Project the work which was most demonstrably successful was in the nursery. It was easier to get a clear picture of just what we were trying to accomplish and likewise easier to determine at the end to what extent we had succeeeded. The questionnaire which follows will set forth more definitely and objectively the aims of character education in the nursery.

QUESTIONNAIRE FOR THE NURSERY

In the square preceding each question write the number, 5, 4, 3, 2, or 1. After each question is a series of five possible answers to the question, numbered 5, 4, 3, 2, and 1 respectively. In the square use the number preceding the phrase which most nearly represents your answer.

Psychological Development

☐ 1. How well does he (she) move about?
5 Runs well, 4 runs some, 3 walks well, 2 walks with difficulty, 1 does not walk

☐ 2. How long does he (she) sleep every day?
5 Sixteen hours, 4 fourteen hours, 3 twelve hours, 2 eleven hours, 1 ten hours or less

☐ 3. Has he (she) a sense of rhythm?
5 Keeps time perfectly, 4 considerable sense of rhythm, 3 tries to keep time, 2 participates in rhythm games with no sense of time, 1 has no interest or ability in rhythm

Trait I

☐ 4. How often does he (she) create imaginary playmates?
5 Constantly, 4 frequently, 3 sometimes, 2 seldom, 1 never

☐ 5. How often does he (she) engage in simple imaginary dramatization?

5 Every day, 4 frequently, 3 sometimes, 2 seldom, 1 never

Trait II

☐ 6. How much baby talk and poor articulation does he (she) use?

5 None, 4 very little, 3 some, 2 considerable, 1 very hard to understand

☐ 7. About how large is his (her) vocabulary?

5 Very unusual, 4 above average, 3 average, 2 below average, 1 very poor

☐ 8. About how many words does he (she) use on the average in a sentence?

5 Usually eight or more, 4 about six, 3 four or five, 2 three, 1 all one or two word sentences

☐ 9. How much curiosity has he (she)?

5 Very much, 4 above average, 3 average, 2 not much, 1 almost none

☐ 10. Does he (she) like to explore with his (her) sense organs; that is, does he (she) enjoy: lots of noise, to smell things, bright colors, to touch soft things, and the like?

5 Constantly doing so, 4 does so a great deal, 3 does so some, 2 not very much, 1 has almost no interest in such activity

☐ 11. Does the child like to explore places outside his (her) own home?

5 Always doing so, 4 very frequently, 3 some, 2 seldom, 1 never

☐ 12. Does the child ask lots of questions about things?

5 Constantly doing so, 4 does so very much, 3 asks some questions, 2 occasionally asks questions, 1 never asks questions

☐ 13. Does he (she) know the correct names of parts of his (her) body?

5 All of them, 4 most of them, 3 some of them, 2 a few, 1 none

☐ 14. Does he (she) know the names of colors?
5 Ten or more, 4 eight or nine, 3 six or seven, 2 four or five, 1 less than four

Trait III

☐ 15. Of how many things is he (she) afraid?
5 None, 4 one or two, 3 three or four, 2 five or six, 1 more than six

☐ 16. Does he (she) tend to shrink from notice?
5 Is quite self-confident, 4 has no such tendency but not aggressive, 3 average, 2 some tendency to avoid notice, 1 constantly shrinks from notice

☐ 17. Does he (she) like to climb?
5 Climbs constantly, 4 climbs a great deal, 3 some, 2 very little, 1 does not climb at all

☐ 18. Is he (she) afraid of the dark?
5 Not in the least, 4 very little, 3 some fear, 2 considerably, 1 very much so

☐ 19. Does he (she) laugh more than he (she) cries?
5 Almost never cries, 4 usually laughs, 3 about equal, 2 cries frequently, 1 almost never laughs

☐ 20. Does he (she) adjust easily to strange situations?
5 At once, 4 quickly, 3 average, 2 slowly, 1 only with greatest difficulty

☐ 21. Is he (she) willing to stay with strange adults?
5 With complete willingness, 4 needs very little adjustment, 3 does so after a while, 2 does so only after repeated meetings, 1 requires a very long time to adjust

☐ 22. Has he (she) developed a fear of failure?
5 Does not mind failure at all, simply tries again, 4 very little bothered by failure, 3 bothered some by failure, 2 definitely tries to avoid failure, 1 refuses to try if there is a possibility of failure

Trait IV

☐ 23. Does he (she) like to drive nails in things?
5 A favorite activity, 4 often does, 3 sometimes does, 2 seldom does, 1 never does

☐ 24. How long can he (she) concentrate on one activity?
5 An hour, 4 forty-five minutes, 3 twenty minutes, 2 ten minutes, 1 less than ten minutes

☐ 25. Does he (she) enjoy using crayons for drawing?
5 Does it constantly, 4 frequently, 3 sometimes, 2 seldom, 1 never

☐ 26. Does he (she) enjoy cutting paper with scissors?
5 Does it constantly, 4 frequently, 3 sometimes, 2 seldom, 1 never

☐ 27. Does he (she) enjoy building with blocks?
5 Does it constantly, 4 frequently, 3 sometimes, 2 seldom, 1 never

☐ 28. Has the child achieved bowel and bladder control?
5 Complete, 4 with rare exceptions, 3 frequent exceptions, 2 rather poor control, 1 almost no control

☐ 29. Does he (she) enjoy constructiveness more than destructiveness?
5 Very constructive, never destroys, 4 builds more than he (she) destroys, 3 somtimes one, sometimes the other, 2 seldom constructs, usually destroys, 1 never builds, always destroys

Trait V

☐ 30. Does he (she) like to be with other children?
5 Very much, 4 often, 3 sometimes, 2 occasionally, 1 never

☐ 31. Does he (she) show the "I want what I want, when I want it" attitude?
5 Very unselfish, 4 fairly generous, 3 average, 2 has this attitude somewhat, 1 very much given to this attitude

Trait VI

☐ 32. Does he (she) enter into activities in which other children participate?
5 Very willingly, 4 often, 3 sometimes, 2 rarely, 1 never

☐ 33. Is he (she) willing to share his (her) toys with other children?
5 Always, 4 usually, 3 sometimes, 2 not often, 1 never

☐ 34. Does he (she) take an interest in new members of the group?
5 Very friendly toward them, 4 usually, 3 sometimes, 2 not often, 1 never

☐ 35. Is he (she) jealous of other children?
5 Never, 4 rarely, 3 sometimes, 2 often, 1 always

☐ 36. Does he (she) blame others for his (her) own failures and wrong doings?
5 Never, 4 occasionally, 3 sometimes, 2 often, 1 always

Trait VII

☐ 37. Are his (her) feelings easily hurt?
5 Not in the least, 4 not much, 3 sometimes, 2 often, 1 very much so

☐ 38. In how large groups can he (she) play without quarreling?
5 Groups of more than six, 4 five or six, 3 three or four, 2 two, 1 prefers to play alone

☐ 39. What is his (her) reaction to frustration by older and stronger children?
5 Accepts it with a grin, 4 takes it philosophically, 3 accepts it on protest, 2 resents it considerably, 1 becomes very angry

Trait VIII

☐ 40. Is he (she) often sullen and angry?
5 Very happy disposition, 4 happy disposition, 3 even tempered, 2 somewhat ill tempered, 1 very bad tempered

☐ 41. How much opportunity does he (she) have for supervised group activity?
5 Daily, 4 weekly, 3 often, 2 sometimes, 1 never

☐ 42. How well does he (she) adjust to routine?
5 Coöperates cheerfully, 4 coöperates willingly, 3 submits without protest, 2 objects to routine, 1 objects violently to routine

☐ 43. What is his (her) usual reaction to authority?
5 Coöperates happily, 4 coöperates willingly, 3 submits without protest, 2 resists authority, 1 extreme negativism

☐ 44. How obedient is he (she)?

5 Obeys gladly when reasoned with, 4 obeys usually without question, 3 complete obedience, 2 obeys fearfully, 1 highly suggestible

☐ 45. Does he (she) show a sense of property rights?

5 Shares toys with other children, 4 does not touch other children's toys, 3 seldom grabs other children's toys, 2 often grabs what he (she) wants, 1 always grabs what he (she) wants

☐ 46. Does he (she) show signs of leadership?

5 Often takes leadership rôles, 4 sometimes does, 3 occasionally does, 2 never does, 1 definitely shrinks from leadership

☐ 47. What is his (her) reaction to minor bumps and bruises?

5 Laughs at them, 4 does not mind them, 3 does not like them, 2 cries a little, 1 cries with terror

☐ 48. Does he (she) show fear with tears?

5 Grins and stands up to it, 4 does not show fear outwardly, 3 very little show of fear, 2 cries some, 1 screams with terror

☐ 49. Is he (she) easily discouraged by slight mishaps?

5 Not bothered at all, 4 bothered very little, 3 bothered some, 2 fairly easily discouraged, 1 completely discouraged at slightest mishap

VII

The Kindergarten Child

Distinguishing Characteristics of the Period

HOW DOES THE KINDERGARTEN CHILD differ from the nursery school child? As it has been pointed out previously, any division into age levels is an artificial one. Characterizing an age level must at best consist of very broad generalizations. However, growth at this early age is so rapid that many changes have occurred. These changes are so significant that the sort of education which can be given to the kindergarten child is extremely different from that which characterizes the nursery. The various functions, physical and mental, which constitute the adult personality have two important stages. The first of these appears when the function first begins to express itself in the growing individual. There is a period when the child simply practices the function as such. The second period begins when the function has become so automatic that the child uses it as a part of his personality to accomplish more remote purposes.

Let us see what some of the functions are which are practiced during the nursery and which become purposive during the kindergarten. The first one is the child's ability to run, jump, and climb. During the nursery he did these things for their own sake. In the kindergarten he does them as a means to an end instead of as the end in itself. He runs to get somewhere and climbs to reach a desired object. The second has to do with talking. During the nursery talking is carried on pretty much for its own sake. At the kindergarten age it becomes a method of communication. The various parts of speech can be used, fairly long sentences are common in the child's conversation, and the spoken word becomes a tool. Other illustrations will present themselves in the course of our discussion of the kindergarten, but these two stand out and underlie most of the changes that occur during this time.

Physical Development

Physically, the child makes another large jump between his fourth and his sixth birthdays. This jump is so large that even the smallest in stature at the age of six are usually taller than the largest when they are four. The absolute growth in inches and pounds is about the same as in the nursery. Obviously, the proportionate growth is somewhat less. The child grows from three feet to about three and a half feet in height, and from a weight of about thirty pounds to a weight of about forty. His hours of sleep diminish somewhat during this time until eleven to thirteen hours are sufficient for most children of this age. His motor activities, which he learned during the nursery, now have become quite automatic and are used purposively to reach his goals. Motor skills begin to appear. Just as walking, running, jumping and climbing are games for the nursery school child, so skipping and hopping become the new acquisitions to the child's motor repertoire in the kindergarten. By the end of this period the child has a great deal more self-confidence in his ability to do things of a motor nature. It is usually during this time that we have the greatest difficulty preventing him from attempting things beyond his capacities. There are wide individual differences, since individual differences become greater as the child grows older. Furthermore, we can measure the child's motor abilities with considerable accuracy. Analysis of the child's motor capacities is extremely important for helping him make his immediate adjustments, and is, therefore, of genuine value in character development.

Mental Development

As it has been pointed out, the chief distinguishing characteristic between the mental behavior of the kindergarten and the nursery child is his use of language as a means to an end. His vocabulary grows very rapidly. He comes to the kindergarten with less than fifteen hundred words in his repertoire and leaves it with approximately three thousand. During this period, girls have a tendency to learn words more rapidly than boys and at all age levels tend to excel them in facility of language use. This superiority in vocabulary, however, does not continue. The child's reasoning ability at this time changes even more than his vocabulary. The what and where questions of the nursery change to how, when and why in the kindergarten, and this contrast, better than any other, characterizes the mental development of the child. In the use of language, the child begins to make generalizations and apply rules although, of course, he is not consciously aware of doing so. The nursery school child simply repeats sentences as he has learned them and, in general, does not create any new ones. The kindergarten child does. When a five-year-old says to his parents, "I throwed the ball," he shows an ability to generalize and transfer which is extremely significant for education. As is obvious, in this he is being more consistent in his grammar than the English language itself is. This ability to generalize is of the greatest importance, and it shows up in a number of different places. He perceives relationships between different things, in acts, antecedents, and consequences. Number concepts begin to appear. The child under four does not really have a concept of number at all. The kindergarten child can count to four or six, and can reproduce groups up to seven or eight. Only when one has considered the place that number plays in human thinking can he realize how much this means in the child's ability to grasp new ideas. This principle of generalization and abstraction is still, however, very primitive.

For the most part, moral concepts are quite impossible. A group of children who had been preparing some baskets for the "poor children" were quizzed as to who the "poor children" were. One or two of them knew some "poor children", but, when the questions were pushed far enough, it became quite obvious that the word "poor" had no connotation remotely approaching the adult conception of it. Kindergarten concepts relate pretty much to specific experiences, and one must not expect the kindergarten child to learn or understand either the Beatitudes or the Ten Commandments. Therefore, when the child asks questions, he should be answered and answered honestly. But a long and abstract answer is of no value whatsoever in contributing to his information.

Special Aptitudes

Expressions of all the special aptitudes flourish during the kindergarten age. This is so much so, that most of his activity seems to center in them. The activity of the nursery is largely in the nature of physical exercise; the activity of the kindergarten is constructive. The nursery school child drives nails in boards just for the sake of driving nails in boards. The kindergarten child builds things. He will have acquired all the color names by five, and his score in color naming and matching will usually be as good at six as it ever will be. Many children show remarkable sensitiveness to color harmony between four and six years of age. A sense of rhythm appears during this period and rhythm games are very popular. All forms of artistic ability express themselves. Clay modelling, water coloring, drawing, cutting out designs with scissors, pasting pictures, and making scrapbooks—all these things fill a large percentage of the child's daily life.

Two problems which need to be solved are still rather obscure as far as our scientific knowledge of them is concerned. One is the problem of measurement. Active as children are at this age in relation to the special aptitudes, the development of good tests for measuring them has been an extremely difficult task. The other problem is in knowing just how prognostic of the adult personality kindergarten aptitudes are. If a child is unusually good in some form of artistic achievement when he is five years old, does that mean that he will be when he is twenty-five? That question we cannot answer too dogmatically. In general, the evidence would seem to indicate that the permanent special aptitudes do not show themselves very clearly until about ten or eleven. They are really different abilities at this period. The kindergarten child draws what he thinks instead of what he sees. It is not surprising, therefore, that when we measure this ability to draw what he thinks, it does not predict very well the later ability to draw what he sees. Musical genius does appear even at this age, but the less outstanding grades of musical ability are still impossible to distinguish. The same is true of mechanical ability. If, however, we continue to measure the special aptitudes as well as we can, making use of the measurements for the immediate adjustment of the child and waiting to see what the future brings forth, these two problems will eventually be solved.

Social Development

From a personality point of view, the social development of this period is the most significant factor in the life of the child. Up to this time, social adjustment in any complete sense of the word simply has not existed. The young child is inevitably self-centered and, if he can learn to tolerate the presence of others who encroach upon his domain, he has learned about all we can expect of him during the nursery period. During the kindergarten period, however, coöperation in the literal sense of that word comes into existence. The imagination which causes the nursery school child to create make-believe playmates brings out in the kindergarten child a fairly highly developed dramatic form of play. This dramatic play involves the coöperation of other actors. Furthermore, a drama of this sort is often constructed coöperatively by a fairly large group of children. When children are not supervised, the size of such groups must be kept relatively small. Otherwise an overabundance of conflict is inevitable. Supervised groups, of course, can be increased in size to fairly large proportions. One social characteristic which seems to have moral significance does come to full maturity during this period, and that is sympathy. Human personality is naturally sympathetic, and the reason why many adults lack this characteristic is because it has been suppressed, not because it was lacking in their native endowment. In spite of this natural sympathy, this is the period, especially with respect to boys, when the "boys don't cry" philosophy is first preached insistently. Its effect is extremely vicious. Instead of developing this sympathy, which ought to become one of the most important traits in our whole social life, it is stunted and often almost completely repressed.

During this period, children learn not only to coöperate with each other but to coöperate with authority more effectively. As much obedience as should ever be required of a child can be secured during this period. But parents and teachers should realize that the child also has developed the ability to make many decisions for himself. He should be given ample opportunity to make decisions and his elders should abide by them. A considerable amount of courtesy can be acquired by the child. "Please" and "thank you" can become a regular part of his social vocabulary. Elders must not mistake their significance, however, and imagine that they represent too much in the way of genuine thoughtfulness. Actually, in the mind of the child they constitute a part of his "ready cash" with which to buy things. That is, he finds that he gets more if he uses these words than if he does not. This is perhaps as it should be for, after all, this is about the only cash that he does have. A similar example is very commonly discovered by grandparents who are forced to buy kisses with good wishes and gifts. A child of this age does not naturally like to kiss, and grandparents should not be too hurt when they find that these kisses do not represent such a complete reciprocation of affection as they had hoped. Finally, social conflicts and more violently aggressive behavior put in their appearance during this period. This is the time when the child is likely to have his first fight, although words are usually a substitute for physical aggression. During this and the primary period which follows, two boys who spend an hour threatening each other, with neither of them making a real aggressive physical act, are learning to make a type of social adjustment which will be important to them in later years when they discover that physical aggressions are largely confined to nations and infants.

Emotional Development

Just as anger is the outstanding emotional expression in the nursery, so is fear in the kindergarten. During the nursery school period the child was just beginning to get acquainted with himself as an individual. Temper tantrums represented an attempt on his part to assert himself. Now his perceptual powers make him much more aware of the world about him. This awareness carries with it the possibility of being afraid of a great many things. A large number of the phobias which later cause so much weakness of personality appear during this age level. One redeeming feature of all this, however, is that this same increase in perceptual ability makes it possible for the child to develop an objective attitude toward these various fearful objects and to evaluate them in rational terms. A problem which has troubled parents considerably is the question of how soon children should learn to face reality in its less attractive aspects. The answer is that this should be a gradual process and certain important aspects of it should begin now. The child is not yet able to understand the social deceit and cruelty that later he must accept as inevitable, but now he can learn to face physical reality as it really is. The cruelties of nature, involving its dangers, can be met with courage by the kindergarten child. It is not good pedagogy to tell a child that a dangerous thing is not dangerous. Such an effort to prevent his developing a fear is likely to lead to a worse fear later on. On the other hand, it is even worse pedagogy to make him emotionally afraid of it. An objective evaluation as far as he is able to understand it is the best form of approach. It should be noted in passing that over-solicitude when children are afraid is a strong temptation to the child to develop pseudo-fears as a way of getting adult attention. When a child is genuinely afraid, he needs encouragement from those in whom he has confidence, but pseudo-fears can be practiced long enough to become real ones in his mind.

Finally, from the emotional point of view, this is the first age of real affection. Affection for parents especially becomes very real during this period. There was a period in the development of certain schools of psychology when parents were urged to withhold any demonstration of affection from their children. Fortunately, this idea was short-lived even among the extremists who proposed it. There is no doubt that a too intense affection by the child for either or both of his parents is undesirable and leads to difficulties and later maladjustments. The fact still remains that the growing child, especially during this troublesome period, needs affection and should have it and have it from lots of people.

The Total Personality

Up to the present time, we have spoken of the child pretty much as if he were a set of habits and attitudes having no unity or individuality at all. Of course, this is not true. Each child has his own personality which is distinguishable from any other almost as soon as he is born. From a practical point of view, however, he could be dealt with at that time as if this were not true. Now, however, as he becomes a social individual, it is important that we treat him as a total personality. A number of studies have been made to discover which of the characteristics of the kindergarten personality are most important in social adjustment. One of the most important of these studies [1] describes nine personality

[1] Roberts, K. E., and Ball, R. S., "A Study of Personality in Young Children by Means of a Series of Rating Scales," *The Journal of Genetic Psychology, 52*:79-149. 1938.

traits and by statistical methods shows their relative importance. In order they are as follows: respect for property rights, the tendency to face reality, a wholesome response to authority, compliance with routine, sociability, attractiveness of personality, independence of adult affection, physical attractiveness, and ascendance-submission. It is interesting to observe that physical attractiveness and aggressiveness, so commonly rated in first place, actually correlate lowest with general personality. If one should seek a set of aims for kindergarten education, probably he could do no better than to choose the first five of this group of nine traits as his goals. To teach the child to have some respect for property rights so that he can distinguish between "mine" and "thine", to train him to face reality, of which we have already spoken, to develop in him a wholesome response to authority, to make him able to comply with routine in the group in which he finds himself, and to develop his sociability and group coöperativeness would contribute substantially to his growth in wholesome personality. In practice, developing these rather general traits consists largely in building specific habits. Most of these habits will appear in the discussion of character development as guided by the eight traits set forth in this study.

Experimental Faith

Vision

Training in vision during this time consists primarily in developing and guiding the now rapidly growing imagination. During this period parents sometimes become unduly concerned about their children's truthfulness. When the five-year-old comes into the house and says that he has seen a cat as big as a cow, parents are often deeply worried. The truth is that his imagination is still new to him and extremely vivid. It is so vivid, as a matter of fact, that he usually has what is called in psychology eidetic imagery. This means that he sees images so clearly that he can describe them as accurately as if he were looking at the real objects. This ability is commonly lost before one reaches adult age. Such vividness of imagination makes it extremely difficult for him to distinguish between imagination and reality. It probably is true that, if put to it, he would not know which cat he really saw, the cat he did see, or the cat as big as a cow which he imagined. As time goes along, especially if this imagination is kept in contact with reality and is made as much a stimulation for his behavior as possible, his ability to utilize it objectively and actively will increase with experience. Parents and teachers should continually broaden the scope of his experience. This gives him more food for imagination, for he cannot imagine things beyond the limits of his experience. Then they ought to leave plenty of time in his daily schedule for carrying out the results of his imaginative planning. As long as the plans of imagination lead to real behavior, imagination and its later forms of daydreaming are sources of power. Among the new fields in which he may go are those of music and art and the beauties of nature. After a child has been subjected to experiences of this sort, watch the next games that he devises out of his imagination and see how fruitful such experiences are in his training. Training in the kindergarten of the sort we have been describing is the very best kind of foundation for the man and woman of social vision. The trouble with a great many adults is that they have never formed the habit of picturing in their own minds social conditions as they are and as they might be, which is the only adequate stimulus for social progress.

Love of Righteousness and Truth

If one thinks of character in terms of strength rather than just the absence of evil, efforts to develop it are quite as desirable to the child as to his teachers. The kindergarten child likes to learn, thoroughly enjoys the tasks that are set before him, and looks forward eagerly to becoming stronger and more grown up. Good teaching should find him an eager learner. Perhaps more than at any other age, by nature he hungers and thirsts after righteousness. It is during this time above all others that parents and teachers must take special precaution that neither learning nor righteousness comes to consist of irksome tasks or inhibited drives. Let character development here be especially positive. If the child does hunger and thirst for righteousness, let us make that righteousness so palatable that this hunger will be augmented instead of satiated. Let us, then, recall that the character of each child is a separate and distinct problem. Its development involves a knowledge of his native endowment and the environment to which he must adjust, as well as of the traits which can be assimilated during this period.

A new concept is almost certain to become an important part of the child's thinking during these years; namely, the concept of sin. Before this time right and wrong are as nonexistent as the concepts of advanced philosophy. To be sure, the ideas of right and wrong which characterize the kindergarten period are very primitive ones. The fact remains, however, that primitive though they may be, concepts of right and wrong do appear. Along with the native ability which makes such moral distinctions possible also goes the possibility of having a sense of guilt and shame. Too many parents feel that morals are quite impossible to teach aside from this sense of guilt or shame. It may be said with considerable dogmatism that guilt and shame are invariably unwholesome and should never be resorted to as methods of moral education. Over-modesty, undue prudishness, which in later years make for so much unhappy marriage, and smallness in personality stature find their beginnings during the kindergarten period. In order to teach a child the appropriateness and inappropriateness of certain types of conversation at the table or before guests it is not necessary to make him have a sense of guilt or shame about those things. In general, adults do not discuss their family budgets with everyone who comes in to call, but that does not mean that they are ashamed of them. Young people in love consider the intimacies of their love-making as quite sacred and private and they do not discuss them in public, but it would be absurd to imagine that they are ashamed of them. Exactly the same principle can be applied to habits of personal cleanliness and the various sex problems that arise. There is not the remotest excuse for the shame and guilt training which has distorted so many personalities beyond wholesome recognition. In this respect, one of the problems which almost inevitably arises during this period, and sometimes much earlier, is that of masturbation. Children discover the sensitiveness of their sexual parts, and it is inevitable that this becomes attractive to them. Such a problem is not solved by the use of guilt and shame. Rather, to avoid excessive stimulation, to provide adequate exercise and good wholesome food, and gradually to give the child a positive wholesome concept of sex is a far better approach.

This elementary development of moral behavior is only one aspect of the trait of hungering and thirsting for righteousness. The other side of it is the desire to learn. The child's interest in things about him during this period grows at an enormous rate and, if his parents and teachers are wise, a great many problems will be presented to him for his own solution. He will come more and more to try to solve his problems for himself before he comes to his elders for help. It is increasingly common for children to attend kindergarten schools. Now is the time to create in the child an insatiable curiosity to learn new things. During the next period, he is to begin his formal education. Many experiments have been performed which show that the child who goes to kindergarten school is a better pupil later on than the one who does not. Undoubtedly the reason for this difference is the broader experience of the kindergarten-trained child and the constant stimulus to his curiosity which he finds there.

Faith in the Friendliness of the Universe

The central concept in Jesus' teaching is the fatherhood of God. No other religious teacher ever conceived the guiding principle of the universe as having the characteristics of a father. Whether or not Christianity will prove to be the ultimate religion probably depends more upon the validity of this concept than upon any other. Interestingly enough, it is the first theological idea that can be given to the child. The basic concept itself can be taught in the kindergarten. The principle of God the father has two important aspects. One is the protectiveness of God; the other is the love of God for all his children and the implied family relationships of his children with one another. Both of these aspects can be taught in the kindergarten period. The first one is the one with which we are dealing in this trait. Something has been said already of the tendency toward the development of fears during this period, such as the fear of water, the fear of the dark, the fear of thunder and lightning, the fear of high places, the fear of strange objects, and the fear of strange people. When one finds a child with a strong sense of insecurity carrying with it a loss of appetite, the inability to relax, nervousness, and often stammering and stuttering, he has a child in whom the protectiveness of a Father-God has not been made a reality. Developing fears in children as a means of disciplinary control is one of the surest ways of destroying forever the possibilty of their learning the fatherhood of God. Ministers and Sunday School teachers to whom the fear of God is the most important element in religion often instill in a child fears that weaken his personality forever. Along with teaching a child the ability to face reality, and indeed as a part of it, one can give the child a very realistic concept of a Father-God which can be made to grow with his intellectual development. Children who are told to say their prayers lest some terrible fate overtake them, who are told that God gives them everything they pray for, are certainly not being trained in a theology that is very helpful in meeting the real problems of life as they face them. The nursery school child is taught to handle objects freely and confidently and to have complete trust in people. The kindergarten child can have this simple, very perfect type of confidence broadened considerably. Such training is very useful in giving the child the notion of all of the factors, both social and natural, which tend to work together for man's happiness. It is not easy to find just the point of stark reality which the child can assimilate into his concept of a Father-God, but it is important that the foundations for this concept be laid and that the earliest steps be taken to make it a realistic concept which conforms to things as he finds them and will find them as he grows older.

Dominating Purpose

The prominence which purposiveness now begins to play in the child's personality makes this trait very much more important than during the two earlier periods. The child's behavior now is definitely purposive—he is building things, actually setting out to accomplish things. To be sure, his purposes are rather short ones. He is not likely to decide on some scheme for world salvation and begin to dedicate the rest of his life to its fulfillment. He is much more likely to initiate fifty or sixty different physical projects in the course of a single day and finish almost none of them. If he begins in the morning to dig a tunnel to China and before noon to dam the ocean, with equally impossible but short-lasting purposes as the day proceeds, we should not be surprised. As a matter of fact, a child's concept of his purposes in life is often more intelligent for his personality development than those his parents conceive for him. The very fact that he is purposive is the important thing.

Two aspects of this purposiveness are especially significant during this period. The first one hinges on the old saying that "Nothing succeeds like success." This is one of the few popular proverbs that psychologically is quite true. It is vitally important that the child experience the pleasure and thrill which come from successful achievement. It is more important now than it has been before to get as good a measure of his abilities as we possibly can and to set up situations and problems for him that will exercise those abilities and give him a sense of achievement. He should work with confidence and pleasure and be able to concentrate for increasingly long intervals on a task which he has conceived.

The other aspect of purposiveness that needs to be learned during this period is the right response to failure. Because he does choose to dig a tunnel to China and dam the ocean, it is inevitable that he will fail many times. Such failures as these are not important, but there are others. He will fail when other children of his age succeed. He will fail when his parents assure him that he ought to succeed. These are the sorts of failure that produce the fear of failure so destructive of strong personality. During this period, then, he needs to be taught how to react to failure. In a very interesting study by Keister and Updegraff,[2] a method for improving children's reactions to failure was devised. In this experiment, numbers of children were found to make undesirable responses when they failed. Some reacted by doing nothing, others by asking other individuals for help, some by crying, and so on. A period of training was established which involved the following features. The children were given tasks to perform, at first very easy and then increasingly difficult, but always of such a nature that success was possible. Simply because children do like to succeed, each new achievement increased the child's perseverance for the next more difficult task. Furthermore, the tasks were of such a nature that the child could see that he was making progress. After a period of time, it was found that when the children came back to the tasks on which they had failed originally and to which they had responded in an undesirable manner, they now made much more effective and persevering types of responses. If to this method is added the training of children in the particular abilities in which they excel, most fear of failure can be avoided.

One of the first symptoms which indicate to the psychologist the presence of a sense of fear of failure in a child is the child's inability to work well under pressure. Many

[2] Keister, M. E., and Updegraff, R., "A Study of Children's Reactions to Failure and an Experimental Attempt to Modify Them," *Child Development*, Vol. 8, No. 3. September 1937.

children tend to go to pieces as soon as pressure is applied. This is more common during this age than at any other. No child should ever be hurried beyond his capacities. He will get as much pleasure from achieving things more quickly than other children, as from achieving them better than other children. If speed becomes an ideal and a stimulus rather than a threat, this tendency to go to pieces under pressure need never appear.

Because of the child's social interests, and especially his innate sympathy, it is also possible during this period to develop the habit of making his purposes social in their nature. When a child beyond six years of age is selfish and self-centered in most of his activities, it is because his parents and teachers have neglected to take advantage of his natural tendencies. A dominating purpose in the service of mankind finds its beginnings during this period, and the child can concentrate now on creating a Christmas card for his mother in exactly the same spirit with which in later years he may give his life to some great altruistic vocation. It is entirely possible that unless he does do it now he is not likely to then.

Fatherly Love

Sensitiveness to the Needs of Others

A good deal has already been said of the child's natural sensitiveness. Fundamentally, this trait is sympathy. During this period the child is easily moved to tears by the suffering of others. Left to his own natural trends, he has a strong tendency to like people in general, and beginning with this period he finds people more stimulating than anything else. This is another phase of the fatherliness of God. The child cannot be taught such abstract terms as poverty and misery, but he can be taught to sympathize with those who are suffering physically. It is far better pedagogy to have children of this age make things for sick people than for poor people. Sickness they understand; poverty they do not. With respect to people who are handicapped, in addition to sympathy they need also to become aware of the pleasant aspects in their lives. An excellent example of this is in learning about the blind. A party in which a group of blind children compete in various games with children of normal vision often becomes a real revelation because it helps them to realize what the blind can do. But above all, this is the period for the development of sympathy and awareness of the needs and sufferings of others.

Forgiveness

Some of the common habits which are the very opposite of this trait will best illustrate how it can express itself during this period. Completely ignoring the feelings of others when attempting to carry out one's own desires, tending to grab the best of everything in sight especially when others grab, being jealous of the popularity of others, the tendency to blame others for one's own wrong doings, being sensitive and having one's feelings easily hurt, the tendency to harbor dislikes for people over a long period of time—these are a few such habits. Traditionally, children have been thought of as being essentially selfish by nature. Such habits as these undoubtedly form the foundation for such an idea. Actually, nothing is easier in child education than overcoming just such habits as these, or rather, preventing their being formulated in the first place. Every one of them can be replaced by a sympathetic, parent-like, protective interest in other children. That is, if children find it necessary to compete with one another, these undesirable reactions are likely to be made. The ideal of brotherly love is difficult to apply satisfactorily to such problems. But if the older children are stimulated to take a protective interest in their younger brothers and sisters, more desirable responses are easily elicited. Dolls and pets are valuable objects for eliciting the same parental drives. Brotherly love, when it is made the central motivation of one's social adjustments, is not easy to learn. Parental love is as natural in the personality of the child as hunger.

Magnanimity

Two important principles, the overlooking of which leads to a large proportion of our human conflicts, can be learned in large measure during the kindergarten period. Both of them were mentioned in the Roberts and Ball [3] study. They are, coöperation with authority and sense of property rights. The nursery child, it will be recalled, conceived of property rights only in the sense of immediate possession. The kindergarten child can definitely learn the notion of "mine" and "thine". This is one of the most important lessons during this age. It is not accomplished as a result of preaching on the part of his elders, but by a process of give and take in his social adjustments, with encouragement and guidance. He is not likely to assert his insistence upon his unsatisfied wishes with temper tantrums. They are fairly rare and somewhat abnormal at this age. They are mostly in the province of the nursery. Along with them he largely abandons aggressive physical conquest as a method for obtaining what he wants.

Together with this sense of property rights comes an increasing coöperation with authority, especially if he is fortunate enough to have thoughtful parents in this respect. There is nothing the kindergarten child enjoys so much as helping around the house, helping with the dishes, sweeping the sidewalk, setting the table or feeding the chickens. These and many other chores, if given to the child as a privilege and responsibility, will be received with delight. These form the very finest foundations upon which a happy and sensible relationship between child and authority can be built. This makes such a relationship more adequate on both sides, on the side of the parent as well as on that of the child. Give every child a certain amount of responsibility around the home, as much as he is capable of taking. Perhaps the most common stumbling blocks for such happy relationships are eating and sleeping habits. The difficulty here

[3] *Op. cit.*

is often due to the unfairness of the adult. A child can learn to understand that a different set of sleeping and eating habits apply to him than apply to his father and mother, but the fact remains that he should have some opportunity for refusals at the table as do his elders. Few adults would like to have the amount and exact specifications of their food set out for them three times a day. It is not strange that the child resents the same thing. Sleep can easily be made a privilege instead of the liability it comes to be in so many homes.

Christian Courage

An aspect of personality which tends to appear during this period is leadership. Every child likes to dominate the group of which he is a part. Too often children come to have this desire so strongly that they will not join a group unless they can dominate it. But this desire for leadership carries with it also the capacity for learning the elements of good leadership. Here is a boy, a natural born leader, whose methods consist largely in physical aggression. He is not especially strong, but his aggressions are so purposeful and his leadership ability so outstanding that other boys naturally follow him. A discussion with him on the qualities of good leadership which would be more helpful than selfish met a remarkably fine response in his mind and changed his whole attitude of leadership very strikingly. Children of this age, then, need training in leadership, but they also need to learn that the best leadership is service rather than mere domination of the group. In drama-type programs, it is essential that children of this age be given adequate opportunities for leading when the activities emphasize abilities which they have in abundance. There will hardly be a child without an endowment of some sort in which he can become an accomplished leader. If he does not have any trait in great abundance, constant practice in the trait with which he is best endowed trains him to become more expert at it and thus provides opportunity for his training in leadership. The child's natural sympathy makes it possible to teach him unselfishness in leadership. His desire for achievement is the basis on which can be built a perseverance that carries him over even disagreeable tasks. Excessive shyness, elementary stage fright, the unwillingness to play with others, the insistence on staying close to an adult can generally be overcome by this sort of training. Several experiments have shown that highly submissive children can be vastly improved in their aggressive reactions by training them along special lines and giving them opportunities for leadership using these new abilities.

Here, then, are the elements in the child's character which can be developed during the kindergarten age. It will be seen that, with the exception of the concept of the fatherliness of God, we have as yet made little or no effort to develop in the child any abstract ideas. We are still laying foundations on which the more abstract ideas can later be built. But it should be equally obvious that these are foundations and as essential to the development of the more mature concepts as any foundation is to the building resting upon it.

Personality Types in the Kindergarten

As we proceed from age level to age level, individual differences become increasingly important. Regimentation is much less possible in the kindergarten than it is in the nursery and it grows less and less so as one approaches maturity. A division into types becomes easier during this period, but it is necessarily an artificial one, based entirely on practical factors. Undoubtedly the most obvious types have to do with the special aptitudes. This is not true in the nursery, where types have more to do with physical activity. But in the kindergarten group there are those children who engage almost entirely in artistic endeavor, such as clay modelling, painting, water coloring, cutting out with scissors, pasting and making scrapbooks. Some children are interested in more than one of these, but any group observed over a period of time can be easily divided into its special aptitude types. There are those given almost entirely to constructiveness. Others like to play in the sandbox. Still others choose rhythm games and singing. In addition to these rather natural divisions into which the children fall according to their abilities, there are those children with outstanding leadership ability and those, not necessarily the same ones, who are conspicuously aggressive. Some will be highly emotional and some rather calm in their reactions. These perhaps are the chief characteristics by which the kindergarten may be divided. It will be seen that this does not constitute a series of pigeonholes into which each child is put, for some children would belong in several of them. But it does point out the most outstanding ways in which children differ, which is vitally important in the development of the drama-type program.

Conclusion

Character consists of intellectual and emotional habits. They are our ways of reacting to the world about us. During the kindergarten age the child's perceptual ability grows so much that he makes his first adjustment to more new things than at any other stage in life. It is obvious, then, that the reactions he learns to make to all this new world will go far toward determining the quality of his character. In the questionnaire which follows, many of the more common reactions are included. To fill out the questionnaire carefully and then to make a list of the reactions which are in most need of development will be of real value in going about this task of character development as purposefully as possible.

QUESTIONNAIRE FOR THE KINDERGARTEN AGE

In the square preceding each question write a number, 5, 4, 3, 2, or 1. After each question is a series of five possible answers to the question, numbered 5, 4, 3, 2, and 1 respectively. In the square use the number preceding the phrase which most nearly represents your answer.

Psychological Development

☐ 1. How many hours does he (she) sleep per day?
5 More than fourteen hours, 4 fourteen hours, 3 thirteen hours, 2 eleven or twelve hours, 1 less than eleven hours

☐ 2. How well developed is his (her) motor coördination?
5 Can ride a bicycle, 4 can ice skate, 3 can hop and skip, 2 can run and jump, 1 can do none of these

Trait I

☐ 3. Does he (she) tell many imaginative stories?
5 Constantly, 4 often, 3 sometimes, 2 rarely, 1 never

☐ 4. Does he (she) engage in imaginative play, creating characters, places and events out of his (her) imagination?
5 To a very large extent, 4 often, 3 sometimes, 2 rarely, 1 never

Trait II

☐ 5. Does he (she) show interest in learning new things?
5 Shows very great interest, 4 above average, 3 some interest, 2 a little interest, 1 no interest

☐ 6. Does he (she) show interest in music?
5 Very great interest, 4 above average, 3 some interest, 2 a little interest, 1 none

☐ 7. Does he (she) show interest in art and the beauties of nature?
5 Very great interest, 4 above average, 3 some interest, 2 a little interest, 1 none

☐ 8. Does he (she) go to kindergarten?
5 Regularly, 4 usually, 3 to church school, 2 to church school irregularly, 1 does not go at all

☐ 9. Does he (she) sometimes solve his (her) own problems?
5 Very often, 4 frequently, 3 sometimes, 2 usually brings them to adults, 1 never solves them

☐ 10. Does he (she) have a good vocabulary?
5 Very unusual, 4 above average, 3 normal, 2 rather small, 1 very meager

☐ 11. Does he (she) ask a great many questions of how, when and why?
5 Constantly, 4 often, 3 some, 2 a few, 1 rarely or never

☐ 12. Does he (she) show a facility with numbers? (Not to be confused with reciting numbers.)
5 Can count objects accurately to twenty-five, 4 to ten, 3 to four or six, 2 two and three, 1 no number ability

☐ 13. Does he (she) tell falsehoods to get himself (herself) out of trouble or to secure something he (she) wishes?
5 Never, 4 rarely, 3 sometimes, 2 often, 1 very frequently

☐ 14. Does he (she) show an inclination to masturbation?
5 No more than normal curiosity, 4 a little, 3 definite tendency to do so, 2 often does so, 1 does so very frequently

☐ 15. Does he (she) have a sense of guilt or shame about matters of personal cleanliness and his (her) sex organs?
5 None at all, 4 very little, 3 some, 2 considerable, 1 a great deal

Trait III

☐ 16. How many fears has he (she) of such objective things as the dark, water, thunder and lightning, high places, strange objects and strange people?
5 No fears at all, 4 one or two, 3 a few, 2 a considerable number, 1 very fearful

☐ 17. Does he (she) show such symptoms of fear as loss of appetite, inability to relax, a sense of insecurity, and nervousness?
5 Shows none of them, 4 shows one or two of them, 3 shows some of them in considerable degree, 2 shows most of them in large amounts, 1 shows all of them in large amounts

☐ 18. Does he (she) stutter?

5 Speaks very clearly, 4 uses a little baby talk, 3 uses a great deal of baby talk, 2 stutters and stammers a little, 1 stutters and stammers very decidedly

☐ 19. Does he (she) engage in motor activities, such as climbing and jumping, with fear or confidence?

5 Complete self-assurance, 4 usually confident, 3 fairly confident, 2 somewhat reluctant in most of them, 1 very fearful

Trait IV

☐ 20. Does he (she) build with hammer and nails?

5 Constantly building things with hammer and nails, 4 frequently does so, 3 sometimes, 2 seldom, 1 never

☐ 21. Does he (she) like to cut things out of paper with the scissors?

5 Constantly does so, 4 often does so, 3 sometimes, 2 rarely, 1 never does so

☐ 22. Does he (she) enjoy clay modelling?

5 Does it constantly, 4 frequently does it, 3 sometimes, 2 rarely, 1 never

☐ 23. Does he (she) like to use water colors?

5 Does so constantly, 4 frequently, 3 sometimes, 2 rarely, 1 never

☐ 24. Does he (she) like to draw?

5 Does so constantly, 4 frequently, 3 sometimes, 2 rarely, 1 never

☐ 25. Does he (she) enjoy rhythm games?

5 Very much, 4 some, 3 indifferent but participates, 2 dislikes them but will participate sometimes, 1 dislikes them and will not participate in them

☐ 26. Does he (she) like to sing?

5 Very much, 4 some, 3 indifferent but tries, 2 dislikes it but will try, 1 refuses even to try

☐ 27. Does he (she) engage in most of his (her) creative activities with confidence?

5 Complete confidence, 4 considerable confidence, 3 rather cautiously, 2 with some fear of failure, 1 with marked fear of failure

☐ 28. What is his (her) attitude toward failure?
5 Try, try again attitude, 4 asks for help, 3 gives up, 2 cries, 1 becomes very angry

☐ 29. How does he (she) react to working under pressure?
5 Is not in the slightest bothered, 4 gets a little hurried, 3 shows some nervousness, 2 tends to get excited if pushed, 1 goes to pieces under pressure

☐ 30. How often does he (she) make decisions for himself (herself)?
5 Makes a majority of his (her) decisions, 4 makes many of them, 3 makes some, 2 makes a few, 1 never makes a decision for himself (herself)

Trait V

☐ 31. Is he (she) quick to show sympathy for suffering?
5 Very sympathetic, 4 usually sympathetic, 3 has sympathy for his (her) friends, 2 shows very little sympathy, 1 no sympathy at all

☐ 32. Does he (she) show a tendency to like people?
5 Likes everybody he (she) meets, 4 likes most people, 3 likes at least half of the people he (she) meets, 2 likes some of them, 1 likes very few people

☐ 33. Does he (she) consider the feelings of others when carrying out his (her) own wishes?
5 Always does so, 4 usually does so, 3 does so for his (her) friends, 2 seldom does so, 1 never does so

☐ 34. Does he (she) have good manners?
5 Very polite for his (her) age, 4 always says "thank you" and "please", 3 average, 2 not very well-mannered, 1 very poor manners

☐ 35. Does he (she) often pretend fears, obviously only to get attention?
5 Never does so, 4 seldom does so, 3 occasionally, 2 frequently, 1 is constantly doing so

☐ 36. Does he (she) help with work around the home, such as drying dishes, etc.?
5 Is constantly doing so, 4 does so very often, 3 sometimes does so, 2 rarely does so, 1 never does so

Trait VI

☐ 37. Is he (she) quite willing to play in groups of children?
5 Does so willingly and confidently, 4 does so usually, 3 sometimes does so, 2 prefers to play alone, 1 is afraid to be in a group

☐ 38. Does he (she) have opportunity for supervised dramatic play?
5 A great deal, 4 quite a lot, 3 some, 2 rarely, 1 never

☐ 39. Does he (she) have a tendency to blame others for his (her) own wrong-doings?
5 Never does so, 4 seldom does so, 3 sometimes, 2 often does so, 1 always does so, never admits that he (she) is to blame

☐ 40. Is he (she) jealous of the popularity of others?
5 Never shows a sign of jealousy, 4 seldom does, 3 sometimes does, 2 frequently does, 1 is constantly doing so

☐ 41. Does he (she) show interest in new members of the group?
5 Always, 4 usually, 3 sometimes, 2 rarely, 1 never

☐ 42. Does he (she) harbor dislikes a long time?
5 Forgets them very quickly, 4 cannot dislike a person for very long, 3 about average, 2 does not find it easy to forget, 1 harbors dislikes a long time

Trait VII

☐ 43. Does he (she) show a sense of property rights?
5 A very clear idea of "mine" and "thine", 4 usually recognizes property rights, 3 wants his (her) own respected but sometimes does not recognize others', 2 some tendency to take whatever he (she) wants, 1 grabs everything he (she) wants and screams if he (she) cannot get it

☐ 44. Is he (she) sensitive, does he (she) have his (her) feelings easily hurt?
5 Very good-natured, 4 not very sensitive, 3 fairly sensitive, 2 has feelings hurt easily, 1 extremely sensitive

☐ 45. Does he (she) find it easy to coöperate with authority?
5 Coöperates with authority regularly and cheerfully, 4 usually does so, 3 rebels occasionally, 2 rebels frequently, 1 almost never accepts authority willingly

☐ 46. How well does he (she) comply with routine in such activities as sleeping and eating?
5 Accepts routine naturally and cheerfully, 4 usually does so, 3 objects to routine somewhat, 2 objects often, 1 rebels violently against routine

☐ 47. Does he (she) show a tendency to over-aggressiveness and fighting?
5 Is always good-natured and cordial toward others, 4 usually is so, 3 does not fight very often, 2 is somewhat over-aggressive, 1 is constantly fighting

☐ 48. Does he (she) maintain his (her) rights in the face of unjust aggression?
5 Always does so, 4 usually does so, 3 does so if the injustice is too great, 2 usually does not resist aggression, 1 never does so, obviously because of fear

☐ 49. Does he (she) have temper tantrums?
5 Never, 4 rarely, 3 occasionally, 2 frequently, 1 very often

Trait VIII

☐ 50. Does he (she) show signs of leadership?
5 Very pronounced, 4 above average, 3 some, 2 very little, 1 none at all

☐ 51. Do his (her) efforts at leadership takes a rational form?
5 Very skilled at leadership, 4 does it reasonably well, 3 uses force as his (her) chief method, 2 accomplishes it entirely by force and loud words, 1 over-aggressive, fighting, angry approach to leadership

☐ 52. Does he (she) show self-confidence when placed in positions of leadership?
5 Completely self-possessed, 4 fairly confident, 3 enough confidence to carry out his (her) purposes, 2 tries to evade leadership if he (she) can, 1 refuses to be put in prominent positions

☐ 53. How well does he (she) coöperate with other leadership?
5 Completely, 4 usually, 3 coöperates sometimes, 2

usually prefers to be in group he (she) can dominate, 1 will not join group he (she) cannot dominate

☐ 54. Is he (she) independent of adult assistance in his (her) social contacts?

5 Completely so, 4 usually, 3 prefers that an adult be around, 2 tends to depend on adult protection, 1 stays very close to adult, showing strong social fear

☐ 55. How does he (she) react to minor bumps and bruises?

5 Laughs at them, 4 does not mind them, 3 rather indifferent, 2 tends to whimper, 1 cries at the slightest pain

VIII

The First School Years

HERE BEGINS THE LONG ROAD of formal education. The shortest period of time usually devoted to this process is ten years, and it may range to as many as twenty or more. How happy and successful these years will be depends more upon the child's first adjustments to this educative process than on any other single factor. And because first impressions are lasting, it is especially important that the first years be happy ones. Most children nowadays go to nursery schools or kindergartens. There they master a few of the more important techniques of school adjustment, especially the social aspect. Usually, however, these are small, carefully selected, and thoroughly supervised groups. Now, especially if he enters the public school, the child is plunged suddenly into the middle of the most democratic of all our democratic institutions. Almost every type of child is there, both of the same age and older. It is not remarkable that the task of making this adjustment should be a difficult and not always a successful one. The church school can do much to make this period a happy one, and an important one in the growth of personality. The difference between the primary child and the kindergarten child is very great. At no other period in life, until the jump from childhood into adolescence, is the change so great. In the case of the primary child, this is not due to any sudden jump in his physical nature, but rather to this sudden change from a home-centered life to a school-centered life. Let us look first, then, to see what natural endowment he has with which to meet this situation, and secondly what contributions we can make to his unfolding development.

Physical Development

Physically, the primary child is still growing very rapidly. Proportionately this is not so much as in preceding years, but there is still a wide gap between the six-year-old and the eight-year-old, the limits of this age level. In addition to increase in height and weight, coördination is the most important feature of his development. At six he is still pretty much a child. At eight, he can swim, skate, and do most of the other complex motor skills. On one test of voluntary control the average performance of eight-year-old children was four times as great as that for six-year-olds. A steadiness test showed an increase of one hundred percent between these two ages. The increase in strength is not nearly so marked. The child still fatigues easily and is still highly sensitive to pain. His energy level is quite as great as it was in the kindergarten. When this is added to his increased coordination, it is natural that it should be a period of great restlessness. Children of this age are quite incapable of sitting still for any considerable period of time. A class of boys and girls at the ages of six and seven, the members of which would sit still a whole lesson period, should be a source of some anxiety to the teacher, and a physician should be consulted. Parents and teachers to whom sitting quietly during long class sessions is the essence of goodness should be kept away from the primary child, for the end result of such discipline must inevitably be harmful.

Mental Development

Learning to read plays a central rôle in the entire personality adjustment of children at this age level. This is not confined to their school adjustment. Its effects will be found in every phase of their behavior. Usually the child makes this adjustment naturally and with relative ease during these first two years. Modern methods of teaching reading have tremendously reduced the incidence of failure. The fact is, however, that there are still many children who do not learn to read easily. Sometimes this is because the factors in their mental development which make reading possible have not matured. But most commonly it is simply because they have not gotten the knack of it. Learning to read involves one important insight which the child must get for himself. It almost always comes suddenly, and until it does come, he does not learn to read. This is true of learning to walk, learning to talk, learning to swim, and many other important skills. About all we can do is to expose the child to many different forms of activity which aid reading and wait until he finds the secret. A most important point, and a difficult one to carry out, is to prevent him from developing serious feelings of inferiority if this insight does not come as early as with most children.

Of all the mental abilities rote memory increases most, and for this reason the child often gets a high sense of achievement from the expression of this ability. The attention span doubles in these years and this means that he can concentrate on a longer task than before. In fact, he will now become interested in a story which continues from day to day, whereas the pre-school child needs to have the complete unit at one time. His vocabulary grows very rapidly. It may range from 800 to 7500 words. The average vocabulary of an eight-year-old child is about 3000 words. Reasoning ability is still very low. Even the most common absurdities which form the basis for many of our simplest forms of humor are quite beyond his comprehension. For example, the following sentence taken from a recent absurdities test was applied to children from eight to fourteen: "A clean-shaven young Englishman, of about 50 years of age, stepped lightly from the train and hurried slowly down the platform with both hands in his pockets, carrying a heavy bag, and curling the tips of his moustache."[1] Almost none of the eight-year-olds were able to detect any of the absurdities in this passage. When we consider teaching the more abstract philosophical principles to children of this age, then we

[1] Burt, C., *Mental and Scholastic Tests,* p. 237 (E. S. King & Son, Ltd., London).

need to recognize the immaturity of their intelligence. Number concepts now begin to appear and the early stages of arithmetic can be begun. It is vitally important, however, that children should not be forced to begin the study of arithmetic until they have reached a maturity of which number concepts are a natural part. To force a child to study arithmetic before this time is simply to develop in him a distaste for it which may never be completely overcome.

Notice the steps through which the child has gone in the growth of his ability to use language. Language is the most important social institution that man possesses but he comes by it very slowly and with many hurdles to be jumped on the way. The process, however, is one of progressive steps each of which can be seen very clearly to lead to the next one higher. During infancy sounds are pretty much the only form of language used. During at least a portion of that period sounds are made for their own sake. Then during the nursery period the sounds are formed into words, and while of course it becomes valuable immediately to use these words as a medium of social intercourse, nevertheless anyone observing the nursery school child discovers that he spends a great deal of time saying words just as words with little regard to their meaning. In the kindergarten this tendency just about disappears and words become purely a way of making social adjustment. During that time, however, he becomes interested in letters and written symbols for their own sake. Now as he comes to the primary this interest gives way to the use of letters as a means to reading. But even here reading is a process which has not yet become a part of him, to be used as a tool. His major interest, however, is in learning how to use the tool. Not until the next level of development will reading reach its peak, and it is the ten-year-old child who wants to read all the time.

Special Aptitudes

Except for the new fields of complex motor skills which now come into being, most of the primary aptitudes are simply a growth from those expressed in the kindergarten. We cannot measure them much better in the laboratory, and when they are measured it is difficult to predict adult characteristics on the basis of their primary status. It is still not uncommon to find a child who rates high in drawing at this level, who at fourteen will show a minimum of artistic ability. To be sure, drawing becomes a little more representative, but the child even at this age is still drawing what he thinks rather than what he sees. This shows itself especially in the relative size of things. A boy drawing the picture of a football outside of his house made the football approximately three times as large as the house. In all probability this represented the relative value of the two objects in his mind at the moment of his drawing. Constructiveness develops fairly rapidly and he can begin to use many of the common tools. This is made possible especially due to the rapid increase in motor coördination. While it is not desirable to permit him to use tools which might be dangerous, yet handsaws, and for that matter most hand tools, can be used with comparative safety. The results in terms of achievement make what little risk there is very much worth the taking. The tendency to collect begins during this period. When this tendency does appear, collections should be made of whatever things there are at hand to collect. Stones, bugs, knives, dolls, and pictures are only a few of the many varieties of collections made. They may show some interest in the more advanced forms of collecting as, for example, in stamps. But this interest is likely to be confined simply to accumulation, and certainly only the cheapest stamps, which can be bought in quantity, should be made available to them.

The social aspects of the special aptitudes begin to appear during this period. In one of our studies we tried to discover what relationship exists between a high or low endowment in the various aptitudes and the presence or absence of problems in social adjustment. Such problems were found much more commonly among children with high musical ability or with low mechanical ability. This would seem to suggest that, at this age, musical aptitude is sometimes a social handicap and mechanical ability an important asset. When one thinks of the strenuous efforts parents often make to persuade their children to practice on the piano, and at the same time how large a percentage of children's games are essentially mechanical in their nature, it is easy to understand these data.

Social and Emotional Development

The most important social adjustment at this age is involved in going to school. Unless one gives thought to it, he is not likely to realize what a tremendous change this does involve. Up to this time, parents choose their children's companions rather carefully and their associations are very likely to be confined to their own social and age level. Now the child goes into large groups of children, both of the same age and older, and from all social classes. He is almost certain to get a considerable amount of bullying and tormenting from his larger and older comrades. Especially if he has some physical handicap, such as being cross-eyed or over-fat, he is certain to come in for a great many jibes and much torture. That this social punishment is painful no one can doubt. But a very important point to remember is that an adjustment to it must be made. To withdraw the child from society and to protect him from this unhappiness is to insure for him a most serious defect in personality. To be sure, every effort should be made to make this social adjustment as easy as possible. If overalls are the socially accepted style of clothes in his school, dressing him in this manner is a real contribution to his happiness. Social conformity during the early years of school adjustment is of great value to the ease and happiness of this adjustment. The boy or girl who is "different" is certain to be in for a great deal of unhappiness.

Emotionally, the child still reacts pretty much to specific situations. If there are evidences of generality, this indicates simply a lack of ability to discriminate between situations and not a capacity for generalization on the part of the child himself. However, a much lower level of negativism and suggestibility makes him more coöperative and objective in his adjustments, especially to authority. Moral vocabulary tests now receive a number of responses on the part of the child. Such words as bravery, love, and cheerfulness are defined by almost all children of this age level, but by very few pre-school children. A study of these definitions, however, reveals how completely specific these moral concepts are: "Bravery is when you jump from a burning building," "Cheerfulness is when you laugh all the time," "Happiness is like at Christmas when you get presents." Abstract concepts are still very much in the future. A very interesting result of this vocabulary test is the definition which the children of this age give to the word "love". It is invariably confined to action. "Love is when you kiss somebody, or hug somebody, or sit by them." The concept of love as an emotional expression of affection is entirely beyond the thinking of the child. Let those who believe that the young child should be taught that God is love consider just what such a teaching means in the mind of the child.

Character Education

Character development now begins to become intentional. Certainly very little can be done to instill in the child of pre-school age a desire for moral growth. Teaching him faith in the friendliness of the universe consists in stimulating him to laugh at his bumps and bruises and does not involve any conscious understanding of its moral significance. In a rather general way, we can describe learning at the pre-school level, both morally and intellectually, as being rather a result of conditioning. If the pre-school child is placed in a sufficient number of situations which bring forth desirable behavior, this desirable behavior becomes part of his personality. Now, however, a moral vocabulary can be begun. Furthermore, it is a usable vocabulary. However much it differs from our mature concepts of goodness, it is important because it means that the child for the first time is beginning to have insight into the development of his own character. Let us examine each of the eight traits, then, to determine specifically how this character education can best be carried out.

Experimental Faith

Vision

Imagination now comes to full bloom. The fact that it is still accompanied by little or no critical refinement leads to the many childhood lies so characteristic of this age and the preceding age levels. Actually, of course, a vast majority of these lies are not only not harmful but actually of positive value in the training of the child's imagination. Their variation from truth is due to the fact that the child still cannot distinguish between what he imagines and what he really sees. As a matter of fact, this inability to distinguish between imagination and reality continues to some extent throughout life. College students often describe experiences which never could have happened and with every confidence that they are telling the truth. Parents frequently tell of behavior and thinking on the part of their children which never could conceivably have taken place at the age level involved. They are not exaggerating or lying—they simply cannot distinguish between imagination and reality. Let us not be too hard on the primary child, then, for his "whoppers". They are the very spice of life and, guided into channels of usefulness and more reality, become the basis for high vision. It seems not unlikely that the ruthless suppression of this imaginative tendency in these early years is partly responsible for the unimaginative lives led by most adults.

Moral concepts are often best taught by use of this same imaginative process. Fairy tales, myths, and fables are the very best tools by which to teach ethical principles. My mother used to tell me that, when I turned over the corner of a leaf in a book or in any other way marred the book, I was killing a fairy. I feel confident that this was a far better method of motivating me to care for my books than any number of sermons on neatness might have been.

The scope of this imagination is in direct proportion to the breadth of one's experiences. It is quite impossible to create anything entirely new. Inventions are always new combinations of old materials. Consequently, if we are to make the child's imagination real and broad, his experiences must be correspondingly broad. Studies have been made which show that the child's concepts are much more accurate where their experience is extensive. They make fewer mistakes about home and food and clothes than about those things which they see outside the home. They do develop some generalities. It is not easy to analyze these generalities nor even to know their unifying characteristics. A child who was playing with blocks kept insisting that a visitor in her home come to see the boat she had made. A whole series of boats were thus exhibited. The visitor found it quite impossible to see any characteristics common to all these boats. Undoubtedly in the child's imagination there was some common feature. What that was, only the child knew. Such generalities are indications of mental development, even though we need to use care in their interpretation.

One other form in which imagination expresses itself is in dreaming. Dreaming is not very common at earlier age levels, but now it becomes a frequent experience. Nightmares are more frequent during this period than during any other period of life. It is not possible to deal with them as such. It seems certain, however, that they grow out of frustration and a sense of failure. Increased experiences with success during the day will most certainly reduce their occurrence.

Love of Righteousness and Truth

Learning to love learning is the great task for this age level in the growth of this trait. At the earlier age levels we have tried to make children love "being good", partly at least, by making goodness lovable. That was important and still is, but the entrance into school and the beginning of formal learning make it the most important aspect of the child's growth during this age level.

Recalling our original diagram of behavior, behavior patterns are adopted only if they reduce tensions and these tensions are desires. Therefore, if school does not reduce some tensions or if it creates additional tensions, the child will not go willingly. Actually, all the novelty involved, the motivation of the fact that older people are interested in education, and the sense of achievement that comes from learning should make this one of the easiest adjustments of the child's life. Unfortunately, this is not always true. Children will go to school with enthusiasm only if the work there is suited to their abilities as well as their needs. A child likes to learn those things which he is capable of learning. But being thrown into hopeless competition and having an endless succession of failures as a reward is not calculated to develop hunger and thirst for learning in any child. This is forcefully illustrated by the fact that feeble-minded children become happy and well adjusted when put into schools geared to their level of attainment.

The three R's are traditionally and logically the three principal tools which the child needs to acquire first if his future education is to be effective. Let us look at each of them briefly. Attention has already been called to the fact that reading requires an insight which comes rather suddenly. If ninety percent of a first or second grade class read well, those few who do not are almost certain to be teased by their comrades because of their failure, and will be very unhappy as a result. Reading opens the door to such a rich variety of experience that the child should and does hunger and thirst for it. Let us be sure that, through patient and understanding help we increase rather than decrease this enthusiasm. Writing, the second of the three R's, is not so important. Most first grade papers leave something to be desired from an artistic point of view. This remains true with many people throughout life. As a matter of fact, if beauty of writing is held up as an ideal and not a duty, much of the disagreeableness that so often accompanies classes in this subject will disappear. Arithmetic is interesting if the child has matured sufficiently to grasp its principles. Certainly, however, maturation here should precede training as in every other phase of development. Will children want these three R's as much as they want toys, money, candy and ice cream? The chances are that if they do not want them a great deal more, this is a sad commentary on the quality of their teaching both at home and at school, and not a lack of natural eagerness for learning on their part. No appetite in life is so strong as the appetite for achievement and it ought to be easy indeed to persuade children to hunger and thirst for learning in their early school years.

Now let us see how a child's growth in righteousness must progress if he is to continue to hunger and thirst for it. The general principle, as ever, is to bring it about that desirable behavior results in pleasantness and happiness. It is equally important to see that undesirable behavior does not reduce tension. To change undesirable behavior in children one must find what tension that behavior is reducing, and look for more acceptable ways of reducing the same tension. A boy who disliked school, was disobedient at home, and extremely anti-social in his neighborhood, is a case in point. His mother wept over him and his behavior. His father threatened and thrashed. Finally a church school teacher, with a clear understanding both of his nature and his abilities, found other types of behavior that gave him a strong sense of achievement and were in themselves satisfying. Because these new forms of behavior reduced more tensions than the old ones, the old ones simply disappeared. It is not often that bad behavior is eliminated from a child's life by paying attention to it as such. If a sufficient amount of punishment is employed, it is possible to set up inhibiting tensions so that the fear of punishment is greater than the pleasure derived from the behavior. But this is not character development. Research tends to show that punishment produces twice as much harm as it does good. Of course, there are individual differences. Some children can be punished physically more effectively than others. It is not probable that we shall ever completely eliminate the need for some physical punishment. But it must always be thought of as a second-choice method rather than a first.

One important moral trait which attracts a great deal of attention during this age is lying. In addition to the imaginative lies, which have already been mentioned, there are also moral lies. The child naturally wants to avoid doing unpleasant things and to prevent punishment for omissions or commissions. It is not at all uncommon for his parents to give him the best possible training in lying along with a high motivation for success. After some act of misbehavior, parents often call the culprit before them with the inevitable question, "Why did you do it?" If he can invent an adequate lie, he may avoid the wrath that is to come. He is quite likely to try, and a few years of such training may produce in him a most remarkable capacity for lying. "Why did you do it?" could very profitably be dropped from the child training methods employed by most parents. In families of several children a similar question which produces the same effects is, "Who did it?" Then the lying not only becomes imaginative, but competitive. It should be obvious that both these questions can be calculated to produce a very much greater hunger and thirst for unrighteousness than for righteousness.

Faith in the Friendliness of the Universe

"God doesn't like boys and girls who are naughty." How often this completely false statement has been made as a motivation for desirable behavior in children. What are the implied conclusions to this statement? The situations which give rise to it almost invariably suggest that the next sentence would be, "Almost everything you do is naughty." The logical conclusion is, as anyone trained in deductive logic can see, "Therefore God doesn't like you." It is not likely that the primary child has sufficient training in formal logic to work out this syllogism consciously. In a rather implied fashion, however, he does react to this implied fact. Not one parent in a million using such an admonition really believes it, but to say the least, it is not very conducive to faith in a fatherly God. There is probably no stage in human development at which the concept of a protective and understanding God is more needed than at this one.

This is the time for the formation of many phobias. These grow out of two rather natural conditions in the personality of the child which predispose him toward them. A phobia is an irrational fear which always has among its causes an experience involving shame or guilt which the individual has tried to forget. This is the first age level at which a genuine sense of guilt or shame is possible. And because it is the beginning of the period of self-condemnation, motivations using it should be avoided. Compelling a child to be good by appealing to a shame motive is like using strychnine to cure disease. There are occasions on which strychnine is the best medicine, but it is never used in large amounts nor without expert advice. Shame and guilt as motivations to good behavior are intimately related to fear. Then too, the child's sudden plunge into a rough and tumble social environment, for which at best he is not very adequately prepared, makes the experience of fear all too common in his everyday life. When these two things are combined phobias are very easily produced.

Fear of failure in the pre-school years is entirely related to general purposiveness. But when the child starts to school, it becomes a basic factor in his faith in a friendly universe. It is certainly good mental hygiene to commend him for successful achievements in his school career. It may be safely assumed, however, that no child is naturally lazy. Furthermore, by nature he keenly desires success. If he fails in school, you may be sure that the very fact of failure itself is a punishment. What he needs at home is not an addition to this punishment, but sympathy, help, and complete understanding. He needs to be shown that one failure is not important and that continued effort is likely to bring good results. When laziness does occur, with the possible exception of physical deficiency, especially in the form of low metabolism, it is a compensation for this fear of failure. A girl had been in the laboratory a short while. For about fifteen minutes all the problems assigned to her were so easy that she knew she could solve them. When she reached the first really difficult one, which was likely to tax her abilities, she said, "I guess I'll have to go home now." This is a familiar expression of this fear of failure.

If the Shepherd Psalm is taught in all its fullness and real human values, it can now become the central feature of a most valuable lesson in the fatherhood of God. The child will not understand all its abstract principles, but its beauty and value lie in the fact that it was written for a childlike people. Most of its concepts are stated in specific and understandable terms, and its philosophy consists in a reaction of confidence. Such a belief will eliminate any necessity for fear and for the corresponding weakness of personality which goes along with excessive fear. It would be tragic indeed if this relatively simple faith were so unrealistic as to keep from the child the real nature of the social problems he has ahead of him. This would be exactly like having parents withdraw their children from the social adjustments they need to make, simply because those adjustments are difficult. Furthermore, this concept of God, if it is to mature into one which is adequate for the normal adult, must be added to from age level to age level as the child is able to comprehend it. College students often insist that they no longer believe in religion. But examination reveals that those things which they think they do not believe are concepts which should have been outgrown many years before. The faith in a Father-God that is adequate to meet the needs of this age level is a desirable source of strength to the child in his present adjustment. It must, however, be as much increased and refined when he becomes a man as any other aspects of his childhood philosophy.

Dominating Purpose

The purposiveness of the child increases markedly during these two years. He is now able to persevere at projects which require a whole day and sometimes a succession of days. This is a conspicuous growth from the minute-to-minute activity of the nursery and the hour-to-hour behavior of the kindergarten. This does not mean, however, that he is yet prepared to set forth on his life work as a project. A gradual increasing in the length of the tasks set before him is important for character building. While it is true that these tasks cannot be longer than the level of his maturity permits, it is equally true that they ought not be shorter. When one sees college students whose perseverance is so small that it is impossible for them to work at a project over a period of even a few days, it is easy to see that their character development in this regard ceased at about the primary level.

Again, emphasis should be placed on the need of having training follow maturation. If the child gets restless or listless, let the teacher or parent take stock of the tasks which he has provided for him, both as to their suitability and their length. The child of this age is extremely active. The right sort of tasks which utilize his abilities and do not overestimate them, which employ all his energies and do not overtax them, makes behavior seem highly purposive in a personality which might otherwise be classified as nervous and restless. The characteristic interests of the primary boys include clay modelling, painting, and building. In addition to these, girls cook and do elementary sewing. The ability to make cookies, apple sauce, and cup custard is an achievement of major importance for this age level. For both boys and girls abundant material should be available for the use of their special aptitudes. They are quite as useful as the three R's in the development of purposiveness. Among the purposive traits which can grow during this time are self-reliance, perseverance, and efficiency. The child can do a great many more things for himself than he ever could before. The process of gradual emancipation from complete parental control should proceed far enough at this time so that there can be no question of a real development in self-reliance. Give him as many responsibilities as he is capable of taking, especially if they do not involve fear. Increasing the length of tasks contributes substantially to his development in perseverance. As for efficiency, he is now willing to be taught how to go about doing things better. For example, he can learn how to hold the hammer in order to hit harder and oftener. A beginning should be made in persuading the child to do some things over again in order to do them better. This is not an easy lesson to learn. It tries one's natural patience a great deal. It is far pleasanter to do new and different things. Nevertheless, if one is to reach a high peak of efficiency in whatever vocation he chooses, many of his tasks will need to be repeated and revised many times. Since it is a difficult lesson to learn, a start should be made as early as possible. It is not likely that the child will want to do things three and four and five times, nor even that he will always want to do them twice. However, when an occasion arises in which the teacher or parent realizes that a second trial will bring about obviously better results, it can be made the opportunity for a lesson in this important habit.

Fatherly Love

Being Sensitive to the Needs of Others

Sympathy is the keyword to the primary child's growth in fatherly love. Sympathy is a natural, inherited attribute in human nature. We tend to sympathize with others not only in their troubles but in their joys. Weeping tends to beget weeping and smiling begets smiling. This natural attribute of sympathy comes to a very high level during this primary age period. Furthermore, the child still has not entered the "hard-boiled" stages which are so characteristic of the next three age periods. Because of these two facts a great many important lessons about sympathy can best be learned at this time. There are other reasons for the appropriateness of these lessons. It is, of course, obvious to everyone that the over-protected world of the pre-school child must sooner or later be made realistic. If this protection is continued to adolescence, the shock which comes from the disillusionment of seeing the world as it really is, is not always easily endured by the adolescent child. It is far better to let this acquaintance with reality come to be recognized gradually, as the child grows. Because of his natural sympathy and his willingness to express this sympathy, this is an appropriate time for him to become aware especially of the suffering of the world. He needs opportunity for, and adult encouragement in, friendly and sympathetic acts. He can be stimulated, especially by means of his natural parental instincts, to do many deeds of kindness for those who are suffering. This sympathy can also be used as a means to a much better social adjustment. Ask any kindergarten child for the names of other children with whom he plays every day. He is likely to know very few. The primary child, likewise, usually does not try to learn the names of many of his playmates. By continued teaching, however, and games devised for that purpose he will learn the names of his friends and will develop the habit of seeking to know people's names. This will be an important social asset to him in later years if it is well established as a habit at this age level. The motivation to learn names may often be built on this natural tendency to sympathy.

Forgiveness

Brotherly love may be a high-sounding ideal for a speech on international good will, but at the primary level it falls on deaf ears. When the primary child is struck on one cheek, the eye-for-an-eye and tooth-for-a-tooth philosophy is much more representative of his actual behavior. A boy was asked in an intelligence test, "What is the thing to do if someone hits you without meaning to do so?" The boy responded, "I would not hit him back any harder than he hit me." No better description of brotherly love at this age could be found than this. In testing, children are often asked, "Toward whom do you lose your temper most frequently?" If their response does not concern their brothers and sisters, it is safe to conclude that they have no brothers and sisters.

Furthermore, and along the same line, the habit of blaming others for one's own wrong-doing becomes a prominent characteristic of children of this age. Their intense fear of blame and of its consequences leads them to shrink from a frank admission of their own guilt. Fortunate indeed is the child whose parents and teachers have managed to keep themselves open to the confessions which are clearly so good for the soul of the child. This can be accomplished only if the child has no fear of such confessions bringing dire consequences.

These two habits may seem to be insuperable obstacles to the development of this trait in the child, but again we can turn for help to the even more powerful parental drives. In the first place, a reverence for the rules of the game can be learned, but much more important than that, a habit of protecting the rights of the younger and weaker members of the group can be acquired. While not as important as it is a few years later, the care of pets may become an important source for developing this trait. Since the child has not yet acquired the social anathema prohibiting affection for younger children, such affection should be the chief emphasis in the training of this trait during the primary age level.

When new children are brought into any group it is excellent character education for the older children to be asked to protect them, help them get acquainted with the group, and see that their rights are respected. They will respond to this with eagerness and efficiency. In few natural situations during their whole lives will there be such abundant opportunity to learn the habit of trying to see that every man gets his chance at happiness and success.

Magnanimity

It has already been pointed out that learning how to get along with people requires practice. While there are natural sympathetic qualities in human personality on which this art can be based, one can no more do it without training than one can speak Latin, play Beethoven or paint like Michelangelo. Because of the various characteristics of the personality of the child at this age level, it becomes an important period for social development. In achieving this, their greatest need is practice and, indeed, practice with a minimum of interference. However, they ought not to be tempted beyond their endurance. Room for excess population and adequate sources of raw materials are even more important in developing this trait in primary children than in solving the problems which a nation imagines it faces. There ought to be enough equipment for every child to have some, and enough floor space for each one to carry out his own creative desires. Given this possibility of complete adjustment, they are likely by a process of give and take and trial and error to learn a great many important lessons about peace-making. They will require each other's help, they will discover the inadvisability of trying to command more than their share, and they are likely to find peaceable means of solution far superior to fighting.

Another important result which comes from the increased maturity of this age, is a new attitude toward their elders. It is the beginning of the period when approval by one's contemporaries is more to be desired than approval by one's parents. The result is the growth of a whole new set of parent-child adjustment difficulties. If, however, the general principle is kept in mind that autocratic authority ought rapidly to be replaced by coöperation with authority, these difficulties should not be great. Too complete obedience on the part of children at this age level is probably to be looked upon with some misgivings. If either extreme is to be chosen, an aggressive rebellion against authority is more to be desired than a weak submissiveness. Neither, of course, is ideal, and coöperation is the goal to be sought. Many of the conflicts which arise through irritation over routine, such as in dressing, eating and sleeping habits, can usually be met by the shift of authority and responsibility in these matters from the parent to the child himself. This becomes even more important when one realizes that the age levels are near at hand in which parents often lose completely the confidence of the child. If the child is made to feel that he is becoming an adult, if an increasing respect for his rights and his opinions is shown by his parents, they may well gain a close fellowship with the child which is never lost and which is so vital to the child himself in those later years when he so much needs adult guidance.

Christian Courage

There are many different kinds of courage, but in the minds of far too many people physical courage is the most important. One of the most vicious types of philosophy that man has ever devised is often used at this, as well as at the preceding age level. This is the "boys don't cry" philosophy. Actually children of this age do not yet have much physical stamina or ability to endure physical pain. When too high a measure of it is expected of them, the inevitable result is a sense of shame and guilt almost certain to produce a strong sense of inferiority. This does not mean that they need to be encouraged in giving in to every little bump or bruise. They should have outgrown this in the nursery. But if the pain becomes too great and tears find expression, sympathy and understanding are the proper attitudes to be taken toward them. As a matter of fact, the "boys don't cry" type of physical courage is mere bravado and has little, if any, relationship to the courage which we hope for them in later years.

A far more positive approach is to develop leadership and followership. Each is important to learn and certainly the former is not learned without having passed its prerequisite course, the latter. The simultaneous training in both is best accomplished by a reciprocal leadership. Each child can be given leadership when activities which correspond to his abilities are being engaged in, and taught to throw his whole energy into good following when the leadership belongs to someone else. This training in followership is not easily acquired earlier than this, and its development is exceedingly important in the strong personality. The willingness to take the responsibility of a leader, on the one hand, or to be a whole-hearted follower, on the other, is an important lesson in the development of real courage. These are far better lessons than to try to develop physical courage which is not adapted to this age level and can be learned much more adequately a few years later.

Conclusion

When we come to the end of the discussion of each age level, the great temptation is to feel that this is the most important period of life. And indeed it is. Each level has its own peculiar problems, as has this one. Each one presents its own opportunities which, if lost, never appear so completely again. Each one makes us understand more completely that their future is now.

The questionnaire in the following pages, suggested for measuring the personalities of the primary children with whom we are dealing, as at all other age levels, should be constantly before us. We know now the general principles of development. Certainly it is obvious that all of them could not be taught to any child, and probably equally obvious that no one child needs all of them. If our teaching, then, is to be effective we must study each child separately and find out which lessons he especially needs to learn. Having done this, we shall find characteristic types of boys and girls which tend to reappear with each new group which comes into our primary departments. Therefore, when drama-type curricular materials are developed which are designed to meet the requirements of any one of these groups, they will fit, with comparatively little change, the groups which come to succeed them. Thus, again, we see that standardized curricula based on this drama-type approach are as possible as the more traditional regimented forms.

QUESTIONNAIRE FOR THE PRIMARY CHILD

In the square preceding each question write a number, 5, 4, 3, 2, or 1. After each question is a series of five possible answers to the question, numbered 5, 4, 3, 2, and 1, respectively. In the square use the number preceding the phrase which most nearly represents your answer.

☐ 1. How restless and fidgety is he (she)?

5 Very stable type of activeness, 4 fairly stable type of activeness, 3 about average, 2 somewhat restless and fidgety, 1 very nervous and restless

Trait I

☐ 2. How much tendency does he (she) have to create imaginative stories?

5 A very vivid imagination, 4 a rich imagination, 3 average, 2 not a very strong imagination, 1 a very poor imagination

☐ 3. How realistic are his (her) imaginative stories?

5 Very closely related to reality, 4 subject only to exaggeration, 3 some tendency to fantasy, 2 unrealistic and fantastic, 1 definitely morbid and fantastic

☐ 4. How much supervision has his (her) imaginative tendencies received from his (her) parents and teachers?

5 Sympathetic and intelligent guidance, 4 some guidance, 3 indifference, 2 efforts made to suppress them, 1 severe efforts to force their suppression

☐ 5. Does he (she) show an interest in fairy tales, myths, and fables?

5 Very great interest, 4 marked interest, 3 some interest, 2 little interest, 1 no interest

☐ 6. What kinds of dreams does he (she) have?

5 Occasional dreams which are very pleasant, 4 frequent dreams usually pleasant, 3 no dreams, 2 occasional dreams usually unpleasant, 1 frequent nightmares

☐ 7. How broad are his (her) experiences?

5 Is constantly meeting new situations, 4 meets many new situations, 3 meets some, 2 very few, 1 almost none

Trait II

☐ 8. How well has he (she) adjusted to school?

5 Very enthusiastic, 4 likes it, 3 goes without objection, 2 does not care much for it, 1 dislikes it very intensely

☐ 9. How much progress has he (she) made in learning to read?

5 Has done unusually well, one of the best in his (her)

class, 4 has learned better than average, 3 is progressing satisfactorily, 2 has not learned much about it as yet, 1 cannot read at all

☐ 10. How well does he (she) succeed in his (her) number work?

5 Does unusually well, 4 can count accurately to one hundred, 3 finds it a little difficult, 2 finds it very difficult, 1 has no concept of numbers at all

☐ 11. Is he (she) in a school or class geared to his (her) level of achievement?

5 Finds his (her) work challenging and possible, 4 is pretty well adjusted to the type and amount of work required of him (her), 3 can do his (her) work with average success, 2 finds his (her) work somewhat too difficult or too easy, 1 is very much bored in school because his (her) work is much too difficult or much too easy

☐ 12. Does he (she) like to collect things, such as stones, bugs, and pictures?

5 Collects constantly, 4 does so a great deal, 3 does some collecting, 2 does very little collecting, 1 never does so

☐ 13. Does he (she) like being "good"?

5 Finds it thrilling, 4 enjoys socially acceptable behavior, 3 does it as a matter of course, 2 does it under protest, 1 dislikes it intensely

☐ 14. Does he (she) enjoy being "bad"?

5 Finds it intensely boring and unpleasant, 4 finds it unattractive, 3 enjoys it sometimes, 2 finds it more attractive than being "good", 1 finds it thrilling

☐ 15. Does he (she) often lie to get himself (herself) out of trouble?

5 Never does so, 4 very rarely, 3 occasionally, 2 frequently, 1 does so very often

☐ 16. How does he (she) respond to physical punishment?

5 Takes it as being just and is wholesomely motivated by it, 4 responds satisfactorily, 3 sometimes is favorably motivated by it, 2 usually responds with sullenness and the effect is not good, 1 is badly frightened or violently angered by it, with no valuable results

Trait III

☐ 17. Has he (she) developed any phobias, that is, irrational fears?
5 None, 4 one or two, 3 a few, 2 several, 1 a number of them

☐ 18. Has he (she) developed a strong sense of shame or guilt?
5 Almost none, 4 a little, 3 some, 2 considerable, 1 very strong

☐ 19. Does he (she) have a strong fear of failure?
5 Never gives up however often he (she) fails, 4 usually willing to try again, 3 usually does not try again, however, with no sense of fear, 2 shows a definite fear of what may happen if he (she) fails, 1 very much afraid of failure

☐ 20. Is he (she) lazy?
5 Very energetic, 4 fairly energetic, 3 average, 2 rather inclined to be lazy, 1 very lazy

☐ 21. What is his (her) concept of God?
5 A father who protects and understands, 4 a father who protects when he (she) is being "good", 3 a powerful being who knows everything he (she) does, 2 a powerful being who will punish him (her) if he (she) is naughty, 1 a terrifying being who will do terrible things to him (her) if he (she) is naughty

Trait IV

☐ 22. Does he (she) like to build things, using several tools?
5 Constantly doing so, 4 very frequently does so, 3 often, 2 sometimes, 1 never

☐ 23. Does he (she) like to draw?
5 Constantly doing so, 4 very frequently does so, 3 often, 2 sometimes, 1 never

☐ 24. Does he (she) like clay modelling?
5 Constantly doing so, 4 very frequently does so, 3 often, 2 sometimes, 1 never

☐ 25. Does he (she) like to paint with water-colors?
5 Constantly doing so, 4 very frequently does so, 3 often, 2 sometimes, 1 never

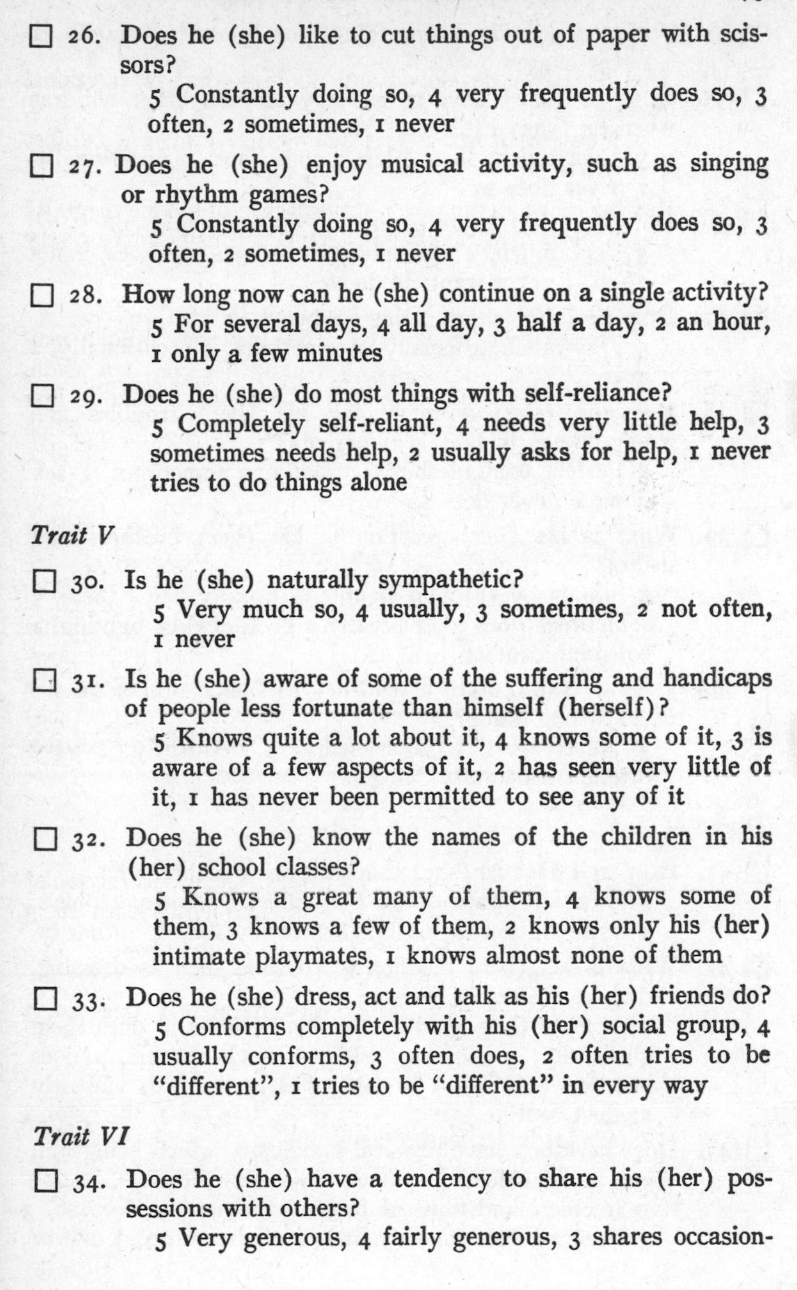

☐ 26. Does he (she) like to cut things out of paper with scissors?

5 Constantly doing so, 4 very frequently does so, 3 often, 2 sometimes, 1 never

☐ 27. Does he (she) enjoy musical activity, such as singing or rhythm games?

5 Constantly doing so, 4 very frequently does so, 3 often, 2 sometimes, 1 never

☐ 28. How long now can he (she) continue on a single activity?

5 For several days, 4 all day, 3 half a day, 2 an hour, 1 only a few minutes

☐ 29. Does he (she) do most things with self-reliance?

5 Completely self-reliant, 4 needs very little help, 3 sometimes needs help, 2 usually asks for help, 1 never tries to do things alone

Trait V

☐ 30. Is he (she) naturally sympathetic?

5 Very much so, 4 usually, 3 sometimes, 2 not often, 1 never

☐ 31. Is he (she) aware of some of the suffering and handicaps of people less fortunate than himself (herself)?

5 Knows quite a lot about it, 4 knows some of it, 3 is aware of a few aspects of it, 2 has seen very little of it, 1 has never been permitted to see any of it

☐ 32. Does he (she) know the names of the children in his (her) school classes?

5 Knows a great many of them, 4 knows some of them, 3 knows a few of them, 2 knows only his (her) intimate playmates, 1 knows almost none of them

☐ 33. Does he (she) dress, act and talk as his (her) friends do?

5 Conforms completely with his (her) social group, 4 usually conforms, 3 often does, 2 often tries to be "different", 1 tries to be "different" in every way

Trait VI

☐ 34. Does he (she) have a tendency to share his (her) possessions with others?

5 Very generous, 4 fairly generous, 3 shares occasion-

ally, 2 usually keeps things for himself (herself), 1 never shares

☐ 35. Does he (she) have a tendency to help other children when he (she) can?
5 Always does so, 4 often, 3 sometimes, 2 occasionally, 1 never does so

☐ 36. Does he (she) enjoy caring for younger children?
5 Very much, 4 willingly does so, 3 sometimes, 2 not often, 1 never wants to do so

☐ 37. Does he (she) enjoy caring for pets?
5 Very much, 4 usually, 3 sometimes, 2 occasionally, 1 never

☐ 38. Does he (she) willingly tell his (her) troubles and wrong-doings to his (her) parents?
5 Perfect comradeship, 4 usually, 3 sometimes, 2 seldom, 1 never does so

☐ 39. What is his (her) reaction to his (her) brothers and sisters?
5 Stands by them in trouble, 4 usually helps them, 3 sometimes does so, 2 usually a good deal of fighting, 1 constant conflict

☐ 40. Does he (she) have a tendency to blame others for his (her) wrong-doing?
5 Never does, 4 occasionally, 3 frequently, 2 very often, 1 constantly doing so

Trait VII

☐ 41. How well does he (she) coöperate with authority?
5 Complete coöperation, 4 usually coöperates, 3 obeys, 2 resists authority, 1 rebels vigorously against authority.

☐ 42. What is his (her) reaction to routine, such as dressing, eating, and sleeping habits?
5 Accepts them gladly as responsibilities, 4 does them cheerfully, 3 conforms without much trouble, 2 does not do them unless he (she) has to, 1 rebels violently against routine

☐ 43. Does he (she) have physical handicaps, which bring him (her) social ridicule, such as cross-eyes, bowlegs, excessive freckles, and unusual fatness?
5 None of these, 4 very little such handicap, 3 one or

two, 2 several such handicaps, 1 very much handicapped physically

☐ 44. What is his (her) reaction to mistreatment by others?
5 Usually willing to forget it if they are sorry, 4 sometimes willing to forget, 3 "eye-for-an-eye" attitude, 2 somewhat revengeful, 1 very bitter, insists on severe retribution.

☐ 45. How does he (she) react to social ridicule and teasing?
5 Takes it cheerfully, 4 takes it pretty well, 3 takes it but does not like it, 2 rebels against it, 1 becomes violently angry in face of it

☐ 46. Does he (she) have ample opportunity for learning to make social adjustments?
5 Very ample both in materials and social contacts, 4 above average, 3 average, 2 not much, 1 almost no opportunity at all

☐ 47. Does he (she) respect the property rights of others?
5 Always does so, 4 usually, 3 sometimes, 2 often grabs for himself (herself), 1 grabs everything he (she) wants without regard to ownership

Trait VIII

☐ 48. Does he (she) have natural leadership ability?
5 Very pronounced, 4 above average, 3 average, 2 not much, 1 none

☐ 49. Does he (she) know how to be a good follower?
5 He (she) coöperates with his (her) leader perfectly, 4 usually does, 3 follows if he (she) can lead sometimes, 2 does not like to go in a group he (she) cannot dominate, 1 refuses to join a group he (she) cannot dominate

☐ 50. What is the quality of his (her) leadership?
5 Leads intelligently and is a popular leader, 4 does fairly well, 3 uses some force and loud talk, 2 tries to lead mostly by force, 1 leads entirely by force and bullying

☐ 51. How well does he (she) adjust to the less pleasant parts of his (her) social environment?
5 Adjusts remarkably well, 4 does fairly well, 3 average,

2 resents social injustice, 1 becomes violently angry at social injustice

☐ 52. How much physical stamina and resistance to pain has he (she)?

5 Can endure pain unless it is severe, 4 reacts to pain without too much crying, 3 cries some, 2 cries violently at pain of any considerable severity, 1 cries violently at even the smallest pain

IX

The Third and Fourth Grades

PHYSICAL PROWESS now becomes to the child the most admirable quality in life. Parents and teachers who expect to command the admiration of their children during the six years following the primary age must have at least an impressive amount of physical strength. Listen to two boys quarreling with each other. They fight more frequently with words than blows, but these words show fully their concept of greatness. They usually start by making dire threats about what each expects to do to the other, and end with a heated discussion of how their fathers would fare in a fight. The primary child, except for the influences of his entrance into formal education, is really more like the pre-school child than like those older. But this child, whom we shall refer to as the secondary child, shows a significant jump in maturity and his activity much more closely approaches that of the next two ages than of his primary brothers and sisters. This is the beginning of the bad boy age which reaches its peak some five or six years later. Goodness, when defined as implicit obedience, keeping out of mischief, being immaculate and cleanly, showing courtesy and thoughtfulness, is a far cry from the normal behavior of the secondary child. It is during this period that the behavior of our children begins to bring alarming numbers of complaints from the neighbors. Windows are broken, minor depredations are wrought upon gardens, garages, and lawns, voices are loud, and, in general, most of the things which the boy or girl of this age finds most desirable to do cause them to be the bane of their elders' existence. Despite this rather dismal picture, it must be kept in mind that where there is power for one kind of behavior there is power for another. These undesirable activities are not necessary in human nature and it only remains for us to find more acceptable ways of utilizing all this energy.

Physical Development

Strength and resistance to fatigue increase enormously during this period. The ability to endure pain is much greater than in the preceding two years. As a result, it is now possible to develop much greater endurance and a higher level of physical courage. There is no decrease in physical activeness, but the child does tend to become less nervously restless. His physical energy is more efficiently harnessed to effective behavior. There is less fidgeting and squirming and more running and fighting. The complex motor skills which are learned during the last year of the primary stage now approach a fairly high level of maturity. Dancing, swimming, skating and bicycle riding are now brought to a point of outstanding performance. In boys, strength doubles between the eighth and tenth birthdays. Although girls do not increase in strength as much as this they are also considerably stronger by that time. Voluntary control, as indicated in a steadiness test, reaches almost as high a point as it ever will. A few children of this age respond well to coaching, but for the most part they are not willing to spend any considerable periods of time trying to master the intricacies of the various skills.

Mental Development

The three R's should now have become an automatic part of the child's personality. To be sure, the growth of ability in mathematics is not very far advanced at this age, and this is very commonly the most difficult of their school subjects. Actually, it should be the very center of their interests, and needs to be made as thrilling an experience as possible.

On the other hand, reading is likely to reach its highest point. Every year, many a parent comes back from a summer vacation reporting that his son or daughter is destined to become a great scholar. When asked the foundation for this prophecy, he reports that the child has spent the entire summer reading. He has read everything he could get his hands on. One boy read a hundred books in a single summer. Parents who are so impressed by this will do well to observe the age of the child. In a large number of cases, they will discover that the period of this enormous reading was during the summer of the child's tenth year. This means that during the third and fourth grades, reading ability should improve enormously. It reaches its peak by the end of the fifth grade. After that, improvement usually consists in vocabulary and difficulty of material, and not in efficiency of the reading process itself. However, this very fact makes another problem important, that is, the child who does not learn to read well. It is not at all uncommon for a child well above average in intelligence to fail to learn to read in the first grade, and sometimes in the second, and then to improve so rapidly as to be quite up to the level of his school grade after he gets the principle involved in reading. But if the child does not show marked progress in this skill by the third grade, professional advice should be sought, and every effort made to discover the cause of this difficulty. Reading is so complex a skill that it is not always easy to discover the factors which retard its development at any age level. A child was brought to the laboratory who was in the middle of the third grade. For all practical purposes it could be said that she had not learned to read at all. Furthermore, she was a constant source of trouble both in school and in her neighborhood. Her parents were being called to the school weekly about one disciplinary problem after another. Experimental analysis revealed the cause of this reading deficiency. She had simply not acquired one very important visual habit which most children learn at a much earlier age level. Because of her increased intellectual maturity it was not difficult to teach her this habit and, once having learned it, reading followed, and in an amazingly short time she was approaching the average level of her school grade. This is typical of the experience of many a child. Some years ago a boy was brought to our laboratory whom teachers had classified as feeble-minded. Performance tests gave no basis for this judgment and experimental analysis of his reading ability revealed the source of the difficulty. He had reached junior high school level without having been taught to read. Any child of normal intelligence can learn to read with some efficiency before the fourth grade. It is important in his social and emotional development as well as in his school achievement.

The voluntary attention span increases now, and a good deal longer task, requiring more concentration and application, is possible. As was pointed out in connection with the primary child, it is of value constantly to increase the length of the tasks set for the child in order to develop this quality as rapidly and as far as possible. A certain amount of reasoning now comes into the scope of the child's performance, especially the capacity for discerning similarities and differences. By this age level discriminations become more possible. In a recent school project, an amateur cast produced a play called "David Copperfield". Groups of children were permitted to see this version as well as the splendid cinema production. Up to the fourth grade level, one production appealed to them quite as much as the other. The fact was they could not tell much difference between them. The discriminative ability, however, becomes much keener before this age level is passed.

Special Aptitudes

The special aptitudes are still pretty much on the child level. It is not until the next period that we can measure them, with confidence that these measurements will predict children's future ability. To be sure, they are able to do much better representative drawing, to carry on a higher level of musical performance and to achieve some creditable results in mechanical fields. Still this achievement does not reach the level of practical efficiency that it will two years later. Two things often happen in this connection. One is that their ambitions to achieve in these fields far outrun their abilities. This makes it all too common for them to start a great many more things than they can finish. Then, too, their newly emerged critical abilities make them, for the first time, aware of the quality or lack of quality of their productions. Many an embryonic artist ceases his career during this period. He may have drawn during every waking hour and on every available spot during his earlier years. But now he suddenly becomes aware of how poor his pictures are, and ceases entirely to engage in this activity. Some help can be given in this respect. Probably very few children could not be taught a measure of artistic skill under good supervision. When they have real talent it becomes especially important that this be done.

Social and Emotional Maturity

During the years from eight to fourteen physical courage is the most desirable of all personality traits. Adjustment difficulties of large proportions are almost certain to come, especially to those boys whose physical endowment is modest. Girls are inclined along this same line of daring and adventure, but they do show a considerably greater interest in the more feminine arts of home-making. This gives them an opportunity for achievement which the boy, who is not physically strong and well coördinated, does not find so easily. Because of the almost inevitable presence of some physical inferiority, every child is likely to experience difficulties in competition and try to develop compensatory mechanisms against them. Hence this may well be thought of as the age level of the inferiority complex. A child's physical deficiencies are very evident on the playground, and his intellectual deficiencies show up with glaring conspicuousness in the classroom. This makes it increasingly important that we know as accurately as we can all of his abilities and aptitudes, so that we can find for him forms of activity and achievement which will keep and develop his sense of self-confidence. With all the difficulties that this emphasis upon daring and adventure creates, the fact is that it also provides the central core of character education. Teachers and parents who can make themselves heroes in the life of the child have an influence not exceeded at any age level in life. A boy who disdained Sunday school and had been the subject of much trouble in his family became much impressed with a new Sunday school teacher. Much to the astonishment of the family, he spent a whole week-end trying to commit to memory the Parable of the Good Samaritan because, as he expressed it, "I cannot let my teacher down." Probably at no period in life is it more important to find the right leadership for the right classes than during this one. At later age levels, when the children are more mature mentally, the teacher simply loses his influence if he makes serious mistakes in his teaching. At this age level, however, if the teacher is the sort the children do not want "to let down," then he actually becomes the criterion of wisdom and the thing is right because he says it. This gives the heroes of children of this age both an opportunity and a responsibility.

Character Development

The dominant tendency to admire physical prowess, which so characterizes this age, continues during the next two age levels. Three words may be used, one to characterize each of these age levels. Courage may be thought of as the keyword for this secondary group, exploration for the junior age, and adventure for the intermediates. It would be forcing age distinctions much too far to suggest that these emphases are as clear-cut as this. There is no doubt that all three are important in all three ages. There does seem to be validity, however, in this distinction between the three age levels. Because this is the first period during which children are capable of enduring pain and fatigue, courage is the most important character trait for them to develop. With this central theme running through all our character education for this age level, let us turn to the eight traits.

Experimental Faith

Vision

This is the first period at which true poverty of spirit can be developed. Imagination of a distinctly creative type can be given much training at the lower age levels, but a recognition of the imperfections in one's performance is not characteristic of children younger than this. It is most interesting to see younger children in a test situation give a solution which is entirely wrong and then sit back in complete satisfaction without the remotest tendency to check up on their results. By no means does this always occur because they do not know the difference. Often, if they are asked to check, they can easily discover their error. Being critical of their performances is simply not characteristic of them. This holds true for the expression of their special aptitudes, such as drawing and singing and building, as well as of their intellectual pursuits. When they reach the secondary level, however, they become self-critical. As has been pointed out, they not infrequently entirely cease some of their activities, because they now realize how inadequate their performances are. Furthermore, as has also been emphasized, they are very likely to attempt to accomplish things which are impossible for them. All of this is a splendid foundation on which to develop poverty of spirit. If their self-criticism leads to such complete discouragement that they cease trying, it is most certainly not strengthening to the personality. But if it becomes a stimulus by which they do the best they can, recognize how much better it could be, and then plan for renewed attempts to reach a higher level of achievement, they are learning the very essence of this trait.

Originality and ingenuity become much more pronounced now. Girls are likely to produce dramas in which paper dolls and puppets are the chief actors. Boys build complex structures with their tools. If care is taken to help them envision performances which are not completely impossible for them but high enough so that they must try several times if they are to achieve success, then the habit can be ingrained in them of always envisioning better things than they have already achieved.

Another outstanding evidence of this more mature vision is seen in the much more extensive daydreaming characteristic of this age level. If they are permitted to envision achievements which are completely impossible for them, it is quite probable that they will learn to become satisfied with achieving them only in their daydreams. This results in daydreaming becoming a retreat from reality and not a stimulus to action. If, however, guidance helps them plan things in their imagination which they can accomplish with persistence even though they are difficult, the habit of making their daydreams become plans for action can be thoroughly ingrained into their make-up.

Love of Righteousness and Truth

As is true at every developmental period, it is of prime importance that ethical and religious teachings be of such a nature that the child can hunger and thirst for them. The notion that goodness consists entirely in not being naughty is a sterile one at any age level. If this is true at other age levels, it is preëminently true during the three of which this is the first. Courage, exploration, adventure—these must be characteristic of any philosophy of life which can be expected to command the respect and admiration and enthusiasm of children during this time. If the teachings of our Sunday school are so over-pious and meaningless as to make this impossible, the fault is with the schools, not with the children nor with the fundamental nature of righteousness itself. Courage rightly directed is not only a good but a necessary trait in strong personality. This is also true of exploration and adventure. It is important, then, to be sure that goody-goody ideals are not held up to the child. To point out the model boy who lives next door is not likely to increase the desire for righteousness. In teaching the life of Christ, one should place as little emphasis as Jesus himself did on negative ethics and should emphasize, rather, the numerous instances in which Jesus so clearly showed his own courage. Throughout the Bible are many magnificent characters who showed this same courage. By winning from the children admiration for these characters because of their courage, many other aspects of their teaching can be brought out. For once they admire a hero, a thing is good because the hero does it.

In continuing their enthusiasm for formal education the emphasis now swings from reading to arithmetic. Reading is rapidly approaching its maturity, but for that very reason it has become a tool rather than something challenging the interest of the child. Arithmetic, however, is only beginning, and both for the adjustment of the child to arithmetic and the further development of this trait itself, it is important that it be made a thrilling experience. This can be accomplished by the use of games, such as playing store, and perhaps even permitting the child during the summer to sell a few items from a sidewalk stand, and other similar intriguing activities which give him the feeling of doing something of an adult nature. Such a method adds zest to the otherwise rather dull task of learning the multiplication table and the rudiments of arithmetic problems.

The thing to keep in mind is that the child is always looking for evidences of individual prowess. He wants to be able to do things that others cannot do. If desirable forms of behavior, either ethically or academically, can be found which bring admiration from his fellows, such behavior will satisfy some of his desires and become a part of his personality.

Faith in the Friendliness of the Universe

The inferiority complex, however much it may be exaggerated in the Adlerian psychology, cannot be over-emphasized at this age level. As has been pointed out, the very nature of the age itself makes it almost inevitable that the child shall have, from time to time, strong evidences of inferiority. If this is met with fear, the results cannot be anything but weakening to the personality. Observe the factors which conspire to this end: obvious individual differences in school, obvious individual differences in motor skills, increased ability to understand the significance and extent of these differences, and as yet not much sense of humor with which to meet them. In our investigations, testing children as we do in all aspects of their personality, we almost never find a child who is not definitely inferior in some part of his personality. Of course, on the other hand, the reverse of this is true. It is also rare to find a child who does not have leadership capacity in some aspect of his native endowment. The principle of positive mental hygiene which we are endeavoring to apply puts the emphasis on this strength. But all too commonly both the educational and the social pressure tend to call attention to one's weakness.

Some of the more obvious types of behavior which are compensations for a sense of inferiority are: a profusion of explorations, alibis for poor work, a period of depression following any failure, the tendency to worry a long time over humiliating experiences, an abnormal fear of examinations, and an undue anxiety about small mistakes. Along with these must also be listed a group of behavior patterns which, while not so obviously related to this inferiority picture, are known by psychologists to be equally significant. They include: becoming easily nauseated even when medical examination can find no organic cause for it, often feeling "just miserable", undue fear of insecurity, a pedantic sense of orderliness, and a tendency to think oneself less noble and good than other people. You may be sure that when these reactions are made, they are evidences of a very unhappy period in the life of the child. They can weaken personality permanently and it is not possible to build a very strong faith on such a fear-filled personality.

The cheerful side of this rather dismal picture is that by utilizing precisely the same factors in personality, it is just as easy and far more thrilling to build a sense of self-confidence and genuine faith in the friendliness of the universe. If emphasis is placed on the strengths and not the weaknesses of children, and if drama-type curricular programs are set up in which each individual has adequate opportunity for leadership and achievement, important lessons can be learned in the development of this trait.

This does not mean that the existence of his weaknesses needs to be entirely hidden from the child. This is not true nor even desirable. If our educational efforts put the emphasis on his strengths, it is far easier for him to acknowledge his weaknesses without getting a sense of inferiority. A series of biographies of men and women who succeeded in spite of great handicaps would be of real value at this age. Beethoven, Jeremiah, Helen Keller, Naaman are only a few of the long list of names which might be included in this series.

Finally, it is possible to utilize all this material in developing the religious concept that God has a will for the life of every individual. Or, to put it another way, however modest one's endowments, there is some field in life in which he can use his talents to achieve something of value to the happiness of mankind.

Dominating Purpose

An intense interest in the problem of vocations is found during this period. It is not a very rational interest but an enthusiastic one. After having tested a group of boys of this age level, we found them very serious about what the tests indicated for their life work. One boy said, "My father says that I am going to be an engineer. I don't know what an engineer is, but he says I must study my arithmetic hard if I'm going to be one, so I guess I had better do that." Perhaps this rather superstitious faith in the ability of tests to predict at this age level one's best possible vocation is not entirely well-founded. It seems, however, that so long as it results in an immediate purposiveness in the life of the child, it is worth while. Furthermore, the prediction is not entirely without foundation. Not all the special aptitudes can be measured with great accuracy this early, but when we examine the profiles of these same children several years later, the changes in the relative measurement of the special aptitudes are not very great. Certainly as a result of these early tests, a good deal of foresight can be used in getting a fairly general view of the type of vocation the individual is likely to be fitted for. The specific nature of it, however, can be determined only at a much later date. But this purposiveness which is so strong at this age level should not be lost. Indeed, the interest in vocations does not become so great again until middle adolescence.

Furthermore, one of the most important factors in personality integration is purposiveness. It is good mental hygiene for young people of any age to have a vocation in mind. The ideal vocation is one which makes them do something about it at the moment. Young children who desire to be policemen, soldiers, firemen and cowboys or nurses and school teachers are choosing far more wisely than their parents, who may envision for them law or medicine or business. If they think in terms of the former it gives purposiveness to their lives at the present, and this purposiveness in turn gives emotional stabilization and greater integration of personality.

The religious ideal of God having a task for each one will meet with vigorous response at this age level. It is a poor teacher who cannot utilize this natural interest in vocation to instill important lessons in the development of this trait. Here, again, the value of obtaining accurate personality profiles of each child and of developing drama-type curricula is obvious. Activity programs in character education are not very easy to develop for this age level. Activities which are at all below the level of the children's abilities are certain to be far below the level of their ambitions. Similarly, projects in line with what they want to do are almost certain to be beyond their capacities. However, this latter choice is more desirable. Teachers who can themselves contribute whatever is lacking, without falling into the temptation of doing it all, are of great value in character education at this age level.

Fatherly Love

Being Sensitive to the Needs of Others

Now, for a period of six years the social attitudes of children are best exemplified by their complete lack of enthusiasm about their baby brothers and sisters. This is a little less intense among girls than boys, and much less socially taboo. However, a rough and tumble life is much more to the liking of both, and the care of babies is very likely to be classified as work for "sissies". This does not mean that the parental drives are not operative at this period. They are quite as strong as they were at the earlier age levels or as they will be later on. It simply means that they find other forms of expression. Perhaps the most wholesome ones are caring for pets, and in the case of girls, dolls. Why a child should be so especially interested in the welfare of a dog or cat and completely indifferent to a baby brother or sister is not easy to see logically. Probably it is due entirely to social traditions, but the fact that it is there makes it important to take it into consideration and to require as little such activity as possible from the child.

Despite all the superficial hardness that shows itself on the surface during this period, children of this age are quite sensitive. Their feelings are easily hurt, and a good deal of their hardness is a compensation for this very fact. In order to make a child realize what another child feels because of his teasing, parents and teachers not infrequently inflict the same thing upon him. Bullying is no cure for bullying, and such methods are almost certain to lead to repeated offenses in the absence of an older person. Actually, to give the child a sense of inner happiness and self-confidence is the surest way of making him sensitive to the needs of others. It stands to reason that the less his troubles cause him to think about himself, the more likely he will be to sympathize with the troubles of others.

Forgiveness

Superficial observers watching the child of this age level are likely to be convinced that he is sensitive to nothing except his own immediate whims and wishes. Frustration of these invariably leads to violent objection on his part. A more sympathetic and understanding insight into the mind of the child finds him much more thoughtful than this would indicate. Teachers and parents and older friends who have a deep affection for him and give of their time and energy in helping him achieve happiness and success find him deeply appreciative and anxious to do something to show that appreciation.

Not infrequently during this period children engage in an undue amount of tormenting and teasing of each other. Bullying is an especially common habit. When it does occur, it is always a compensation for an inferiority complex and its cure is not found in dealing with the habit itself, but rather in helping the child find better forms of achievement. Occasionally, a very shy child who has been unduly submissive will suddenly discover his capacity for inflicting pain on others and go into an energetic period of bullying. This is a fairly natural compensation for that earlier period of submissiveness and will almost certainly disappear as soon as the pendulum has had time to swing back to normal. Almost always, this is due to conscious or unconscious jealousy. When a child attempts to prevent other children from doing things or insists upon forcing his will upon them, it is because he has not found any other sources of achievement. A measurement of his personality will make it possible to provide activities which utilize his best abilities, and it will be much easier to teach him to admire the abilities of others and to give them opportunity for expressing these abilities.

Magnanimity

Obedience is likely to be conspicuous by its absence during this period. The child is almost certain to feel that a good many of the parental commands imposed upon him are unjust and unfair, and many of them are. To be sure, his intelligence does not make him capable of understanding all of the implications of the parental will. And there are undoubtedly many occasions on which father and mother do know best. But there are also a great many other occasions on which this knowledge is not nearly so profound. Coöperation with authority is best gained in the child when parents and teachers plan to make it a two-way process. When one sees an extremely disobedient child, close examination usually reveals some unfair tyranny. As a matter of fact, the child of this age level has as keen a sense of fair play as at any age in life. He respects severe discipline, when he recognizes its justice, but he most certainly does not respect discipline which is not just. Furthermore, when his elders require of him responsibilities which give him a sense of importance and achievement, the problem of authority is not likely to be important. There seems little question that this is the most important habit to learn at this age level: that is, how to coöperate with authority. What has been said does not mean that the child can always understand what is best for him, but if every effort is made to explain to him why various requirements are made, and especially if the requirements made on his elders are pointed out to him, he is likely to be more willing to conform to their desires even when he cannot fully see the justice of them. What an important lesson this can be! Often by appealing to the parental instinct, the significance of having confidence in the greater insight of one's elders can be brought forcibly to the child's mind. It is easy to show him how many of the desires of a still younger child are quite foolish even to him, although the younger child does not perceive that fact.

Christian Courage

Physical courage is not very common among children younger than this. Indeed, it is nothing short of cruelty to endeavor to elicit it. But now a much greater capacity for enduring pain and fatigue makes possible a challenge to continue one's work or purpose even in the face of hardship. This does not mean that the "boys don't cry" philosophy is the best method to gain that end. It is a far healthier procedure to pay no attention to crying as such, but rather to praise the child's ability to carry through what he sets out to carry through even when pain and fatigue interfere. Longer hikes which are almost certain to involve thirst, extreme fatigue, and perhaps blisters, are good lessons in learning such a trait.

At this age level, "I dare you to" is life's greatest challenge and at the same time life's greatest terror. Not to be willing to take a dare is one of the most difficult things to face. When dares are proposed by his contemporaries, the child often has to refuse to take them because the capacities required for their performance are limited only by the imagination of the proposer. Not infrequently this limitation is still further increased by returning the dare with interest. An interchange of dares may well be an important relationship between father and son, and even mother and daughter. If the father chooses the dare intelligently and does not get beyond the bounds of safety or the child's capacity, it may well be a strong motivation for courageous performance. Care must be taken, however, to be sure that the dare is not one which the child will refuse, and through it gain an even greater sense of inferiority than before. The child can now learn the necessity of doing unpleasant tasks for the good of the whole. He can see the justice of such duties when shown that even mother and dad have similarly unpleasant tasks to perform. He can be shown, furthermore, that they regularly perform these tasks even when they do not want to or do not feel like it. It is not quite right to say that the child of this age can be made truly magnanimous, but he can learn a quality of justice which is an important part of this trait.

Furthermore, the child needs less and less protection from the justice and injustice and the give and take of the world as it really is. Learning this lesson is a difficult experience in life, but a necessary one if the child is to be happy in the face of it. It is all well and good to work for justice and to insist upon justice, but the fact remains that there is an abundance of injustice in the world and if a person spends his whole life bemoaning it, nothing is gained except his own unhappiness.

An ever-increasing amount of leadership training should be taking place. Pubic speaking can now become a part of the child's activities. The courage to stand on his feet and express his views to an audience is far more easily accomplished if begun at an age level as early as this. The child is certain to get a great deal of achievement satisfaction from such an accomplishment, and by means of it there can be instilled in him a desire for good articulation, a wider vocabulary, and an increased capacity for formulating ideas.

Conclusion

Consider, now, some of the important lessons that are possible to teach during this age level: learning to get satisfaction from doing things well, the ambition and desire to speak well in public, reliability in carrying out one's responsibilities, keeping one's promises, the ability to keep on going even through minor illnesses and physical pain and great fatigue, the willingness to suffer in the service of someone he loves, the habit of doing things promptly however disagreeable they may be, and an insight into the hero qualities of the Cross. Certainly the teaching of such habits to children of this age level should be a thrilling challenge to anyone who desires to contribute to the happiness and success of our boys and girls.

Finally, we come to the questionnaire for the measurement of personality at this age level. It should be applied carefully through the coöperation of both parents and teachers in order to gain an accurate estimate of what each child needs to learn. Then, in view of these specific needs, prepare character education programs designed to produce these results. Finally, go over the questionnaire again at the end of the training period to discover how much has been accomplished as a result of these efforts.

QUESTIONNAIRE FOR THE THIRD AND FOURTH SCHOOL YEARS

In the square preceding each question write a number, 5, 4, 3, 2, or 1. After each question is a series of five possible answers to the question, numbered 5, 4, 3, 2, and 1, respectively. In the square use the number preceding the phrase which most nearly represents your answer.

☐ 1. Does he (she) now seem poised and deliberate in his (her) physical activity?
5 Very much so, 4 above average, 3 about average, 2 somewhat nervous and fidgety for his (her) age, 1 very nervous and restless in activity

☐ 2. How steady in motor control is he (she), as shown by his (her) ability to use tools requiring such steadiness?
5 Unusually good motor control, 4 above average, 3 about average for his (her) age, 2 rather poor motor control, 1 very poor control

Trait I

☐ 3. How much imagination has he (she)?
5 Very vivid, 4 above average, 3 average, 2 below average, 1 little or no imagination

☐ 4. How realistic and creative is his (her) imagination?
5 Very realistic and creative, 4 closely related to reality, 3 very little tendency to fantasy, 2 somewhat bizarre and fantastic, 1 very fantastic and bizarre

☐ 5. Has he (she) acquired the habit of trying things over and over again, in an effort to make them better, even though they are acceptable the first time?
5 Does so frequently, 4 does so sometimes, 3 does so occasionally, 2 does so rarely, 1 never does so

☐ 6. Is he (she) critical of his (her) solutions to problems, so that he (she) realizes his (her) errors?
5 Examines his (her) work carefully, 4 usually, 3 sometimes, 2 rarely, 1 never

☐ 7. Does he (she) often create dramatic activities from his (her) own imagination?
5 Constantly doing so, 4 often does so, 3 sometimes, 2 seldom, 1 never does so

☐ 8. Does he (she) spend much time daydreaming?
5 A normal amount, 4 very little, 3 more than average, 2 too much, 1 constantly doing so

☐ 9. Are his (her) daydreams stimulating or retreats from reality?
5 Very stimulating to action, 4 usually stimulating, 3 sometimes one, sometimes the other, 2 usually day-dreams of wishes which are impossible in reality, 1 always retreats from reality

Trait II

☐ 10. Does he (she) like to read?
5 Reads constantly, 4 reads a great deal, 3 average interest in reading, 2 reads only what is required, 1 reads little or none

☐ 11. Does he (she) enjoy his (her) work in arithmetic?
5 Very much interest, 4 likes it a good deal, 3 average interest, 2 dislikes it, 1 dislikes it very intensely

☐ 12. What is his (her) attitude toward being good?
5 That it is courageous and adventurous, 4 desirable, 3 rather dull, 2 undesirable, 1 very goody-goody and infantile

☐ 13. Does he (she) usually tell the truth, even when it may involve his (her) receiving punishment?
5 Very truthful, 4 fairly truthful, 3 average, 2 will falsify to avoid punishment, 1 very untruthful

☐ 14. Can he (she) be trusted with money?
5 Completely, 4 usually, 3 if not too much, 2 not very trustworthy, 1 not at all

☐ 15. Is he (she) enthusiastic about his (her) school work?
5 Very much so, 4 likes it, 3 goes willingly, 2 rather bored, 1 dislikes it intensely

Trait III

☐ 16. Has he (she) developed feelings of inferiority?
5 None at all, 4 very few, 3 some, 2 a number, 1 an unusual number

☐ 17. Does he (she) have a sense of inferiority in his (her) school work?

5 Perfectly self-confident, 4 usually confident, 3 average confidence, 2 feels inferior, 1 has strong sense of intellectual inferiority

☐ 18. Does he (she) have a sense of inferiority on the playground?

5 Plays games with complete confidence, even if he (she) does not do them well, 4 usually confident, 3 sometimes a little hesitant about joining in, 2 has to be urged to participate, 1 very much afraid of playground participation

☐ 19. Does he (she) display some of the aggressive reactions to feelings of inferiority, such as disciplinary problems in school, changing activities frequently without finishing any of them, giving numerous alibis for poor work?

5 Shows none of them, 4 very few, 3 several, 2 many of them, 1 exhibits them very strongly

☐ 20. Does he (she) exhibit some of the fear reactions to feelings of inferiority, such as depression from failure, worry over humiliations, fear of examinations, fear of insecurity, tendency to think himself (herself) worse than others, and over-anxiety over small mistakes?

5 Shows none of them, 4 very few, 3 several, 2 many of them, 1 exhibits them very strongly

☐ 21. Is he (she) ever a subject for school discipline?

5 Never, 4 seldom, 3 occasionally, 2 frequently, 1 is a constant source of trouble

☐ 22. Is he (she) inspired by the stories of great men who have succeeded in spite of physical handicaps, such as Beethoven, Lincoln, Helen Keller, Steinmetz, Naaman, and Jeremiah?

5 Very much so, 4 gives him (her) some confidence, 3 somewhat, 2 a little, 1 not at all

Trait IV

☐ 23. Does he (she) exhibit marked vocational interests, such as being a policeman, soldier, cowboy, nurse, or school teacher?

5 Very great interest, 4 above average, 3 some interest, 2 a little, 1 none

☐ 24. Does he (she) show an interest in vocations about which he (she) knows nothing except that his (her) father or some adult friend is in them?

5 Very strong interest of this sort, 4 some such interest, 3 a little, 2 none, 1 does not even know what vocation his (her) father is in

☐ 25. Does he (she) have a long attention span?

5 Can concentrate on a task a long time, 4 above average, 3 average, 2 cannot concentrate very long, 1 very marked inability to concentrate

☐ 26. Does he (she) often attempt to do things much beyond his (her) abilities?

5 Usually adjusts his (her) choice of tasks to his (her) abilities, 4 sometimes tries things a little beyond him (her), 3 frequently does so, 2 very often does, 1 always does so

☐ 27. How does he (she) react to failure in a difficult task?

5 Tries it repeatedly until he (she) succeeds, 4 tries at least twice before giving up, 3 gives up and tries something else, 2 develops some feelings of inferiority, 1 shows marked symptoms of an inferiority complex

☐ 28. Does he (she) often engage in such activities as selling things, helping about the house, etc.?

5 Very often, 4 often, 3 sometimes, 2 seldom, 1 never

☐ 29. Does he (she) like to write poetry?

5 Constantly doing so, 4 often does so, 3 sometimes does, 2 seldom, 1 never

☐ 30. Does he (she) often give expression to musical aptitudes?

5 Very often, 4 frequently, 3 sometimes, 2 seldom, 1 never

☐ 31. Does he (she) often give expression to artistic ability?

5 Very often, 4 frequently, 3 sometimes, 2 seldom, 1 never

☐ 32. Does he (she) often give expression to mechanical ability?

5 Very often, 4 frequently, 3 sometimes, 2 seldom, 1 never

Trait V

☐ 33. Does he (she) like most other children he (she) meets?

5 Likes everybody, 4 usually does, 3 many of them, 2 some of them, 1 very few of them

☐ 34. Is he (she) careful not to hurt the feelings of his (her) playmates?
5 Very considerate, 4 usually, 3 fairly considerate, 2 not very thoughtful, 1 very unkind to them

☐ 35. Does he (she) have good manners for his (her) age?
5 Unusually good, 4 above average, 3 average, 2 not very good, 1 very poor manners

☐ 36. How well does he (she) take care of his (her) own dress, toilet, and the like?
5 Does so completely, 4 most of it, 3 average, 2 lets mother do some of it, 1 lets mother do almost all of it

☐ 37. Does he (she) show appreciation for things done for him (her)?
5 Very appreciative, 4 fairly appreciative, 3 shows good manners about it, 2 indifferent, 1 rude and greedy

Trait VI

☐ 38. Does he (she) engage in bullying, tormenting and teasing?
5 Never, 4 seldom, 3 sometimes, 2 often does so, 1 constantly doing so

☐ 39. Does he (she) have a strong sense of fair play?
5 Very much so, 4 considerable, 3 average, 2 rather selfish in play, 1 very selfish and unfair in play

☐ 40. Is he (she) jealous of other children?
5 Never displays jealousy, 4 occasionally is, 3 sometimes is, 2 frequently is, 1 extremely jealous

☐ 41. Is he (she) willing to take care of younger brothers and sisters?
5 Enjoys such responsibility thoroughly, 4 does so willingly, 3 does so without objection, 2 does not like it, 1 refuses to do so

☐ 42. Does he (she) enjoy caring for pets?
5 Very much, 4 likes it, 3 indifferent to pets, 2 rather dislikes pets, 1 very much opposed to caring for pets

☐ 43. Does he (she) blame others for his (her) own failures and wrong-doings?
5 Never, 4 rarely, 3 sometimes, 2 often, 1 always

Trait VII

☐ 44. How does he (she) react to frustration of his (her) own wishes?

5 Evaluates the situations rather objectively, 4 does not like it but does not display anger, 3 with some anger, 2 with considerable anger, 1 with temper tantrums

☐ 45. How does he (she) react to authority?

5 Splendid coöperation with authority, 4 fair coöperation, 3 tends to be either stubborn or too submissive, 2 very stubborn or submissive, 1 extreme negativism or suggestibility (In answers 4-1, underline which)

☐ 46. Is he (she) unusually sensitive, that is, are his (her) feelings hurt easily?

5 Not at all, 4 very little, 3 some, 2 rather sensitive, 1 very sensitive

☐ 47. Does he (she) have a strong sense of property rights?

5 Very complete, 4 usually, 3 sometimes, 2 not very good, 1 takes whatever he (she) wants if he (she) can get it

☐ 48. Does he (she) have confidence in the superior wisdom of his (her) elders, when his (her) own wishes are refused as being undesirable?

5 Accepts such judgments wholeheartedly, 4 accepts them confidently, 3 accepts them doubtfully, 2 usually doubts wisdom of parents, 1 perfectly sure of his (her) own judgment against theirs

Trait VIII

☐ 49. Are his (her) social reactions confident or shy?

5 Completely confident, 4 fairly confident, 3 average, 2 has some tendency to withdraw from social contacts, 1 very shy

☐ 50. Does he (she) have a large measure of physical courage?

5 A great deal, 4 above average, 3 average, 2 not much physical courage, 1 is very cowardly

☐ 51. Is he (she) willing to continue his (her) tasks in the face of some fatigue and pain?

5 Has marked perseverance, 4 above average, 3 average, 2 gives up rather quickly, 1 gives up very easily

☐ 52. What is his (her) reaction to a dare?

5 Reacts with rational courage, 4 reacts irrationally with bravado, 3 does a good deal of bluffing, 2 shows some fear, 1 is very much a coward in such matters

☐ 53. Is his (her) hero-worship directed toward a person or persons who exert a wholesome influence on him (her)?

5 His (her) heroes exert a splendid influence, 4 good influence, 3 not very helpful, 2 rather harmful, 1 very bad influence

☐ 54. Does he (she) show evidences of good leadership?

5 Is a fine strong leader, 4 shows good leadership, 3 occasionally acts as a leader, 2 seldom does so, 1 never does so

☐ 55. Is he (she) a good follower?

5 Gives splendid coöperation to his (her) leaders, 4 fairly coöperative, 3 follows with indifference, 2 rather non-coöperative, 1 refuses to be led at all

☐ 56. Is he (she) willing to do some unpleasant tasks for the good of the whole group?

5 Does so willingly, 4 does so usually, 3 sometimes, 2 rarely, 1 never

☐ 57. Does he (she) keep his (her) promises even when they are difficult to keep?

5 Always does so, 4 usually, 3 sometimes, 2 not if difficult, 1 not trustworthy at all

☐ 58. Can he (she) speak in public with some confidence?

5 Complete confidence, 4 some confidence, 3 average, 2 does so only with urging, 1 afraid to speak in public

☐ 59. Is he (she) willing to accept responsibilities?

5 Does so gladly, 4 willing to do so, 3 does so sometimes, 2 dodges responsibility if he (she) can, 1 never takes responsibility

☐ 60. Does he (she) have a sense of humor?

5 Very heartily enjoys humor even at his (her) own expense, 4 enjoys it except at his (her) own expense, 3 has some appreciation of humor, 2 does not enjoy humor very much, 1 has no sense of humor

X

Middle Childhood

THIS MAY BE THOUGHT OF as the age of exploration. While again the reader must be warned against too literal a following of such single-word characterizations, it is true that if parents and teachers set up curricular programs which involve exploration, they are certain to find eager followers among their boys and girls of this age. There are a great many remarkable similarities common to this age, the one preceding it and the one following it. These three together constitute the period in which children are very much individuals of action rather than individuals of ideas. The middle group, to which we shall refer as the junior age, has, however, many characteristics all its own which distinguish it from the other two.

Physical Development

This seems to be the healthiest period of life. There are fewer cases of disease, both contagious and otherwise, during these two years than at almost any other. This may be because it is also a period of slow physical growth. Toward the end of the period, girls enter the stage of their most rapid growth. And during the intermediate period which follows they are likely to outgrow boys. For boys this period of rapid growth does not come as a rule until several years later.

The capacity for complex motor skills increases, and now team games begin to replace purely individual play. Specialization in athletic competition begins, and each boy or girl chooses not only his games, but which position on the team he wishes to play. This is because he is beginning to recognize the need of coöperation if the greatest enjoyment is to be forthcoming. It is still a long time, however, before individual superiority ceases to be a much greater motivation than team success. Anyone who observes team games during this and the next age level is likely to conclude that children get a great deal more pleasure from arguing than from playing the game. In a recent contest between two baseball teams of boys eight to fourteen years of age, the proportion of time spent in arguing was approximately fifty percent greater than that spent at playing. This occurred despite the fact that it was supervised by a playground director and held under the most favorable conditions for smooth running. In attending a professional baseball or football game and listening to the remarks of the crowd, one may be inclined to wonder if there are not a great many adults who have never outgrown this age level. The specialization which is necessary for true team play also brings about a willingness to practice in order to acquire excellence. This is the first period during which children will do this to any very great extent. Previously they are much more anxious simply to play, however poor the performance. High school and college athletes will find an extremely appreciative group if they devote part of their time to coaching children of this age level. Perhaps the most important element in athletic activity now is the tremendous growth of the competitive spirit. Furthermore, this competitive spirit makes them eager to measure their performances. Races that are timed and jumps that are measured are far more attractive than they have ever been before, and the desire to establish records begins during this period.

Mental Development

This is the great age of reading. During the earlier school years the mastery of the process of reading has been going on but has not advanced far enough so that reading has become a natural part of the individual's personality. Now it has, and because it does open up such a wide and interesting world which has been closed to the child before, it is not remarkable that the tenth summer should often be a period of the most intense reading. Unfortunate indeed is the child who has not acquired the art. The point has already been emphasized that if the child comes to the third grade without having made marked progress, he ought to be given professional advice on how to overcome this handicap. Probably there is not a child of normal intelligence who cannot be taught to read effectively and with considerable rapidity. Boys are especially interested in books of adventure and in mechanical magazines and books. They like to make things, and books which tell them how to do so are unusually attractive. Girls read both the so-called girls' books and boys' books because they, too, like action and adventure. Boys acquire a great deal of skill with their hands and are especially adept in the use of a jackknife. Girls show an increased interest in dolls' clothes and the more advanced phases of cooking. However, a number of investigations give adequate grounds for the assumption that girls have quite as much mechanical ability as boys. Many of them undoubtedly would work in a shop and use tools if they were permitted and encouraged to do so.

Handwriting reaches its highest level of efficiency at this age. On the whole it tends to decline from this time on. One study using a scale of legibility showed that the average legibility score for children of this age was sixty, whereas the average adult was fifty, and the average professional man thirty-five. The modern child is no longer handicapped by the tremendous effort that was made in the last generation to produce artistic writing. Writing has become what it should be, a means of communication. This does not mean that children should not be encouraged to use legible and attractive handwriting. But certainly a beautiful hand should not be made the indispensable goal that it was thirty years ago.

Dual personalities begin to show themselves now, especially in the use of language. Most people realize that their writing vocabulary and style are usually different from their spoken language, but it is not so commonly recognized that children's classroom grammar may be very different from their playground grammar. One boy who regularly received excellent marks in his English classes was heard to make this remark on the playground, "I ain't never got nothing no way." This is not so great a cause for concern as parents often make it. When situations arise in later years which call for the use of good English, they will find that it comes to them almost as naturally as did the playground language which is not appropriate to the situation.

Special Aptitudes

The growth of mechanical ability has already been pointed out. Musical aptitude, as far as the basic elements are concerned, is now almost as good as it ever will be. Our methods for measuring the special aptitudes are further advanced with respect to musical ability than to any other. It is important to distinguish between those children who resent music lessons because of lack of ability and those who do so because of social pressure. A sense of rhythm, the discrimination of tone, and associative memory are almost as good as they ever will be, and children with marked ability should be given musical training with or without their enthusiastic coöperation.

Artistic aptitude is also maturing rapidly. However, the child's critical ability is maturing even more rapidly and his estimates of his artistic creations often lead to a discontinuance of all interest in drawing. As in athletics, this could well be a period of coaching. There are many tricks, especially those which deal with perspective, which would contribute substantially to the child's capacity for satisfactory artistic achievement. For example, teaching the child to draw a box which looks solid, simply by drawing two squares so that the sides of one intersect the sides of the other and connecting the corresponding corners, is one of these tricks. There are many such tricks which could be taught which would help the child do things that he had not believed possible before. In other words, previous to this time, not much training in drawing can be given.

Imagination develops now at a very rapid rate and it is at the base of the adventurous spirit which so predominates this age. Imagination here expresses itself in an intense curiosity which, in turn, leads to the desire for exploration.

Social and Emotional Maturity

Clubs and gangs now come into their own. They are always uni-sexual in their nature and tend to be quite spontaneous and somewhat accidental. Leadership in them shifts depending on the purpose at hand. This purpose is invariably one of action. Whether this action turns out to be social or anti-social depends considerably upon the guidance it receives. The number of different things children do is limited only by the number of things there are to do. Studies of the number of different play activities show that they reach their peak during this period. It is to be expected, therefore, that this period will be characterized by the appearance of many serious delinquencies. It has been referred to by one psychologist as the period of "competitive socialization." This competition leads to extremes in almost any direction it takes. The word "dare" comes to have even more significance, and what the child does is often determined by the character of the daring. During this and the following period, boys and girls tend to avoid each other as completely as possible. Each is somewhat shy in the presence of the other and each, at least on the surface, tends to have considerable contempt for the other. Actually, the sexes probably do hate each other as groups, but secretly experience about as many attractions individually as at any other age. To be sure, the methods of love-making are somewhat different here, since they take such forms as pulling hair, kicking, and making uncomplimentary remarks about each other. As groups, however, children of this age must be kept entirely separate. Girls now go in for distinctly feminine things and boys stick to the masculine activities, especially when their masculinity eliminates any possible suspicion of femininity. Most girls would like to do the things that boys do, and most boys would be much intrigued by some of their sisters' activities. Neither dare show these interests, however, because of social pressure. This is especially true of the boys, where the slightest suspicion of femininity would almost certainly result in social persecution.

When inquiries come to a psychologist about problem children, the chances are that the child is in this or the next age level. These problems are usually of an aggressive nature. This is because parents and teachers commonly tend to regard disciplinary problems and problems of obedience as the most serious. Actually, an over-submissive, over-obedient child is far more of a problem than one whose activities bring numerous phone calls from the neighbors. In either case, however, the solution is positive and not negative. On the one hand, excessive energy needs only guidance to make it highly acceptable. Suppression, whether by threat or shame, is not a solution to the problem at all. On the other hand, challenge is the key to bringing out aggressiveness where it is lacking. Most problems are due to the failure to find acceptable forms of achievement.

Character Development

Perhaps the best single key to the character development of the child during this period is in keeping him so busy doing good that it does not occur to him to do evil. This is not as simple as it sounds, for "good" must be of such a nature as to appeal to him. If we keep in mind our keyword, exploration, we may find many of the problems of this age level easier to solve. Prevention is much better than cure. Far too many parents confine their character education to a series of inhibitions. They wait until the child gets into mischief and then urge him to "be good". It would be a very beneficial thing for parents if their children should ask them on such occasions, "What is good?" The child has boundless energy and a keen curiosity. These must be expressed. We shall not solve his problems until we find acceptable ways for expressing them.

Experimental Faith

Vision

An enthusiasm for life's possibilities, so predominant during this period, makes growth in this trait especially easy. If a child is to develop vision, he must have a breadth of experience as a basis for it. If he does not have this broadening of his horizon, it will most certainly not be his fault. Every waking moment of his life is likely to be spent in searching for new experiences. Fathers may be certain that their sons will welcome explorations anywhere that they have not been. Mothers will find their daughters intensely interested in new activities, both inside and outside the home.

Hero-worship is also a vital factor. During this age level, the hero is still likely to be an actual person. The quality which inspires the worship is usually physical prowess. This is quite as true of girls as boys. A boy of this age was being urged by his family and the family doctor to eat spinach. This he refused to do in spite of all the warnings they gave him. A football captain in a near-by college was invited to his home. At dinner he ate great quantities of spinach and commented on its significance in becoming a great athlete. After that no difficulty was experienced in motivating the boy to do likewise. He wanted spinach three times a day. (In this connection it is interesting to note that inquiries among about five hundred children found only a handful who did not like spinach. A large number of them gave it as their favorite food. This is interesting in view of the traditional notion of children's attitude toward spinach.) When the child's hero has fine character, he may have an incalculable influence upon the child. The child is likely to imitate him in all characteristics, both in appearance and behavior. A boys' baseball team had been built around the personality of an adult leader. He was the idol of the members of the team. He often found himself arguing about the decisions of the umpire. He suddenly became aware of the tremendous influence this was having with these boys. He then adopted the policy of defending the umpire's judgments even when he was certain that they were wrong. He was astonished to discover how rapidly the members of his team came to do the same thing. This is even more remarkable considering the disposition of boys of this age level to argue. Men and women who are chosen as heroes by boys and girls of this age level should recognize their power with them and utilize it to the best advantage.

The child is somewhat poor in spirit during this time. He does recognize his shortcomings and his inabilities. Even more than in the preceding age level, he realizes how small his achievements are and he dreams of the future when he can do greater things. It is important that these dreams be kept in some contact with reality, and be stimulating not only in their visions for the future, but in their relationship to the present. He needs to be poor in spirit, but at the same time he needs to recognize that continued effort now is likely to result in more effective performance later on. Therefore, when he talks of the high achievement he expects to reach when he is a man, it is important to help him discover effective steps he can take in that direction now.

Love of Righteousness and Truth

If you hear children talking pig-Latin to each other, the chances are pretty good that their ages will not vary many years from eleven. This is much more significant than appears on the surface. All popular statements to the contrary notwithstanding, this should be one of the most enthusiastic school ages of all. Curiosity is at its highest peak and the desire for learning should accompany it. However, such learning needs to be exciting and no one who looks at some of the curricula which are given to the children of this age level in our schools can, by the longest stretch of the imagination, classify it as exciting. Compound interest problems, using huge sums of money, are quite unrealistic even to most adults, much less to a ten- or eleven-year-old child.

Nevertheless, trading back and forth, utilizing practical sums of money and such articles as they have for exchange, provides the foundation for an arithmetic which is both practical and interesting. Reading, if it consists in stories—biography or fiction—which gives the child fascinating glimpses of new fields, is almost certain to be of interest to him. When lack of interest is found in school work, it is due either to the nature of the school curriculum itself or to the inability of the child to do the work required, and not to laziness. Hartshorne and May [1] found a reasonably high correlation between the intelligence quotient and the amount of cheating done in the classroom. This means that cheating is a compensation for a form of achievement which otherwise seems impossible. The best way to deal with cheating is not by moral lectures, but by finding more adequate ways of satisfying the desire for success. A child may prefer cheating to failing, but no child prefers cheating to genuine success. A good deal of attention, therefore, needs to be paid to study habits during this period. If the child recognizes that a mastery of these methods of study will increase his skill, he will spend a considerable amount of time practicing, just as he will in athletics or in the expression of his special aptitudes.

Furthermore, he is now ready for some genuine religious insight. The elements of abstract reasoning begin to appear. Thus, at ten he cannot define such words as revenge, justice, purity or charity. At twelve he can. This does not mean that he will have a profound insight into all of the philosophical implications of these terms, but he will begin developing a moral vocabulary upon which can later be built a deeper understanding. However, the method of teaching must be exploratory. There are two teaching sins which ought to be avoided. The first is the tendency to tell a good story and then ruin it with a moral. The other, and really a worse one, is to ruin the good story by pointing out the moral first. Thus a teacher may say, "This morning we

[1] Hartshorne, H., and May, M. A., *Studies in the Nature of Character,* I: Studies in Deceit (Macmillan, 1928).

want to study about self-control," and then tell numerous stories to illustrate this concept. But the very fact that the stories are being told to illustrate a moral concept destroys all their interest to the child. It is a far better thing to tell the story in which this quality is prominent and let the child discover the quality for himself. If enough stories are told and incidents cited, sooner or later he will discover the moral and it will be a far more thrilling experience than having it pointed out to him in pre-digested fashion.

Finally, it is important now to instill in the child a keen and burning desire for his future adventures in the fields of learning and achievement. A boy watching his father do what seems to him miraculous forms of arithmetic achievement, as in one case adding three columns simultaneously, will study his arithmetic with much greater eagerness in the hope that some day he can equal this performance. By this method one can build the habit of having an insatiable hunger for more knowledge. This is a habit of mind which is of great value in the personality of every child.

Faith in the Friendliness of the Universe

The child's natural curiosity and desire for exploration make this period an ideal time for acquiring another lesson about God in nature. Not all those who profess to worship God in nature indulge in much worship. But explorations into the woods and fields to study flowers, birds, insects, and animals, not only for the purpose of recognizing them but also for discovering their interdependence and mutual assistance, provide one of the best lessons that can be learned about the lawfulness of the universe. Because this is one of the ages for collecting, a very good form of activity in character education is the collection of different kinds of natural living objects by members of class groups. If someone who is well informed in nature study is directing this project, he can create an extremely interesting and valuable period for boys and girls of this age level. A drama-type curricular unit can well be made around this theme. Bring in a biologist, if possible, who specializes in ecology. A plant and animal population study could well be made of some near-by woods. Assignments could be made from week to week, perhaps letting the girls specialize in flowers, birds, and plants, the boys in animals and insects. A period of common discussion and report of progress should be held each Sunday morning with interpretations and new assignments by the leader. The leader should be constantly alert to find and point out instances of interdependence and mutual assistance. Where no trained biologist is available, there are numerous books which can be used by anyone willing to invest the necessary time and study.

A belief in the friendliness of the universe is more easily held if the child inherits some capacities through which he can gain self-confidence and keep the respect of his fellows. This, in turn, is much easier if we have accurate measurements of his special aptitudes so that we know how best to utilize them. In any particular group, the differences in aptitudes make possible a comprehension of how important and necessary mutual assistance is in human society. Perhaps the concept that God has created a friendly universe, in the sense that if men obey his laws happiness will result for all, is a little too abstract for this age level. Such lessons as these, however, are important foundations upon which to build that more abstract concept in later years.

Dominating Purpose

Does your child, or even more probably, does your neighbor's child seem bent only on mischief if he is about this age? Why do children seem so determined to keep everyone in the neighborhood in a constant state of turmoil? The answer is not difficult. His mischief is his concept of the height of achievement. Purposiveness has now come to a point where it is the chief hunger in his life. Purposiveness can be defined psychologically as the gaining of a sense of achievement which satisfies the appetite for achievement. Something must seem important, thrilling, and a little bit dangerous if it is to give him complete satisfaction for this appetite. The fact that he may be caught is a part of the pleasure. A boy in one of our slum districts was describing to his club leader one of his experiences. "Gee, mister, we had a grand time last night. We threw rocks through the windows of the old factory. We broke a hundred before a cop came, and it was lots of fun when he chased us!" It was easy to see from the eagerness of his report and his enthusiasm in it that, for him, this was the very acme of achievement.

The first important thing to recognize is that, in itself, this desire for achievement is not wrong. The second factor to recognize is that it must not be suppressed. The third thing is that if we are to eliminate socially undesirable expressions of it, we must replace them with socially desirable ones that are just as satisfying to the child. Simply to tell such a boy how wrong all this is, and that he must stop doing it, is no solution to the problem. Unless there are forms of adventurous religion which make possible the use of this dynamic force, we may as well give up to begin with. But there are many of them.

During this period a tremendous increase in self-reliance and dependability is possible. Many boys during this time have paper routes and carry them with complete dependability, however many difficulties of weather may interfere. Selling cold drinks, cookies and the like are fine activities for children of both sexes. Children now have the capacity to become absorbed in creative work. For boys, model airplanes, radios, chemistry sets, art, music, and even poetry are common forms of expression. For girls, in addition to art, music, and poetry, there come interior decorating, sewing, cooking, and gardening. Every child should have some hobby of this sort and an opportunity for an adequate expression of it. This opportunity should include not only the place and materials for expression, but also whatever agencies for training are available. On the basis of all these things, it is easy to see what extensive projects could be undertaken in church schools to serve some useful purpose.

It is now important to begin to think seriously about actual vocational guidance. The special aptitudes are mature enough for us to measure them accurately and gain a pretty good idea of the general type of vocation for which the child is suited. During this and the period which follows, however, it seems desirable to have the child gain a very broad picture of all the vocations. Vocational guidance tests are often given to college students designed to find out how well-informed they are about the possibilities in various fields. And the lack of information they have about a vast majority of them is quite astonishing. It is important for an individual not only to know his own vocation but those of his fellow-men. The orientation of one's job into the total social structure is quite as important as having an enthusiasm for it. It seems desirable, therefore, to take three sightseeing trips through all the vocations. The first one, which should be taken at this age level, should be one of pure exploration. It is entirely probable that the average boy or girl of this age level has little, if any, concept of what people in various vocations do. No better task in character education could be carried out than one which took children into various offices, factories, schools, farms, etc., to find out what people do. Drama-type projects could be constructed in which children set up model communities, each adopting one of these vocations, the purpose of the whole project being to show the effects of coöperation as compared to the lack of it. Skillful guidance could make this one of the finest lessons these children will ever learn in the art of getting along together. This can be accomplished most successfully if we know what their aptitudes and abilities are and place them in the parts of this model community which fit these measurements.

The competitive spirit is so characteristic of this age that it forms a powerful and useful motivation to be used in all phases of education. It will be recalled that rote memory is the first of the mental abilities to reach maturity. There are many things, both in secular and religious education, which need to be committed to memory. Contests in which children compete are always attractive. Bible verse memory contests, therefore, add substantially to the attractiveness of religious education. It is important that goals of achievement be set. It is impossible to jump as high in empty air as over a pole. The difference comes in the fact that the pole constitutes a goal. This needs to be kept in mind in all phases of the child's activity. When long projects are undertaken, work is generally better when children have clear and visible measures of progress and success. For example, teachers find that large piles of student papers are more easily and efficiently graded if they are graded in groups of ten. This principle ought regularly to be applied at the junior age level. Finally, let us look back on our original question. Are children of this age naturally mischief-makers? The answer is clear. The reason why they have ever been is because we have not taken the trouble to find for them fields for using their abilities just as exciting and thrilling as these less desirable ones which they find for themselves.

Fatherly Love

Being Sensitive to the Needs of Others

This is a period when being sensitive to the needs of others is one of the child's most predominating traits, although this is not always obvious to the superficial observer. During this period he is likely to form intense personal friendships. Both boys and girls have chums to whom they swear eternal allegiance. For the first time in their lives they find a devotion and affection which challenges them to make sacrifices. These friendships are almost as intense as their love affairs will be five or six years later. For example, they are now willing to play what someone else wishes to play even if that is against their own wishes. This is a period in which "brotherly" love can really be taught; that is, if brotherly love is not made to apply to brothers but to others of the same sex. Although not infrequently brothers do become chums, and sisters likewise, if they are very close to the same age level.

It is important now to leave the child a great deal of freedom to work out his own social adjustment. Parents and teachers who interfere with what may seem to them to be cruel treatment on the playground are almost certain to augment that treatment instead of helping it. If there is enough adult supervision to prevent too great damage being done, the best thing to do is to let children fight their own battles. One observing such battles discovers that most of them are entirely verbal. Apprehension for the safety of the participants is not to be gauged by the threats that arise during these verbal battles. Actually, children have a much greater interest at this age level in each other's activities, and much greater willingness to help each other. But since they never have tried it much before, it is not surprising that their social technique needs a lot of training. If the ideal of getting along together can be stimulated in them so that they feel it to be a sense of achievement, they are likely to progress more rapidly toward this ideal than otherwise.

Forgiveness

This is a difficult but very important trait to be developed during this period. It is easy to persuade children to forgive their chums. They are not only determined to give them an opportunity for happiness and success, but they may even use violence if necessary in an effort to do so. The competitive spirit which now becomes so strong is both a source and an obstacle for acquiring this trait. To win by fair means or foul is a strong temptation. Their sense of fair play is still at a fairly infantile level. The parental concept of forgiveness is not easy to learn. A boy in a summer camp, who was from a very poor family and had no spending money, stole some firecrackers from a tentmate just before the Fourth of July. The latter, being somewhat smaller physically, appealed to a camp leader for assistance in meting out punishment to the thief. The leader pointed out to him the motivation for the stealing and suggested that a far better punishment would be to give the boy even more firecrackers. With some misgivings he finally acceded to this suggestion and carried it out. As a result of this experience the two became fast friends. There can be no doubt that both of them grew in character through the process.

This is a period during which democracy in its true sense is especially important. Children ought to have contacts with all kinds of people. Race and class prejudice may have some defense socially but it has none psychologically. It is certainly true that character grows fastest and most completely when children are taught to be interested in the welfare of every social class. It seems probable that many of our social problems will be more easily solved if those trying to solve them have had this opportunity. Among the good influences of motion pictures, the very common tendency to make heroes of men and women from the lowest as well as the highest walks of life undoubtedly does much to create a mutual tolerance which ought to be helpful in solving some of our social problems. No one who has ever studied labor problems or class problems denies that a major factor in all disputes is lack of understanding between the two sides of the quarrel. A democracy of contacts at this age level will go far toward engraining the type of tolerance so much needed in the solution of these problems.

Magnanimity

One of life's most valuable possessions, a sense of humor, is likely to show itself first during this age level. Whether or not having a good sense of humor, as opposed to overserious-mindedness, is an inherited mental capacity is still very much an unsolved problem in psychology. There can be little question, however, that even if a sense of humor is a special aptitude, it can be definitely improved or retarded by life's experiences during these early years. Perhaps the most important element in a good sense of humor is the ability to appreciate a joke on oneself. Of course, this ought to begin back in the nursery when the child is learning to smile at his own bumps and bruises. It seems probable that the chief reason for not laughing at a joke on oneself is a sense of inferiority which makes one over-sensitive. If through these years the child is taught to laugh at his own failures and react to them with the "try, try again" philosophy, he will have learned an important lesson toward developing a good sense of humor. Over-seriousness seems to be largely a matter of over-estimating the importance of things. The things that happen to us in the immediate present are almost certain to seem more important than they really are. It is now possible gradually to teach the child to evaluate things in terms of their significance over a longer period. This is another important lesson in developing a high sense of humor. A good sense of humor is much the most important element in eliminating anger from personality. When this capacity is combined with the strong tendency to form personal friendships, the child can learn some important lessons in the growth of magnanimity.

One of the most important aspects of conflict which comes into the experience of the junior child is his reaction to authority. The solution to the problem consists in more and more coöperation and less and less coercion. Punishment may produce conformity, but it almost never produces self-direction and self-control. Eighty percent of the children of this age put the blame on the one who punishes. Furthermore, they are quite sincere in this. Problems are not solved by conversions which are not sincere. This does not mean that punishment is never desirable or possible. Sometimes it is. There are individual differences in the way children respond to it and situations differ. If the child understands clearly the justice of the situation, he is likely to respect the punishment rather than react to it too bitterly. On the more positive side, the solution lies in giving the child increased responsibility, plenty of space for expression, and possessions of value which are very much his own. One boy of eleven was given entire charge of the family accounts—this after it was discovered that he had unusual mathematical ability. He made a most remarkable success of his new responsibility and, according to the reports of his parents, did a far better job than they had ever done themselves. By way of interest, according to the father it was significant that when it came time to make pledges to the church, community chest and the like, the boy's recommendations were far more generous than their pledges had been in the past. This was simply carrying out the principles which the parents themselves had taught him. As the father expressed it, he had never before realized how far he missed practicing what he preached. Space is important. A large attic room finished off sufficiently well for habitation can be of tremendous value to the growing boy for his numerous activities. Because now he is beginning to appreciate the cost of things, a few reasonably valuable possessions need to be a part of his sacred domain. No one else in the family, whether adults or other children, should have the right to interfere with this domain or to touch these possessions. When these three requirements are fulfilled, the problem of developing coöperation with authority will be found much simpler.

The need of intimacy between parents and children becomes both increasingly difficult and increasingly important. So many new fields are opening up to the child about which he ought to ask questions of his parents. The problem of sex, if it has not already become prominent, is almost certain to do so during these two years. Will the child ask his parents for advice? That depends a good deal on whether or not he thinks his parents are willing to discuss the question frankly and honestly, and if he has confidence that they know the answer. As one girl expressed it, "I don't talk things over with Mother because she never suggests anything that works." If parents are to gain and maintain the honor of their children's confidence, it is necessary that they be highly respected by their children. A very difficult task for parents is to avoid the holier-than-thou attitude. It is not likely that the children will do or say things any worse than they did themselves at the same age level. If they remember this and are increasingly tolerant, their opportunity for helping their children is infinitely greater.

Christian Courage

The religious challenge that appeals during this and the next period is to meet life courageously. More and more now the child needs to become aware of the realities in life, adjustment to which demands courage. As has been pointed out before, over-protection now brings too great a measure of disillusionment in adolescence with too little courage to meet it. Undoubtedly, the challenge to make great sacrifices for one's friends is the best clue to developing this trait.

A very common undesirable behavior reaction for this age level is bullying. It is especially characteristic of larger children. There can be no question that the tension to which this behavior is a reaction is a desire for leadership. They get a sense of power out of tormenting weaker and younger children. The very fact that they desire this leadership, however, makes them especially susceptible to training in more intelligent types of leadership. Numerous investigations have been made which show that the best leaders are those who like and are liked by the largest number of their associates. Simply to point out this fact to the child and help him realize that true leadership comes through this means is almost certain to meet with a strong response. Leadership is likely to be based on physical prowess during this period and, as has been pointed out before, it changes from occasion to occasion depending on the purpose at hand. This provides adequate opportunity for using the drama-type approach in developing this trait. Activities can be suggested which require different abilities, and different children will assume leadership positions who have those abilities.

Conclusion

This, then, is the age of exploration. This desire for exploration can be mental and moral, quite as well as physical. Because of the strong tendency to personal hero-worship, remarkable influence can be exerted upon the child during this period by those who achieve this recognition. This, of course, represents for the hero both a challenge and a responsibility. The creative tendency becomes much more prominent and the achievements of children of this age are of considerable significance. Many other evidences of maturity begin to appear, including the first steps toward an intelligent choice of a vocation. Again, if we look at this age level, it seems that it must be the most important one in life.

In the questionnaire which follows, the steps in growth that need to be taken by the junior child will be set forth. When parents and teachers have estimated the calibre of their children by means of it, they will also see in it the specific steps in character development that need to be taken.

QUESTIONNAIRE FOR THE FIFTH AND SIXTH GRADES

In the square preceding each question write a number, 5, 4, 3, 2, or 1. After each question is a series of five possible answers to the question, numbered 5, 4, 3, 2, and 1, respectively. In the square use the number preceding the phrase which most nearly represents your answer.

In a few questions, some other information is desired. The nature of this and how to indicate the answer are included in the question involved.

Psychological Development

☐ 1. How healthy is he (she)?
5 Is the picture of health, 4 never sick, 3 seldom sick, 2 often sick, 1 always sick

Trait I

☐ 2. How much curiosity has he (she)?
5 Very great, 4 above average, 3 average, 2 not very much, 1 almost none

☐ 3. How well chosen are those who inspire his (her) hero-worship?
5 They are splendid influences, 4 a good influence, 3 of no value, 2 rather harmful influence, 1 very bad influence

☐ 4. How much tendency has he (she) to daydream?
5 A normal amount, 4 very little, 3 more than average, 2 too much, 1 constantly doing so

☐ 5. Are his (her) daydreams stimulating?
5 Are really plans for action, 4 usually lead to some action, 3 not closely related to his (her) behavior, 2 consist of imaginary activities which he (she) cannot do in reality, 1 very fantastic and unreal

Trait II

☐ 6. Does he (she) enjoy his (her) school work?
5 Very keenly, 4 considerably, 3 rather indifferent to it, 2 dislikes it, 1 hates it

☐ 7. Does he (she) have efficient study habits?
5 Studies very efficiently, 4 better than average, 3 fair study habits, 2 poor, 1 very bad study habits

☐ 8. Does he (she) read well?
5 Very rapidly, 4 above average, 3 about average, 2 rather slowly, 1 very slowly

9. Does he (she) like to read books? (Rate each type separately)
5 Is constantly doing so, 4 reads many, 3 reads some, 2 very few, 1 none

☐ Books of adventure
☐ Mechanical books and magazines
☐ Travel books
☐ Biography

☐ 10. Does he (she) ever cheat in school work?
5 Never, 4 once in a while, 3 sometimes, 2 often, 1 very frequently

☐ 11. Does he (she) ever cheat on the playground?
5 Never, 4 once in a while, 3 sometimes, 2 often, 1 very frequently

☐ 12. Is he (she) good in handwriting?
5 Has very legible, attractive hand, 4 fairly good, 3 average, 2 not good, 1 very poor

☐ 13. Does he (she) use pig-Latin?
5 Constantly, 4 often, 3 sometimes, 2 rarely, 1 never

☐ 14. Can he (she) use good English when he (she) wants to?
5 Very easily, 4 fairly well, 3 average, 2 not very well, 1 very poorly

☐ 15. Does he (she) look forward to his (her) future years in school with enthusiasm?
5 Eagerly, 4 with pleasure, 3 thinks little about them, 2 rather dreads them, 1 longs for school days to end

☐ 16. Is he (she) interested in religion?
5 Very much so, 4 some, 3 rather indifferent, 2 dislikes it, 1 dislikes it very much

☐ 17. Does he (she) like being good?
5 Considers it a thrilling achievement, 4 does so willingly, 3 considers it dull, 2 thinks it is infantile, 1 much prefers being bad as being more exciting

Trait III

☐ 18. Does he (she) have self-confidence?
5 Complete self-confidence, 4 a great deal, 3 some, 2 very little, 1 none

☐ 19. Does he (she) know of the interdependence of plants and animals?
5 Has had a great deal of such training, 4 knows a considerable amount, 3 an average amount, 2 very little, 1 nothing

☐ 20. Does he (she) on the whole enjoy life?
5 Very much so, 4 considerably, 3 some, 2 very little, 1 considers life very unhappy

☐ 21. Does he (she) have a rational recognition of the general extent of his (her) abilities?
5 Very objective and wholesome recognition of them, 4 fairly objective, 3 tends to underestimate them, 2

shows feelings of inferiority, 1 pronounced inferiority complex

Trait IV

☐ 22. Is his (her) activity in general characterized by purposiveness?

5 Is very purposive, 4 usually so, 3 sometimes purposive, 2 not very purposive, 1 seldom or never acts with intelligent purpose

☐ 23. Does he (she) have any vocational interest?

5 Very much, 4 some, 3 a little, 2 almost none, 1 no interest in vocation at all

☐ 24. Is he (she) willing to practice to gain excellence in various skills?

5 Will practice indefinitely, 4 practices a great deal, 3 practices some, 2 practices very little, 1 refuses to practice at all

☐ 25. Does he (she) have outstanding mechanical skill, such as using a jackknife, making model airplanes, building radio sets, and the like?

5 Quite marked skill, 4 above average, 3 some, 2 not much, 1 none

☐ 26. Does he (she) engage in such activities as gardening, cooking and sewing?

5 Very often, 4 frequently, 3 sometimes, 2 rarely, 1 never

☐ 27. Does he (she) enjoy painting, drawing, clay modelling, wood carving, interior decorating?

5 Very much, 4 frequently, 3 sometimes, 2 rarely, 1 never

☐ 28. Does he (she) like to write poetry?

5 Very much, 4 often, 3 sometimes, 2 rarely, 1 never

☐ 29. Does he (she) like to dance?

5 Very much, 4 quite a lot, 3 some, 2 not much, 1 dislikes it

☐ 30. Does he (she) have many responsibilities around the home?

5 A great many, 4 some, 3 a few, 2 one or two, 1 none

☐ 31. Does he (she) enjoy music by playing an instrument or singing?

5 Very much, 4 considerably, 3 some, 2 a little, 1 not at all

☐ 32. Does he (she) engage successfully in such activities as carrying a paper route or running a roadside stand?
5 Does so very successfully, 4 considerable success, 3 moderate success, 2 does not try much, 1 never does so

☐ 33. Is he (she) well informed as to the nature of the various vocations?
5 Very well informed, 4 knows considerable about them, 3 knows something, 2 knows very little, 1 knows nothing about them

☐ 34. Does he (she) do a lot of collecting, as stamps or coins?
5 Constantly doing so, 4 spends lots of time at it, 3 does some, 2 not much, 1 never does

☐ 35. Is he (she) dependable in carrying out what he (she) agrees to do?
5 Completely, 4 very, 3 fairly, 2 not very, 1 not at all

Trait V

☐ 36. Does he (she) show genuine interest in what others are doing?
5 Very active interest, 4 considerable, 3 some, 2 not much, 1 none

☐ 37. Is he (she) willing to do things for his (her) chum?
5 Will sacrifice anything, 4 does a great deal, 3 does some things, 2 not very much, 1 demands that the chum do things for him (her)

☐ 38. Is he (she) generally sympathetic?
5 Very much so, 4 quite, 3 somewhat, 2 not much, 1 not at all

☐ 39. Is he (she) always willing to help when needed?
5 Very much so, 4 usually, 3 sometimes, 2 rarely, 1 never

☐ 40. What is his (her) attitude toward the opposite sex?
5 Normal wholesome reaction, 4 deals with them rather indifferently, 3 avoids them where possible, 2 pulls hair, etc., 1 torments and teases incessantly

Trait VI

☐ 41. Has he (she) come to specialize, in the various team games, as to what position he (she) prefers to play?
5 Very completely, 4 in most of them, 3 in some of them, 2 not much, 1 not at all

☐ 42. Is he (she) often jealous of other children?
5 Never, 4 rarely, 3 sometimes, 2 often, 1 very often

☐ 43. Does he (she) often blame others for his (her) own wrong-doing?
5 Never, 4 occasionally, 3 sometimes, 2 often, 1 always

☐ 44. Is he (she) willing to care for or protect younger children?
5 Quite willing, 4 usually, 3 indifferent, 2 dislikes it, 1 hates it

☐ 45. Does he (she) like pets?
5 Very much, 4 more than average, 3 some, 2 not much, 1 not at all

☐ 46. Does he (she) have a sense of fair play?
5 Very keen, 4 above average, 3 average, 2 not much, 1 none

☐ 47. Is he (she) snobbish or democratic in his (her) social contacts?
5 Very democratic, 4 usually democratic, 3 democratic with many people, 2 somewhat snobbish, 1 very snobbish

☐ 48. Does he (she) show race and class prejudice?
5 Not at all, 4 very little, 3 in a few cases, 2 quite a lot, 1 very much so

Trait VII

☐ 49. Does he (she) react magnanimously to injustices done to him (her)?
5 Splendid wholesome reaction, 4 usually fair about it, 3 an eye-for-an-eye attitude, 2 tends to repay it with interest, 1 is very revengeful and bitter

☐ 50. Is he (she) more interested in the success of the team or of himself (herself)?
5 Very much a team player, 4 will sacrifice his (her) own interests for the team, 3 about average for age, 2 pretty

much an individualist, 1 entirely interested in his (her) own achievements

☐ 51. Is he (she) a good club or gang member?
5 Very popular in clubs or gangs, 4 fits in quite well, 3 fairly good, 2 not very good, 1 very poor club or gang member

☐ 52. Does he (she) have a good sense of humor?
5 Very much so, even at his (her) own expense, 4 above average, 3 some, 2 not much, 1 none at all

☐ 53. How does he (she) react to authority?
5 With splendid coöperation, 4 usually coöperates, occasionally rebels, 3 sometimes rebels or is too obedient, 2 usually rebels or is over-obedient, 1 negativistic or submissive (Underline which, in answers 3, 2, or 1)

☐ 54. How does he (she) react to physical punishment?
5 Very wholesomely, 4 fairly well, 3 it does little good, 2 resents it somewhat, 1 becomes sullen and defiant

☐ 55. Is he (she) much given to fighting?
5 Never does so unless attacked, 4 seldom does so, 3 sometimes, 2 often fights, 1 constantly doing so

☐ 56. Does he (she) have some worthwhile possessions which are his (her) own?
5 A generous amount, 4 a number, 3 some, 2 a few, 1 none

☐ 57. Is he (she) intimate with his (her) parents?
5 Very much so, 4 more than average, 3 somewhat, 2 not very, 1 not at all

Trait VIII

☐ 58. Does he (she) have leadership capacity?
5 Very outstanding, 4 considerable, 3 some, 2 little, 1 none

☐ 59. Is he (she) selected as the leader of his (her) group?
5 Always, 4 often, 3 sometimes, 2 rarely, 1 never

☐ 60. Does he (she) show a good many over-submissive reactions?
5 None, 4 very few, 3 some, 2 many, 1 is very submissive

☐ 61. Does he (she) ever act as a bully?
5 Never, 4 rarely, 3 sometimes, 2 often, 1 constantly

☐ 62. Is he (she) a good follower?

5 Coöperates perfectly with his (her) leaders, 4 usually coöperates, 3 is a fair follower, 2 usually prefers to dominate the group, 1 will not join a group he (she) cannot dominate

☐ 63. What is his (her) reaction to a dare?

5 Objective and rational, 4 usually takes the dare, 3 hesitates to accept it, 2 shows considerable fear, 1 very much afraid

☐ 64. What is his (her) concept of the Cross?

5 An act of great courage, 4 admirable, 3 does not think much about it, 2 resents it, 1 morbid attitude

☐ 65. How does he (she) react to life's injustices?

5 Accepts them normally as part of life, 4 reacts to them fairly well, 3 resents them somewhat, 2 becomes somewhat angry, 1 becomes very violently angry

XI

In Junior High School

IF THE AGE GROUP which includes the seventh and eighth grades in school often seems to be the most difficult with which to deal in our homes and church schools, it is because of the lack of adventure there. Just as exploration is the keyword to the fifth and sixth grades, so is adventure to the seventh and eighth. No age level in the entire developmental scale shows such great sex differences as this one does. Junior high school boys are still much more like fifth and sixth grade boys than they are like their high school brothers. Activity is still their major characteristic. Meditation and philosophical reasoning are not only beyond them mentally but quite outside the range of their interests. They are very much doers of the word, and no program which does not involve action with a capital A will interest them very deeply. While girls are also interested in adventure, read adventure stories and listen to adventure programs on the radio, they are coming into maturity and begin to have considerable thoughts of romance. They are much more likely to be thinkers. In one intermediate department, a group of children were sought out to form a Bible class which was to study rather deeply some of the more difficult portions of the Bible. When the whole department had been thoroughly combed, seven girls and one boy were found who fitted into this group. This is a condition which can well be expected because of the very nature of the two sexes. Activities in common, because of their great incompatibility, are almost impossible and should be attempted only on the rarest occasions. However, while we must recognize this increased maturity of the girls and take it into consideration in our dealing with them, the fact remains that adventure is still the keynote to the age.

Physical Development

Physically, this is the age of the greatest difference between the sexes. Girls, in general, outgrow boys during this period and mature, on the average, about two years earlier than do their brothers. One may expect that approximately a tenth of them will be physically mature when they come into this department at twelve years of age, and eighty percent of them will be when they leave it at fourteen. This means that, especially on the girl's side, sex education should be completed during this time. It needs to be a wholesome, strictly honest, very positive and genuinely inspiring type of discussion. The first menstrual period can be pictured in the mind of the girl as God's ordination of her into womanhood, and a fact of which she can be justly proud. This is far more wholesome than if it is pictured as something to be dreaded, ashamed of, and a handicap to be borne during most of her life. In the past, a great many unfounded fears and unnecessary precautions were added to this part of the girl's life. Actually, unless there is a physical defect, there need be little, if any, curtailing of her activities during this time. She can run, play tennis, and do all of the other things which she normally does. A good deal of this change of attitude is probably due to a real change in our physical hygiene. A comparison of physical tests given to the modern bare-legged, outdoor girl shows that she is from twenty-five to fifty percent healthier and stronger in every respect than her grandmother was at the same age.

While sexual maturity comes somewhat later with boys, one can be certain that some of the boys in any group of this age level will have reached this stage. Every one of them will be experiencing a very active curiosity about all the physical aspects of his life, and most especially this one. It is quite as important, then, that boys, too, have a thorough, complete and wholesome sex education. During the last few decades a great deal of thought has been given to the problem of how best to accomplish this side of the child's education. To be too free and open about it has seemed to some to endanger the child's moral development, but to be too secret and mysterious about it is almost certain to do so. Probably the best single cue to sex education is to tell the truth and to describe it as normal and wholesome. Sexual morality is best achieved by presenting it as a source of strength and an evidence of achievement. Shame and guilt motivations are as harmful here as in any other aspects of personality.

This is the last period in which girls have any chance of competing physically with their brothers. By the end of this period, boys begin to outgrow them, both in strength and in size, and this superiority increases rapidly during the whole adolescent period. During this one level, however, girls may be taller and quite as strong as their brothers. Not infrequently boys meet this embarrassing competition with various manifestations of poor disciplinary reactions. Bad boys at this age level are for the most part reacting either to this competition with their sisters or expressing energy for which no other outlet has been discovered. There can be no question but that such activities as the Scout Movement have tremendous value in this phase of the child's development. Motor skills now reach their maturity. Both the boy and the girl have almost as good coördination as they will ever have. Only an increase in strength and size makes greater achievements possible in the future.

Mental Development

The school is not so handicapped by sex differences as those agencies which deal with character development. For, mentally, the difference is not so great. Their intelligence is at the same level, and in general their intellectual growth finds boys and girls on a par with each other. As a result, they do not need to be segregated into different classes, or to be subjected to different types of teaching.

The great event here for most of them is the entrance into junior high school. Before this time, they have had one teacher each year. That teacher taught them everything and their only adjustment was to her methods of teaching. This very fact compelled her to teach children rather than subject matter. Now, however, they begin the years of specialization, and are likely to have a different teacher for each subject they study. This means that they must adjust to different methods of teaching and different attitudes toward classroom behavior. Furthermore, because they are subject specialists, the teachers are much more likely to put their emphasis on the subject rather than on the study of the individual children, who are usually so numerous as to make such individual interest almost impossible. Sometimes children adjust well to this change, and sometimes very poorly. If, during the preceding years, they have acquired good methods of study and have achieved normal levels of performance, they are likely to find this new adjustment stimulating and very challenging to their abilities. If, on the other hand, they have not made a good adjustment to school in the earlier years, and especially if they have not learned to read well, their adjustment here may prove to be a very difficult one. Up to this time good teaching and individual attention can make promotion from grade to grade possible, even if the child has not learned to read too well. But when he reaches the junior high school level, written instructions replace much of the individual teaching, and a handicap which is almost insurmountable will be found by the poor reader.

Rote memory and arithmetical reasoning have now about reached their peak. A good deal more abstract reasoning is possible by the junior high school child. What may be termed philosophical reasoning still remains for a later developmental period. However, intelligence in general is approaching maturity, and books written for this age level will not be found too juvenile for adults to enjoy them. In the old-fashioned Sunday school, where the same lesson was used throughout the school, the lesson material was selected primarily because of its appeal to this age level. As a result, senior departments and adult classes rarely came into contact with the richer, more philosophical portions of the Bible, especially the Prophets and Paul's Letters. To teach these at the junior high school level would be quite foolish. To omit them in the later periods is depriving the individual of some of his finest experiences.

Special Aptitudes

The special aptitudes develop so rapidly during this period that, by the end of it, we can determine with considerable precision what a child's endowment is in each of them. We may not wish to choose his vocation or to encourage him to do so as early as this, but the fact remains that we know how much he has of imagination, artistic ability, musical ability and mechanical ability, as well as the various aspects of his intellectual capacity and his physical endowment. We can be reasonably certain as to where his field of vocational choice must lie if it is to be intelligently chosen.

Two things are important with respect to these aptitudes. One is that we must measure them. To "know thyself" is possible for the first time in the history of the world. And the best period of life for making such measurement is this one and the one preceding. Parents should take every available opportunity for finding out as much as they can about their children during this period. The information that can be gathered from psychological measurements will be of the greatest value at the high school level when the child is actually selecting his vocation.

The second fact is that these aptitudes must now be given a great deal of training. Because boys and girls of this age so much more frequently act like children than adults, it is difficult for us to realize what high levels of achievement they are capable of reaching with respect to these special aptitudes. Very remarkable performances in all of these fields are to be found. Our more modern schools give abundant opportunity for this training. Many of our church schools which emphasize activity programs need to be sure that the programs for this age level are of a calibre capable of utilizing these abilities to their fullest extent. If the church does not have the equipment or the leadership to do this, it ought not to attempt activity programs at all. For it is almost certain to bring contempt on itself, in the mind of the child of this age, by doing an inferior task. In Chapter XIV of this book, a curricular unit has been worked out in some detail. The age level used is this one. A study of that unit will illustrate these points fully. The home, too, should provide abundant opportunity for the expression of these special aptitudes. Stamp collecting, model airplane building, junior chemistry sets, radio sets, as well as musical instruments should be available to both boys and girls with appropriate abilities. It is unfortunate when these opportunities are found only at the upper high school level, where they take away interest from the more important high school studies. The junior high school level is the period for such activities and they should be encouraged and fostered to the fullest extent.

Social and Emotional Maturity

This is the period in life in which the widest sex differences occur. Boys are still in the all-boy anti-girl period. They read boys' books and boys' books only. One may examine them and never find an iota of romance. It is interesting to notice that girls also read these boys' books, but in addition to that, read girls' books and begin to show some interest in the more romantic types of fiction. However, their proximity to the adventure level makes them choose a type of love story of the more blood-and-thunder type. Both boys and girls form close-knit gangs or groups which have the utmost contempt for each other. For boys, team play now comes into prominence. While the junior boy would practice long periods of time to increase his individual performance, he was still pretty much incapable of team play. During this age level, however, teams become common, and while the desire for individual excellence still plays an important part in athletic activities, a much higher level of coöperation is possible than in preceding periods. Fishing, camping and hunting are all activities which challenge and interest boys of this age very much. This, of course, accounts for the enormous popularity of the Boy Scouts. Girls, likewise, show a great deal of interest in these activities, and nowadays they are permitted to do these things.

Emotionally, boys and girls are now becoming a great deal more critical, and as a result, correspondingly more self-conscious. They become more keenly sensitive to failure in competition and deeply depressed if this failure is too marked. Certainly a contributing factor to bringing about this state of mind is their intolerant cruelty to each other. Their overwhelming praise of physical prowess makes life unhappy for those whose endowments do not render it possible for them. Their thirst for adventure makes them dare things sometimes far beyond their ability, and the social contempt heaped upon the boy or girl who will not take a dare ranks among the cruelest of man's inhumanities to man. When a boy or girl simply cannot make the grade in this respect, there is not much we can do to help them except to let them become a few years older, when their attitudes toward each other are a little more intelligent. However, it is of the greatest importance for us to discover any special abilities they may have and help them find forms of expression for them which are socially approved by their contemporaries.

Character Development

It goes without saying that the junior high school student will choose those morals which are associated with adventure, or in the case of girls, with adventure and romance. It seems obvious that moral lessons which have no relationship to these two factors are entirely lost on children of this age. Teachers and parents may as well save their breath as to attempt them. Perhaps the most important personality trait which can be developed during this period is self-reliance. Because of their love of adventure and their willingness to dare, they seek experiences in which they have to stand alone without the assistance of their elders. Perhaps the outstanding characteristic of the American boy of this age, as compared to his European contemporary, is in this very fact. Parents who are over-concerned about the safety of their boys and girls should bear in mind that a price in strength of personality will have to be paid for too great a caution. It is, of course, true that our numerous accidents do make us anxious to protect our boys and girls as much as possible, but this should not be carried to the extreme of keeping from them the opportunity to take care of themselves. Let us turn now to the eight traits and see how each of them can be developed during this period.

Experimental Faith

Vision

What could inspire vision so much as the spirit of adventure and romance? When we think of vision as having an enthusiasm for the achievement of one's purpose, it seems to carry with it the very spirit of this age level. Since this is the period in which we are laying the immediate foundations for choosing a vocation, it is important to have the child see the adventurous phases of the various vocations. A boy whose father was a banker and who had all of the necessary qualities for following in his footsteps did not wish to do so, because banking seemed to him so dull and uninteresting. His father made it his business for some time to give his son an insight into the many thrilling experiences that beset the life of a banker. Before he had finished, the boy saw the vocation as the very essence of adventure itself. It is not always possible or even desirable to choose a vocation at this age level, but it is possible to have young people discover the thrill and the possibilities of all vocations.

Hero-worship is still as strong as it ever has been. But

whereas the junior child, for the most part, chooses as his heroes people of his own acquaintance, hero-worship now begins to swing to historical characters. Reading interests shift accordingly, and both boys and girls become interested in biographies in which the spirit of adventure is the central theme. Probably no successful life is dull. Every vocation has its exciting moments. Much could be done to give young people a clear vision of the whole social structure of civilization by means of biography and the study of the thrilling aspects of the various vocations. Some of the Bible heroes who are ordinarily little known, such as for example, Jeremiah, Nehemiah, and Hosea, as well as many of the church heroes, including Augustine, Luther, Wycliffe, Huss and Wesley, were men whose lives were so filled with danger and excitement that good biographies could be made the means of a great deal of character education during this age level.

The inevitable result of hero-worship is daydreaming. It is perfectly natural for one to picture himself accomplishing the same things as his hero. But daydreaming can be either helpful or harmful. If daydreams become visions of future achievement which stimulate the youth to do something toward that achievement now, they are of inestimable value. If, on the other hand, they are retreats from a rather dull world in which the youth lives in an imaginary fairyland which has no contact with reality, then they are anything but desirable. One of the values of Scouting is that it gives the boy or the girl opportunities to do some of the thrilling things which their story-book heroes have done.

In character education generally, both in the home and in the church, it is important to know who are the youth's heroes and to discover ways in which admirable phases of their lives can be brought into reality. A father who discovers that his son has become intensely enthusiastic about Abraham Lincoln is not being over-sentimental when he permits him to do some of the things the boy Lincoln did at his age. A good rule to follow at all ages is never to let a daydream end in a sigh. Make them be real and be a stimulation to action.

Love of Righteousness and Truth

Being good is certainly not the most prominent characteristic of the normal boy or girl of twelve. In fact, a good deal of evidence could be produced to substantiate the claim that it is the greatest period of moral depravity. Behavior problems of all sorts reach their peak during this time. Aggressively antagonistic behavior, disobedience and disrespect, school difficulties, truancy, excessive daydreaming, lying, and stealing are only a few of the many evidences of this fact. To them, Hallowe'en is the great holiday of the year. How shall we hope to teach such a group to hunger and thirst for righteousness?

Recalling the basic principle of learning presented in the first chapter, it will be remembered that only those forms of behavior become habitual in human life which reduce tensions, that is, satisfy desires for achievement, social approval, and the satisfaction of appetites. Not all that goes by the name of righteousness has the capacity for doing any of these things. Some of the duller and more prosaic notions of goodness consist primarily in the things one ought not to do. We preach with enthusiasm to our youth about hungering and thirsting for them. But when we are honest, we are likely to admit that only a perverted appetite could work up a genuine enthusiasm for doing nothing. Most of us recognize this really. It is not at all uncommon for a father in a severe and somewhat pious voice to order his son not to be too energetic on Hallowe'en, and then follow up this order with an enthusiastic and perhaps slightly enlarged description of his own escapades when he was at the same age. Some years ago, an ex-convict was going about among our colleges telling students that crime does not pay. While talking to a class one day, he was asked a question about one of our prisons. Immediately his face lighted up, and, in the next half-hour, he gave a very fervent description of the various prisons: which were the hardest to break out of, which were the severest in discipline, and he even named the one of which he would be proudest to be an alumnus. It became quite obvious that his piety was rather superficial and that, deep in his heart, he still had a preadolescent enthusiasm for misbehavior. Unless righteousness, then, has some of the qualities of adventure, it is completely beyond the interest and scope of this age level. If adventurous religion is to be an ideal in our churches, this is the time to start it. There can be no question but that a good deal of the enthusiasm of youth for evil is due to the unattractiveness of goodness. If a boy of thirteen who never gets into mischief, who is completely obedient to his parents and teachers, who never misses school and never does any of the "dangerous" things, is held up before a normal boy of this same age level as a "good" boy, the results for both are likely to be disastrous. Goodness must be made attractive to the spirit of the boy and the girl. A judge was reprimanding a young delinquent who had broken his arm while hanging on to a moving truck and asked him this question, "Don't you realize that that is dangerous?" The boy responded, "Of course I realize it's dangerous—that's why I did it." As long as a good share of our moral admonitions contain, "Don't do that because it's dangerous," we are not likely to appeal to this age very strongly. When we find a type of righteousness in which the logical command is, "Do that although it is dangerous," then we shall have a righteousness for which this age level will genuinely hunger and thirst. If we would eliminate the types of undesirable behavior from life which are so characteristic of the age, the best method is to make them seem weak, dull, and prosaic. If we wish to substitute for them types of behavior which can be called genuinely righteous, they must be strong, thrilling, and adventurous.

Let the children, then, have abundant access to stories of invention, biography, travel, popular science, and for the older girls, good inspiring love stories. These love stories, however, need in them the spice of adventure if they are to appeal to this age. Find activities which will challenge the courage and daring of the boy and the girl, as well as use all of their abilities to the utmost. When this kind of righteousness is produced, the behavior of our youth will improve and the quality of our own concepts of righteousness will have been enriched. For none of us quite outgrows this desire for adventure.

Faith in the Friendliness of the Universe

Up to this time, the concept of God which has been given to children is for the most part one of care and protection. During the preceding age level, but more especially in this one, a very different element in the growing concept of God must come into existence if youth is to continue a wholehearted worship of Him. The youth at this age level will be inspired by the courage of Jesus at Gethsemane. Let him realize completely that God did not protect him from the danger which he was to face, but rather, gave him strength with which to face that danger. Jesus at Calvary will show him the same sort of strength. The kind of prayers that Jesus prayed on both those occasions ought to be pointed out to him and the kind of answers Jesus got to those prayers. When the youth has been shown these two episodes in the life of Jesus, he will have learned a far more challenging concept of God and a more forceful and dynamic concept of prayer. Self-reliance is not likely to be increased by a concept of God which makes Him overprotective, or by a concept of prayer which, to the youth seems strangely like cowardice. But give him a concept of God which carries with it the high courage and adventure of Jesus during his last week of life, and he will be challenged by it now as he never can be at any other period in his life.

It has been pointed out that one of the evidences of weak personality is disintegration, of which the most conspicuous symptoms are emotional excesses. When an individual loses his head entirely, or goes into a temper tantrum, or in any other way gives up the whole of his personality to the satisfaction of a single impulse, he is giving evidence of weak personality. Developing strong personality, then, consists in the integration of all these drives and motives so that they act together, and so that no one of them can ever gain control of the total personality to the exclusion of the others. Through this method, which we have just described, of giving to the child a concept of God and prayer which helps him to face danger with courage, we have contributed enormously to the total integration of his personality. Only when he comes to adolescence and learns an equivalent lesson about anger can he learn a more important one. Worship, which ordinarily is not very conspicuous in the life of boys and girls of this age, can be made a real part of their personalities if taught in this way. The average college student, and for that matter, the average adult of today never seems to feel much need of worship. How can the problems that face youth be adequately thought out in their own minds unless they have periods of quiet meditation when they can think objectively? If the youth at this age level can be taught this concept of prayer and come to use it in his own life, he will learn some of the sources of power that come from genuine worship.

Dominating Purpose

Choosing the right vocation is probably the most difficult and, at the same time, the most important single task in a man's life, so far as character and strong personality are concerned. Purpose is the strongest integrating force in the personality picture. The ideal age for this vocational choice is during the high school level, but, if it is to be done intelligently, the preparation for it must be made now. This preparation consists largely in a second sight-seeing trip through the vocations. The first, during the preceding period, was a trip of exploration, satisfying their curiosity as to what all the vocations were about. This one goes deeper than that. Each vocation should be studied to discover its adventurous qualities. Every child knows the adventurous qualities of aviation, Arctic exploration, the army and navy, but how many feel an equal enthusiasm for farming, law, and the ministry? Carrying out this second sight-seeing trip through the vocations is an important task for a character education program at this age level. It should not be confined simply to those vocations in which the individual concerned has a personal interest, but should include all vocations. A study made a few years ago showed that for a vast majority of high school boys and girls, ninety-eight percent of the vocations seemed dull and uninspiring. This is a tragic commentary on our vocational guidance, for a very large majority of these same boys and girls must go into these very vocations which to them seem drab and uninteresting. If during this period we can give them an enthusiasm for every vocation, then every one of them will go with enthusiasm into whatever vocation his abilities and opportunities bring him. This broad understanding is important for another reason. Too many men, who do have the good fortune to get into a life work of genuine interest and challenge to them, have too little respect for many of the other vocations around about them. A far greater measure of social coöperation would be brought about if every man saw, not only the thrill of his own life work, but that of his neighbor as well.

This should not be thought of as being confined to boys. It can be quite as much a feature of the girl's education. To be sure, she may look with interest into a different group of vocations, although in many of them both sexes are found. It may seem on the surface that this is not so important for girls since such a large proportion of them marry and have home building as their central task. As a matter of fact, probably no vocation either among men or women is so difficult, hazardous, and adventurous as home building. Nor is there another which requires so much preparation, especially with the increasing complexity of our modern life.

But, in addition to this forerunner of vocational choice, there are other elements in the child's life which are purposive or should be purposive in their nature. The collecting tendency reaches its peak during this level and can be made as creative and adventurous as almost any other phase of his life. The search for a missing stamp or coin or picture may well be a thrilling experience for any boy or girl. Probably as much or more is learned by such activities and hobbies as in their formal school work.

Then, too, for those who have any language capacity, this age is likely to be one when a great deal of creative writing is done, especially poetry. Both boys and girls tend to create verse during this period. Not all boys will admit it because it does not always conform to the social approval standards of their contemporaries. Actually, poetry of considerable merit has come from children of this age, and such activity should be encouraged and stimulated by both parents and teachers.

All the special aptitudes should be encouraged. Every opportunity should be provided, in the form of tools and equipment, for the expression and training of whatever abilities are found in the personality profile. With all their evils, few stages in the growing personality can become as purposive as this one.

Fatherly Love

Being Sensitive to the Needs of Others

When one observes the deliberate coarseness, excessive practical joking, ill manners at the table and the general level of thoughtlessness which so frequently characterize the behavior of youth of this age, being sensitive to the needs of others seems quite out of keeping with their whole attitude toward life. However, when we study the natural characteristics of their make-up, we find an intensity of friendliness which leads to chumships which are almost unbreakable, a quick sympathy which makes them great lovers of animals, and a warm impulsiveness which finds them quick to respond when they are stimulated to do so. In the face of these facts, one wonders why this seemingly anti-social behavior is so common. The answer is not difficult to find. In the first place, they have an intense fear of being sissies. This disdain for sissiness in boys is finding its counterpart in girls nowadays in their contempt for what they call wholesomeness.

If one visits a typical boys' school in England, he is struck immediately by the remarkably good manners and gentlemanly conduct of English boys between the ages of twelve and fifteen. They do things and wear clothes which the American boy would not do if his life depended on it. Why the difference? The difference is entirely in what each considers to be manly. To the English boy, this quality of neatness and good manners seems to be a part of growing up. He feels that he is becoming a man in so doing. To the American boy, the same characteristics constitute being a sissy. It is interesting to see how inconsistent children's logic is in this regard. Two boys, one twelve and one eight, were walking along a sidewalk after a rain. The older one was trying to persuade the younger one to splash through the muddy water at the side of the walk as he was doing himself. His strongest argument was, "Do you want to be a baby?" He wished also, of course, to leave the impression that doing so was manly. Actually, he was doing precisely what a baby would do and the younger boy precisely what a man would do.

The important thing is that their apparent coarseness is quite superficial, and, underneath the surface, the youth of this age level are as sympathetic and sensitive to others' troubles and pains as at any other age in life. If somehow we can make this natural conduct seem manly, we shall now contribute immensely to the development of this trait.

Another important point in this connection needs to be brought out in connection with this age level. It has been emphasized again and again that during this period the child is a person of action. Ideas to him are for the most part stimuli to do things. Sometimes the ideas and resultant actions are not as socially desirable as they might be, but this very dynamic feature of his personality is a source of learning an important lesson. It is a characteristic of many adults that they have many good impulses but do not carry them into action. With his keen insight into strong personality, William James gave as one of his major admonitions, "Act on your good impulses." This he felt to be an essential factor in the development of will power. Since this is the natural thing for the child to do at this age level, a little encouragement on the part of his elders may well make this a permanent feature of his personality.

Forgiveness

In Chapter XIV, the illustrative curricular unit is devoted entirely to teaching twelve-year-old boys some of the lessons of this trait. Because it is dealt with so extensively there, it seems hardly desirable to dwell upon it at too great length here. The most important point is to recognize that, as has been true with most of these trait concepts, a very much enlarged vision of what forgiveness means can be learned during this period. The average child of this age level, and for that matter the average high school or college youth, is likely to think of *forgive* and *forget* as synonymous terms. Forgetting is fairly easy if he is a normal youngster, but that is about as near to forgiving as he usually comes. However, because this is an age in which the attractiveness of a thing is in proportion to its difficulty, and because he has such contempt for mere platitudinous piety, it is the right time to enlarge his concept of forgiveness. Forgiveness, which involves the courage to do things for those who despise him, and to befriend unpopular contemporaries in the face of social disapproval, can be a challenging source of achievement during this period. There is nothing in his natural make-up which prevents it from happening. The parental drive is there, as it has always been. It happens that caring for pets, instead of for one's baby brother or sister, and standing up for his rights and fighting like a man are more approved than turning the other cheek and forgiving.

At no age level is his sense of fair play and his insistence upon rules stronger than at this time. And while it may require a little suggestion on the part of his parents and teachers, it is easily possible for him to be stimulated to see to it that games are played and rules are made which give everyone, even those of less endowment, a real chance to succeed.

Because of their greater maturity, girls can be taught a more mature form of forgiveness than boys, especially toward the end of this age level. On the one hand, they are not so bound down by the he-man ideal and their more mature point of view makes possible a more profound understanding of the full concept of forgiveness. They can be stimulated directly, both from the parental point of view and from the point of view of social vision, to acquire completely the concept of being determined to give everyone his chance at happiness and success.

Magnanimity

Righteous indignation is one of the most common forms of emotional expression during this period. At no period in life after the nursery does anger play so prominent a part as it does here. The chief difference is that, in the mind of the child at least, the anger is always righteous. The tyranny with which some parents treat their boys and girls would be just grounds for rebellion in any social institution. Because it is an age during which these children sometimes act like adults and sometimes like children, it is rather natural that their parents treat them sometimes like adults and sometimes like children. Unfortunately, far too many parents treat them like children but expect them to act like adults. However young they may seem, and however foolishly they may act, the fact remains that they are approaching maturity very rapidly, that they are capable of a great deal of responsibility, and ought to be able to make a vast majority of their decisions for themselves. Their immaturity may lead to mistakes from time to time, but the mistakes constitute a very small price to pay for the growth in strength which will result from giving them these responsibilities.

If anger is thought of as manly, it is not likely that they will abandon it. A father who frequently and conspicuously speaks of "standing up for his rights" and a mother who permits her own temper to be aroused because of "the principle of the thing" are not likely to be good influences toward teaching a boy to control his temper. Given good examples in the home, many fine attitudes can be built about this trait, if the attitudes seem to the child to be manly. The ability to take minor insults without anger, to hold one's temper in the face of bad decisions in athletics, and the ability to do one's best against a vastly superior opponent are all splendid lessons if well taught.

Girls often show an intense religious fervor during this period. This does not often appear in boys until some years later. This religious fervor if guided into channels of stability and wholesomeness can become a source of power. If permitted to be morbid and over-emotional, it can become one of the principal factors of a weak, over-sentimental personality. The boy's attitude toward religion is quite likely to be patterned after that of his father and his heroes. If his father's table conversation never touches on religion, and if his Sunday morning occupation consists of reading the sport page and financial news instead of attending church, his son is not likely to hold a very high regard for religious activity. Only if the father lives the rôle that religion is important and manly will the son do so.

Christian Courage

The place of the Cross in the religion of Jesus can be taught at no other age level so well as at this one. To teach it earlier is likely to produce fear to a dangerous degree. To teach it later does not find such natural responsiveness as during this period of adventure. The concept of a leader who had the courage to face inevitable arrest, torture, and execution for what he believed to be right is the very epitome of heroism to the boy or girl of this age level. This is not a period during which the Cross should be a gilded symbol, but a grim reality in the life of Jesus. For parents who want their children to have courage not based on fear and powerful enough to carry them through any emergency, no finer method can be chosen than through the lesson of the Crucifixion.

Leadership now begins to appear in its mature form. Especially in those children whose natural endowment is great, opportunities for speaking in public, for heading up committees, for initiating and carrying out enterprises of their own should be found. Their notions of social approval and disapproval often make them do things that give the appearance of indifference to such opportunities, but actually they genuinely desire leadership training.

They can now reach the peak of the self-discipline that makes them endure hard work and pain to gain proficiency in any field of activity. In hero-worship also can be found the stimulation to face danger and elements of hardship without wincing. An important point needs to be gotten over to them, and that is that courage consists not so much in the elimination of fear as in the control of fear. Most football players are very much afraid just before the whistle blows for the game to begin. Most public speakers are afraid when they face their audience. Most soldiers are afraid as they go into battle. There is nothing to be ashamed of in this natural fear. It is a far more wholesome thing to recognize it, to admit it frankly and throw all of its energy into increased activity, than to try to teach a child that he is not afraid of anything.

Conclusion

Here, then, is an age level as full of possibilities as any during the entire period of growth. If it seems to be a difficult age to those whose job is character development, it is because of the ways in which the task has been undertaken. The secret of success depends upon the ability to utilize the forces that are operating in the children and not to try to inhibit them. One who makes character, religion, and righteousness a source of adventure will meet success with boys and girls at this age. Those who attempt to thwart this adventurous spirit in them are destined to failure.

The following is the questionnaire for estimating the maturity of the personalities of this age with which we are dealing. As has been true at the other levels, such a painstaking analysis as this, carried out by parents and teachers of each child, will go far toward giving a clear picture of what can be accomplished for each one. The examination of this questionnaire will demonstrate its purpose and how it is to be used.

QUESTIONNAIRE FOR JUNIOR HIGH SCHOOL AGE

In the square preceding each question write a number, 5, 4, 3, 2, or 1. After each question is a series of five possible answers to the question, numbered 5, 4, 3, 2, or 1, respectively. In the square use the number preceding the phrase which most nearly represents your answer.

In some questions some other information is desired. The nature of this and how to indicate the answer are included in the question involved.

Psychological Development

☐ 1. How much time is spent in athletic and physical activities?

5 Very much, 4 much, 3 some, 2 little, 1 none

☐ 2. How successful has he (she) been in this?

5 Very successful, 4 successful, 3 moderately successful, 2 little success, 1 no success

Trait I

☐ 3. Does he (she) daydream much?

5 Very much, 4 frequently, 3 average, 2 seldom, 1 never

☐ 4. Are his (her) daydreams stimulating or rather quiet and retiring?

5 Very stimulating, 4 stimulating, 3 average, 2 rather quiet, 1 very introverted

☐ 5. Is he (she) much given to hero-worship?

5 Very much, 4 frequently, 3 average, 2 seldom, 1 never

6. How heroic does he (she) consider each of these? Rate each.

5 Very heroic, 4 heroic, 3 interesting, 2 dull, 1 very unattractive

- ☐ Movie actors or actresses
- ☐ Famous athletes
- ☐ War heroes
- ☐ Aviators
- ☐ Scientists
- ☐ Doctors
- ☐ Musicians
- ☐ Lawyers
- ☐ Writers
- ☐ Religious heroes of the past
- ☐ Biblical characters
- ☐ Teachers
- ☐ Parents
- ☐ Artists

☐ 7. How strong, constructive, and well-trained is his (her) imagination?

5 Very much so, 4 better than average, 3 average, 2 not very constructive, 1 not much imagination

Trait II

8. Which of the following are characteristic of him (her) and how often?

5 Very often, 4 frequently, 3 average, 2 seldom, 1 never

- ☐ Aggressive and antagonistic behavior
- ☐ Disobedience or disrespect
- ☐ Failure to coöperate
- ☐ School maladjustment
- ☐ Truancy
- ☐ Lying
- ☐ Stealing
- ☐ Fighting

9. What is his (her) attitude toward the following?

5 Thrilling, 4 exciting, 3 all right, 2 dull, 1 infantile or undesirable

- ☐ Obedience
- ☐ Good marks in school
- ☐ Being good
- ☐ Helping at home

☐ Religion ☐ Good manners
☐ Helpfulness ☐ Neatness in dress

☐ 10. How much sex curiosity has he (she) indicated?
5 A great deal, 4 much, 3 some, 2 little, 1 none

☐ 11. How much accurate and detailed sex information has he (she) been given?
5 A great deal, 4 much, 3 some, 2 little, 1 none

☐ 12. How much interest does he (she) show in books of adventure?
5 Very much, 4 much, 3 some, 2 little, 1 none

☐ 13. How much interest has he (she) shown in love stories?
5 Very much, 4 much, 3 some, 2 little, 1 none

☐ 14. How well adjusted is he (she) to school?
5 Very well adjusted, 4 well adjusted, 3 average, 2 not well adjusted, 1 badly maladjusted

Trait III

☐ 15. What is his (her) concept of God?
5 A creator of the universe, 4 a Biblical character, 3 moral disciplinarian, 2 a divine Santa Claus, 1 believes there is none

☐ 16. What is his (her) concept of prayer?
5 A source of strength in time of danger, 4 a source of help in trouble, 3 asking for what you want, 2 a formality, 1 has no concept

☐ 17. What is his (her) notion of God's will for him (her)?
5 That God has a particular place and job of great importance for him (her) to do, 4 to be a minister, 3 to go to church, 2 to be good, 1 has none

☐ 18. How much self-reliance does he (she) have?
5 Completely self-reliant, 4 has much self-reliance, 3 average, 2 little, 1 none

☐ 19. Does he (she) have feelings of inferiority?
5 None at all, 4 a few, 3 some, 2 more than average, 1 very strong

☐ 20. Has he (she) stayed away from home all night this year?
5 Very often, 4 frequently, 3 occasionally, 2 seldom, 1 never

☐ 21. Has he (she) gone alone on a train or bus trip this year?
5 Very often, 4 frequently, 3 occasionally, 2 seldom, 1 never

☐ 22. Has he (she) taken a trip alone to a distant place this year?
5 Very often, 4 frequently, 3 occasionally, 2 seldom, 1 never

Trait IV

☐ 23. How much does he (she) know of the various vocations?
5 Unusually well informed, 4 knows many of them, 3 average, 2 knows very little, 1 almost nothing

☐ 24. Has he (she) chosen a vocation for himself (herself)?
5 Very enthusiastic about one, 4 definite about one, 3 talks about one, 2 vague about it, 1 has no idea about it

☐ 25. Is it in line with his (her) abilities?
5 Suits him (her) perfectly, 4 well chosen, 3 all right, 2 not well chosen, 1 completely impossible for him (her)

☐ 26. Does he (she) collect anything and how much? (What? ———)
5 Very enthusiastic collector, 4 active collector, 3 average, 2 an occasional collector, 1 never collects

☐ 27. Does he (she) do any creative writing? (What? ———)
5 Very often, 4 frequently, 3 occasionally, 2 seldom, 1 never

☐ 28. Does he (she) engage in imaginative activities as, for example, story telling? (What? ———)
5 Very often, 4 frequently, 3 occasionally, 2 seldom, 1 never

☐ 29. Does he (she) do any artistic work? (What kind? ———)
5 Very often, 4 frequently, 3 occasionally, 2 seldom, 1 never

☐ 30. Does he (she) participate in musical activities? (What? ———)
5 Very often, 4 frequently, 3 occasionally, 2 seldom, 1 never

☐ 31. Does he (she) do mechanical things? (What? ———)
5 Very often, 4 frequently, 3 occasionally, 2 seldom, 1 never

☐ 32. Has he (she) had a job this year? How often?
5 Very often, 4 frequently, 3 occasionally, 2 seldom, 1 never

☐ 33. Has he (she) taken care of family accounts this year?
5 Very often, 4 frequently, 3 occasionally, 2 seldom, 1 never

☐ 34. Has he (she) done any of the responsible family business this year?
5 Very often, 4 frequently, 3 occasionally, 2 seldom, 1 never

Trait V

☐ 35. Does he (she) have close chums or intimate friends?
5 Very many, 4 many, 3 some, 2 a few, 1 none

36. Which of these are characteristic of him (her) and how much so? (Rate each separately.)
5 Very characteristic, 4 fairly characteristic, 3 average, 2 occasionally so, 1 not at all

- ☐ Deliberate coarseness
- ☐ Excessive practical joking
- ☐ Constantly teasing others
- ☐ Constantly imitating others
- ☐ Grabbing at table
- ☐ Thoughtlessness of others' wishes

37. How does he (she) regard each of these?
5 Manly, 4 desirable, 3 all right, 2 weak, 1 infantile

- ☐ Good manners
- ☐ Kindness to brothers and sisters
- ☐ Thoughtfulness of others
- ☐ Obedience to parents and teachers
- ☐ Use of good English

38. Is he (she) impulsively sympathetic to each of these?
5 Very sympathetic, 4 above average, 3 average, 2 has little sympathy for them, 1 not at all

- ☐ Animals
- ☐ Chums
- ☐ Younger children
- ☐ Older persons
- ☐ Mothers and sisters

Trait VI

☐ 39. Does he (she) have friends of the same sex?
5 Very many, 4 a number, 3 some, 2 a few, 1 none

☐ 40. Does he (she) have friends of the opposite sex?
5 Very many, 4 a number, 3 some, 2 a few, 1 none

☐ 41. Is he (she) kind to animals?
5 Very much so, 4 above average, 3 average, 2 not kind, 1 very cruel

☐ 42. How keenly is he (she) devoted to fair play?
5 Very much so, 4 above average, 3 average, 2 below average, 1 not at all

☐ 43. How good a loser is he (she)?
5 Splendid sportsman, 4 above average, 3 average, 2 below average, 1 not at all

☐ 44. What is his (her) attitude toward younger children?
5 Very affectionate, 4 likes them, 3 indifferent, 2 avoids them, 1 torments them

☐ 45. What is his (her) attitude toward less endowed children?
5 Helps them, 4 likes them, 3 indifferent, 2 avoids them, 1 despises them

☐ 46. What is his (her) attitude toward queer children?
5 Helps them, 4 likes them, 3 indifferent, 2 avoids them, 1 despises them

☐ 47. How much interest has he (she) in such activities as gangs, Scouts, radio clubs, teams, etc.?
5 Very much interest, 4 lots of interest, 3 average, 2 little interest, 1 no interest

Trait VII

☐ 48. What is his (her) reaction to injury from others?
5 Returns good for evil, 4 turns the other cheek, 3 forgives and forgets, 2 retribution or retaliation, 1 intense revenge

49. How frequently does he (she) lose his (her) temper toward the following?
5 Very often, 4 frequently, 3 occasionally, 2 seldom, 1 never

☐ Brothers and sisters
☐ Father

☐ Mother
☐ Playmates
☐ Teachers
☐ Strangers

☐ 50. What is his (her) attitude toward injustice?
5 Returns good for evil, 4 endures it, 3 average, 2 becomes angry, 1 becomes very angry

☐ 51. What is his (her) attitude toward bad decisions in athletics?
5 Accepts them in good spirit, 4 accepts them, 3 average, 2 dislikes them, 1 becomes very angry

☐ 52. What is his (her) attitude toward superiority in an opponent?
5 Wholehearted admiration, 4 some admiration, 3 average, 2 dislikes it, 1 very jealous, tends to discount it

Trait VIII

☐ 53. What is his (her) attitude toward the Cross in religion?
5 Considers it heroic, 4 considers it admirable, 3 thinks of it as a symbol, 2 does not give it much thought, 1 hardly aware of it

☐ 54. How much opportunity does he (she) have for practice in leadership?
5 Very much, 4 above average, 3 some, 2 little, 1 none

☐ 55. How good a follower is he (she)?
5 Very coöperative, 4 good, 3 average, 2 non-coöperative, 1 very poor

☐ 56. How much is he (she) able to endure pain to achieve his (her) purpose?
5 Has great endurance, 4 has some endurance, 3 average, 2 avoids pain, 1 is much afraid of pain

☐ 57. How much will he (she) sacrifice for his (her) chums?
5 Will make great sacrifices, 4 will sacrifice some things, 3 average, 2 makes very little sacrifice, 1 none at all

☐ 58. How much will he (she) sacrifice for his (her) brothers and sisters?
5 Will make great sacrifices, 4 will sacrifice some things, 3 average, 2 makes very little sacrifice, 1 none at all

☐ 59. How much will he (she) sacrifice for his (her) parents?
5 Will make great sacrifices, 4 will sacrifice some things, 3 average, 2 makes very little sacrifice, 1 none at all

☐ 60. How much will he (she) sacrifice for his (her) classmates?
5 Will make great sacrifices, 4 will sacrifice some things, 3 average, 2 makes very little sacrifice, 1 none at all

☐ 61. How much will he (she) sacrifice for younger children?
5 Will make great sacrifices, 4 will sacrifice some things, 3 average, 2 makes very little sacrifice, 1 none at all

☐ 62. How much will he (she) sacrifice for strangers?
5 Will make great sacrifices, 4 will sacrifice some things, 3 average, 2 makes very little sacrifice, 1 none at all

XII

The High School and College Age

THE PROBLEMS OF ADOLESCENCE, as the youth of today faces them, are quite new in civilization. One can read the wisdom of antiquity and realize that the difficulties which beset every other age level are much alike, in ancient times and ours. But with adolescence, it is a different story. Can you change human nature? Biologically, adolescence is exactly as it has always been. Human nature cannot be changed in that sense, but the adjustment problems of adolescence never existed before except in very rare instances. Even our grandparents went directly from childhood into maturity through the medium of marriage. Within the last two generations the length of the adolescent period has increased from one or two to ten or fifteen years. Let those who hark back to the "good old days" for methods of child training keep in mind that here is an instance, in America at least, in which human nature has been changed. A whole new epoch has been added to it; namely, adolescence.

Since 1880, the number of pupils in our high schools, in proportion to the population, has now increased one thousand percent. If the same proportion of youth had gone to high school in 1930 as in 1880, our high school population would have been approximately half a million. Actually, it was four and a half million. Today, at the age of twenty-one, less than one-fifth of our boys are married and fewer than one-half of our girls. Then, when one looks at the changes which have been wrought in civilization by science during that same period of time, he is immediately faced with the fact that for once the oratorical statement, "We are living in a new age," is indeed true, especially for our youth. Most of us now in middle life or beyond had very little of radios, airplanes, or even automobiles to complicate our adjustment during this same period. It is difficult for us and impossible for our children to realize what tremendous social problems they have set up.

Furthermore, and this is the most important thing, these very agencies have not only increased adjustmental difficulties but they have decreased the resources of our youth to solve them. A few generations ago, adequate time to think was available to every young man and woman. Good or bad though the results might be, he was very likely to develop something of a philosophy of life. Nowadays, although we travel much faster, we have much less time to spend thinking. To those whose contacts do not bring them often into the social groups of adolescents, it would be a revelation to discover how busy they are. One high school sophomore in reporting her activities indicated that she was a member of fourteen different high school organizations which, on the average, met once a week. When all these are added to the curriculum of her school work, her athletic responsibilities, her other social obligations, her church activities and the "must" movies, one wonders how she finds time to eat and sleep, much less time to think. Yet here is an age in which the mind is just reaching maturity and at which philosophical reflection is possible for the first time. Probably nothing else in the life of an adolescent is so important as to think through life's problems and become intelligently oriented to meet them, but for this task there is no time.

If the church has a golden opportunity for shaping the leadership of the future, it is during adolescence. Idealistic as young people are, a religious program that meets their rigorous requirements for thoroughness, honesty and idealism can become one of the most powerful influences in their lives. This is not easily accomplished because even parents nowadays, as they look with some misgivings on the busy lives of their children, insist on Sunday being a day of rest. Let us look, then, at this interesting age and with full recognition of the limited data available upon which to make our judgments, endeavor to face honestly the problem of adolescence.[1]

Physical Development

Adolescence is a period of extremely rapid growth and change. Weight increases more during the years from twelve to seventeen than in the preceding ten years. Furthermore, these growth changes are not always regular and consistent. The bones, muscles, glands, heart, lungs, brain, and viscera all grow at somewhat different rates, each producing problems of considerable significance. Of course, a great many of the problems which arise because of the asymmetries in growth are problems which are best solved by time; that is, they are simply outgrown. A boy may grow as much as twenty-five pounds in a single year. One boy at the beginning of a year weighed 112 pounds, and at the end 137 pounds. Thus, as has been said, he had gone from the flyweight class, according to boxing regulation, through the bantamweight, the featherweight, and into the lightweight class. It is little wonder that physical adjustments are difficult under these conditions. In the early years of adolescence, girls are usually an inch or so taller than boys. This is especially important at the extremes. The unusually tall girl and the unusually short boy often have reason to believe that fate has not been kind to them. At dances, this particular problem comes to a head. The short girl is pronounced cute, which is all well and good for her, but it leaves the implication that the tall girl is not cute. The tall boy is spoken of as manly. This is kind enough to him, but it implies that the short boy is not manly. In very few phases of our adult life are young people so cruel to each other as they are with regard to their physical endowment. The girl with outstanding physical attractiveness is rushed by all her

[1] Cole, L., *Psychology of Adolescence* (Farrar and Rinehart, Inc., New York, 1936). This is one of the most thorough volumes dealing with this age level. It is written especially for the use of teachers and can be highly recommended for a more thorough treatment of adolescent problems than is possible in this chapter.

boy associates. The girl with more modest endowment in this respect is not only simply left to suffer in silence, but often subjected to the cruelest sort of ridicule. It requires a good deal of faith, magnanimity, and patience for the boy or girl of little physical attractiveness to achieve the popularity of their more fortunate companions. The most important thing is, it can be done. There is probably not a single condition of physical endowment so small but that popularity can be achieved. The methods by which this can be accomplished will be discussed later in this chapter.

Modern youth is a good deal better equipped physically to meet life's problems than their ancestors. This is especially true of girls. A good deal of criticism has been focused on the bare-legged, boisterous, active girl of today, but as has been pointed out, she is from thirty-five to seventy-five percent stronger than her grandmother was at the same age.

As for her morals, they are certainly not so prudish as her grandmother's. She meets life a good deal more frankly and discusses problems openly that her grandmother would never have mentioned even privately. But the fact is, modern youth is probably as fine morally, if not finer, than in any preceding generation. There can be little doubt that the social morals of the last two generations were unrealistic and poorly adapted to the needs of human nature. It will not be at all astonishing if this young generation, with all its breath-taking frankness, solves the problem of a more adequate and healthier standard of morals.

Many factors conspire to make boys desire athletic achievement more than anything else. Because they have come to the age when falling in love is one of life's most important experiences, it is inevitable that they dream of performing great feats. The best opportunity for this is in athletics. However, boys are really much less ready for strenuous athletics than girls are. Girls mature earlier and are much further developed physically than their brothers are. Hence the very common experience of high school athletes being burned out before they go to college. This does not mean that they need to be over-protected, but it does mean that frequent physical examinations, and not their ambitions, should be the limiting factor of their athletic endeavors.

One of the most unruly things the adolescent has to control is his appetite. His stomach becomes much larger and he seems to have an endless capacity for food. Furthermore, this appetite is likely to crave all sorts of rich and undigestible foods. Since in many cases he is likely to be eating his lunch away from home every day, on money provided for that purpose, care needs to be taken that it does not consist entirely of hot dogs and hamburgers, washed down with ice cream sodas or milk shakes, followed by banana splits, doughnuts, or cream puffs. The various skin infections which follow such a procedure set up social problems of considerable magnitude, at least in the mind of the youth.

This is the age when perspiration is likely to be more abundant than during any other period, just in the very nature of the physical organism. This does not contribute to the social poise and comfort of either sex. There are many ways, however, in which the acuteness of the problem can be dealt with. Its cure comes, of course, in growing up. A few years later this excessive tendency to perspire is likely to decrease.

Far and away the most important physical development of adolescence is sexual maturity. Girls mature somewhat earlier than boys, but there is a wide range of individual differences in both sexes. The following table will show the rate at which maturity occurs.[2] This means that girls should

Percentage					Age					
Mature	9	10	11	12	13	14	15	16	17	18
Girls	1	1.5	4	12	(50)	80	90	97	99	99.9
Boys	0	0	1	3	15	35(50)	65	85	94	99.9

be given fairly adequate sex education by ten years of age and boys by twelve. Most sex education of the more elab-

[2] Adapted from Cole, L., *Psychology of Adolescence*, p. 36 (Farrar and Rinehart, 1936).

orate and thorough-going character is given between fifteen and seventeen, but by the age of fifteen, ninety percent of girls and sixty-five percent of boys are already sexually mature. Sex education would be more timely at an earlier age level.

The achievement of sexual maturity is of great importance and can be made a dynamic event rather than one involving shame and guilt. The whole problem should be made one of achievement and pride, not one of sin and repression. The problem becomes many times more acute due to the postponement of marriage in our modern civilization. The older methods of assuring sexual purity on the basis of fear and guilt are no longer possible with the average intelligent boy or girl. Other motivations need to be used. It has often been said, "Sex is strength." It can be wasted or it can be conserved and thrown into more dynamic living. Among the notions of the past, the idea that total sexual abstinence is physically dangerous is quite as unfounded as that masturbation will lead to insanity. Parents and teachers who expect to participate in the fundamental sex education of their children need to be correctly informed on all of these questions. The youth of today learn so much from other sources that they quickly detect ignorance on the part of their parents.

Secondary sex characteristics are often as much a source of embarrassment as the primary ones. In boys, the two most conspicuous are the change in voice and the growth of hair on the face. The former is likely to be a real ordeal. When a boy cannot confidently predict whether his utterances are to be squeals or bellows, he is likely to worry considerably about the necessity of talking at all. The growth of hair on the face is almost invariably looked forward to with a great deal of anticipation. For some curious reason, it has become one of the outstanding evidences of manhood. So, many a boy can be found using his father's razor long before his parents admit the necessity for it. In girls the secondary sex characteristics are much less violent and embarrassing. As has been pointed out before, too much emphasis has been put on avoiding physical activity during the menstrual period. Actually, in a normal, healthy girl about as much physical exercise can be engaged in during this time as during any other. Changes in body contours are much more likely to be sources of attractiveness and therefore welcome rather than embarrassing.

Mental Development

During adolescence, intelligence reaches its peak. Only wisdom, not the capacity for acquiring wisdom, increases from now on. However, the range of individual differences is enormous. In one school for the feeble-minded, an adult woman making rugs can complete approximately four a year. These sell for one dollar apiece. She has an I.Q. of approximately fifty. This is the earning capacity of this mental level. Average intelligence falls at about the borderline between unskilled and skilled labor. A 100 I.Q., average by definition, is not sufficiently high to warrant optimism about a college education. Of course, colleges differ in their requirements, and other qualifications often play an important part (especially outstanding football ability). It seems more intelligent, however, to think of a college education as quite as specialized as art or music or mechanics. It is, therefore, adapted to those who have the inherited qualifications to assimilate it. It is no more to be thought of as a disgrace to lack the abstract intelligence necessary for this sort of education than to lack musical ability or artistic ability.

The most important mental ability which comes during this period is what may be termed the capacity for philosophical reasoning. Junior and intermediate boys argue incessantly about an umpire's decisions. High school and college youth argue much more enthusiastically about the existence of God. Discussion groups are extremely popular at this age level, and almost any young people's society can reach some size if it devotes most of its time to abstract and profound discussions. As has been found characteristic of new abilities at the other age levels, it is inevitable that they exaggerate their importance. Actually, their rote memory is quite as good and a little bit better than it ever has been before. College students speak with contempt about the rote memory courses as compared with the courses requiring thought, but this is much more an expression of their desires than it is a statement of true value.

All along the line mental capacities are increasing. The capacity for concentration approaches maturity. The difficulty it meets is in the overwhelming competition it receives from the many activities which tend to distract the youth. Favorable conditions for concentration may well be prepared for the adolescent. But the kind of conditions which are favorable differ enormously from individual to individual. One wishes a quiet room with no distractions, while another prefers the radio going full blast. Perhaps the best definition of a favorable environment is the one which yields the best results. Imagination not only increases in quantity, but changes considerably in quality. The romance which is the colorful center of the adolescent's social life is likely also to be the guiding motif of his imagination. The value of this for developing some of our eight traits is obvious.

Finally, the capacity for organization now reaches maturity. This capacity has been growing steadily and almost uniformly from about six years of age. Its usefulness in study habits is, of course, large. Many of the methods for efficient study have been impossible to teach or to learn until this age level. They can be now, however, and should be. It is interesting to note that in one large group of young people where five discussion courses were offered, the one devoted to study habits proved to be the most popular. This, of course, is because it met a real need.

Emotional Development

Since emotions constitute the best criterion of mental health, no phase of personality can be discussed which does not involve them. All of the eight traits are fundamentally emotional attitudes. No one acquainted with adolescence can fail to recognize that, emotionally, this is the most unstable age. So many new interests come suddenly into the focus of activity that the youth necessarily over-emphasizes their importance and indulges in many emotional excesses. Many a girl cries her heart out and feels that life is not worth living because she has not received an invitation to an important dance. Many a boy is quite ready to end it all because of his failure to win the affection of some particular girl. One girl showed the most violent reaction to being asked to walk in a procession in which there were young children. She felt that this would almost certainly bring her social ridicule. To be sure, a much greater stability is eventually achieved and these things gradually assume their proper proportions. The fact remains that they are exceedingly important for immediate adjustment. Indeed they are just as important as the adolescent thinks they are.

Emotions, especially excessive fear and anger, are always significant factors in personality. They are not simply mental experiences; they have far-reaching and violent physical reactions in the body itself. Faith cures have sound, physical bases. Fear or anger influences the digestive processes, the secretion of the endocrine glands, and the flow of blood so extremely that health is greatly endangered when these emotions occur too frequently.[3]

Furthermore, the causes of emotional outbursts change. Anger, for example, during the pre-school years is largely a result of restraint, or of taking things away from the child, or otherwise causing him to do things he does not wish to do. During the elementary school years, injustice, real or imagined, is the most important point. It is almost invariably restricted to specific situations. But during adolescence, injured vanity becomes the outstanding source of irritation. "The principle of the thing" and "standing up for one's

[3] Cannon, W. B., *Bodily Changes in Pain, Hunger, Fear, and Rage,* 2d Edition (D. Appleton Co., 1929).

Those who are interested in a more complete description of this phase of our make-up should look into this book, which is one of the most readable and accurate accounts of it.

rights" are causes of a great deal of unhappiness, as well as of an enormous amount of indigestion due to anger. During adolescence, fear is likely to be more social than physical. The infant is afraid of noise and things happening to him physically; later he acquires a fear of snakes, water, dogs, etc. At a still later age, fear of failure and inferiority become important, but at adolescence sarcasm and ridicule are far more dreaded. Fear is always destructive of personality. Anger is at least aggressive. But personality in general would be far healthier with a minimum of these two emotions.

Social Development

Tradition tells of epoch-making events which are destined to happen in the twinkling of an eye. Whether this be true or not, such events do occur in the lives of thousands of our adolescents in the form of falling in love. It is not always so sudden as that, but whether sudden or gradual, such experiences are essential to normal development. Like every other phase in life, these love affairs carry with them their dangers, but it should be understood by parents that none of these dangers is so difficult to escape from as those that beset him or her who does not fall in love. Neither state is insuperable, but the point is, one cannot avoid the one without involving the other. In general, several such love affairs can be thought of as more desirable than just one. Each one produces its harvest in terms of experience, maturity, and emotional depth. This is the center of adolescent social life from which all other aspects are derived. Even when a boy or girl is not in love at the moment, nevertheless all social activities are constructed on the assumption that he either is or wants to be. The gang of the junior and intermediate ages composed of only one sex disappears almost entirely and the crowd of the adolescent age takes its place. There is a vast difference between the two. The crowd is very heterosexual. Indeed, one of its prime requirements is that its membership shall be very nearly equal in the two sexes. Furthermore, their motives are quite different. The junior and intermediate gangs are always up to something. What mischief they may think up next is always a source of some foreboding by the entire neighborhood. But nothing could be more harmless than a crowd. As a matter of fact, to the superficial observer, the crowd often seems to do nothing at all but just sit and talk. This does not seem very adventurous to the child, but it is the very height of adventure to the adolescent. He is learning a lot of important lessons by means of it—how to get along with people, the various social skills, how to judge people, and perhaps most important of all, experience in love making. Crowds have their disadvantages. One is that they almost inevitably become cliques which erect solid walls against the outsider. Young people's groups in churches may discuss ways and means of making strangers feel at home, and evolve all sorts of methods to bring this about, but careful examination of results is not very promising. Cliques still remain and still tend to bar outsiders.

This is the period during which there are the largest number of organized social activities. Schools almost always take advantage of the adolescent social tendencies in the actual propagation, or at least encouragement, of all kinds of social societies. Student self-government is perhaps the outstanding example of this. Churches, feeling the importance of developing in their youth a love for the church, try to make it a social center. Not infrequently, they duplicate social organizations of the schools and only multiply the already over-crowded activities of their young people. That there is a place for organized social activities no one can deny. Certainly, left to their own devices, young people often set up social activities which are neither intelligently constructed nor in many cases socially helpful. In our large, modern, heterogeneous high schools there is room for a great many social organizations. There ought to be activities for everybody, and this, of course, means that fairly accurate knowledge of the aptitudes and abilities of the individuals forming these groups is important. Athletics ought to be as broadly inclusive as possible. The value of highly organized intercollegiate and interscholastic teams is still a question. But whatever its ultimate solution, the fact is that intramural athletics, including, as they do, much larger numbers, are probably far more beneficial in the growth of character. Of course, there is a place for the person of high endowment in the more specialized teams, and indeed there should be. Of what value is endowment in any field if opportunity is not provided for its expression? The pity of it is that there should not be equal social recognition of outstanding achievements in music and art and mechanical ability as well as in scholastic and athletic prowess. It is quite as great an achievement to be all-American in the one as in the other.

Character Development

There is a real need for a book on a theology for youth. Those who have had the privilege of a theological education and who then listen to high school and college young people discuss all these same philosophical problems in their naïve uninformed groups realize how enthusiastically these same young people would receive training in a theology prepared especially for them. This may not sound very thrilling at first reading, but theology consists of a concept of the universe, and its major problems include: the nature of the universe itself, the being and nature of God, immortality, sin and evil, the problem of suffering, and many other similar problems. Listen to bullpen sessions among college students or to arguments within a crowd, and many of them center around precisely these same problems. The great contribution of any religion is its concept of the universe. Christianity is no exception to this, and youth ought to know its fundamental tenets.

When we ask young people what their immediate problems are, their answers are varied. One large group gave as their most difficult problems these: vocational guidance, parental authority, school adjustment, religion, health and food, friendship, race and national prejudice, sex, leadership, and popularity. There were a great many sex differences. Among the boys vocational guidance was far the leading problem, whereas with the girls parental authority took first place. A little thoughtful consideration of the everyday questions of youth will show how true to life this distinction is. It is very interesting to observe that, with the boys, religion came second, whereas, with the girls, it was sixth. In one Sunday school class composed of high school students, the proportion of boys to girls was almost two to one. With the girls, school adjustment proved to be very important, but with the boys, less so. The others of these ten problems ranked about the same in both sexes. One may choose these ten problems and build around them a discussion group which will attract most of the young people for an almost unlimited period of time. They do like to argue. The use to which this arguing has been put by such organizations as the Y.M.C.A. and many young people's church groups is adequate evidence of its power. Let us now turn to the eight traits and see what the church can offer to the development of character and personality during adolescence.

Experimental Faith

During the entire life of the child, from the time he is born until now, character education has been possible toward the development of each of these eight traits. Yet, until this time, an understanding by the child of the concepts involved has been largely impossible. It would be quite difficult, even during the intermediate age level, to explain to children what is meant by poverty of spirit, meekness, and peacemaking. These concepts are so abstract and difficult that it requires all of the mental facilities of mature intelligence to comprehend them. Yet this very comprehension is the final and important step in bringing them to fruition. If young people are to acquire an enthusiasm for the philosophy of Jesus, it is important that they comprehend clearly all that is involved in the teachings which Jesus gave about human personality. This, then, is the most important task in the religious education of adolescents; namely, a clear comprehension of Jesus' teachings themselves. It is especially important that the problem of prayer be given complete discussion. Prayer, as Jesus used and taught it, constitutes one of the greatest sources of power on which human beings may draw. It is indeed a sad commentary on the quality of our religious education when so many of our college young people show by their discussions that they still hold concepts of prayer which they ought to have outgrown when they graduated from the kindergarten.[4]

Vision

This is preëminently the age of vision. Idealism reaches its peak. It has never before been so prominent nor will it ever be again. To be sure it is often unrealistic and impractical, and the disillusionments that inevitably come with the first years of complete self-determination are likely to cool its ardor somewhat. For this very reason, it is important that all its values to the mature personality be gained while it is prominent. A corollary of this idealism is found in ambition. Unless parents and teachers have spent a great deal of time during his early years drilling the child in the necessity of financial security, the adolescent is not likely to be too mercenary. Not a few of those who pretend to be sophisticated and disillusioned, are, beneath the surface, quite as idealistic and have quite as high visions as their companions. There is hardly an adolescent boy who does not secretly imagine that he is going to be a great man. Nor are there many girls who do not have equivalent dreams.

The unfortunate part of all this comes in the fact that, at least as youth defines greatness, only a very small percentage of them can become great. It is all well and good

[4] Ligon, E. M., *The Psychology of Christian Personality*, Chapters VI and VII (Macmillan, New York, 1935). In these two chapters will be found a discussion of Jesus' teaching about prayer and its value in personality.

for every American mother to look upon her new-born son as a future president of the United States. It is quite another thing to instill in him through the years the feeling that unless he does achieve this or some other prominent position in life he is a failure. Actually, every one of them can be great. The greatest man I have ever known lives in a small town, has received only an elementary school education, has never accumulated great wealth, nor been acclaimed by thousands of people. His vocation has been that of running a lumber yard. But the vision he had for his task, as one of the builders of a vast new empire and for inspiring youth to achieve things to the best of their abilities, has made him truly great. It is not the objective size of the vocation chosen, but the vision one has for that vocation which determines whether it shall be great or not. It now becomes a necessity for boys and girls to know as accurately as science can tell them what their aptitudes and abilities are and, on the basis of this information, to select a vocation, but most important of all to get a vision for that vocation. The groundwork for this should have been laid in the junior and intermediate departments by means of the two sight-seeing trips which they have taken through the vocations, one by way of exploration, the other by way of adventure. If this preliminary work has been well done, it will not be difficult for the adolescent to get a vision for his job, whatever it may be.

But vision is not confined to one's job. It includes a recognition of the importance of everyone else's job and a clear understanding of the social structure of which the youth and his friends are a part. At commencement time, chosen speakers invariably tell high school and college graduates about the world they are to build. These speeches are sometimes inspiring, and these young people go out actually expecting to build that world. Most of them go all the way through their lives without ever even finding it. Their jobs and the various political and social issues that they meet seem entirely unrelated to this idealistic world, and they never find this great task of which they were told when graduating from school. During these adolescent years, it is necessary for them to get a clear picture of the whole social structure and the importance of each little part of it, so that they recognize the significance of their own contribution, however small it may be.

Daydreaming may now become a source of power. Nothing stimulates daydreams more than falling in love, and no daydreams are so stimulating to activity as these very ones. When a young man, driven by such an affection, thinks of future achievements with which to impress his beloved, he at the same time seeks to find ways of doing something about it now. Again, a difficulty arises when the things he has been taught to consider important are beyond his possibilities. Then, all too frequently, he tends to retreat into a world of unrealistic daydreams where these native handicaps are no longer insuperable. Such daydreaming is inevitably unhealthy and, if carried to too great an extreme, may actually become a form of mental disease. Again, the solution lies in getting a vision of greatness within the limits of one's power of achievement. It seems probable that more unhappiness in human life is caused by over-ambition than by any other single cause. This is especially characteristic of our American life. The bound-to-rise philosophy which tells of going from a log cabin to the White House is inspiring to youth, but the cold facts are that a vast majority of us do not get there. Such a vision can only lead to failure. We can be proud of the ambition of our American boys and girls. This is a quality of Americanism which certainly ought not to be lost; but it must be retained without, at the same time, paying the price of so great an amount of unhappiness.

The broader one's experiences, the more realistic and well-oriented will be one's vision. Wide experiences, interests and activities are valuable in the growth of this trait. Travel, adventures in the business world, clubs and hobbies, books and lectures are all food for the development of constructive imagination.

Finally, it is important again to recognize that the trait

of which we are speaking is a habit of mind. This habit of mind is that of always looking for greater achievements and for better things. It is not a habit or an appetite which is satiated by achievement, because each new achievement should in turn become a stimulus to a still better one. "Our old men dream dreams, our young men see visions." There is good psychology in this. Some men are young at eighty because of this mental habit of always looking forward. Others are old at thirty because of the unfortunate habit of dreaming about the "good old days". The basic elements of this habit of mind should have been formed through the years from infancy up. A clear comprehension of its full significance is the final step in its development. Nothing in the life of Jesus is more stimulating to adolescent youth than this trait. His own high vision, which made him enthusiastic about the future even when he was giving his life for it, can be a source of inspiration which may well be given to every high school boy and girl.

Love of Righteousness and Truth

The Christian philosophy of life can be understood for the first time during this period. This is evidenced by an investigation which was made to discover at what age it is possible for children to understand the various teachings in the Christian philosophy.[5] The Parable of the Sower, the Parable of the Two Foundations, and such teachings as the one which begins with "What shall it profit a man," "Men love darkness when their deeds are evil," "Judge not," and "Love God and keep his commandments," were used. Such a concept as "Judge not that ye be not judged" was incomprehensible to children under fourteen, and even at sixteen about one-fifth of them could not give a reasonable interpretation of it. None of these teachings can be thought of as being appropriate for children until the adolescent pe-

[5] Cole, L., *Psychology of Adolescence*, pp. 215-217 (Farrar and Rinehart, 1936).

riod. And adults, as a rule, are not usually characterized by their enthusiasm for Bible study and theological discussions. Their love of righteousness and truth is much more likely to be confined to business, bridge, and golf. But, during adolescence, it can be taught in such a way as to command the interest of young people. Their intelligence has just matured and they are interested in using it. Philosophy is a new field for them. It is like opening an entirely new treasure house to them. It is not remarkable that they should thoroughly enjoy these mental experiences.

This desire to philosophize has already been mentioned as expressing itself in the tendency to argue. Discussion groups are by far their most popular form of activity. It matters not whether these discussion groups are organized, for wherever two or three adolescents are gathered together, an argument on the profound problems of life will be found. The too prevalent tendency to devote our entire adolescent program to discussion, however, has about run its course. Adolescents are beginning to realize that, however pleasant it seems, usually it does not accomplish much. To deny them the right of discussion would be fatal to any organization which expects to hold their interest, but every discussion ought to be prefaced by some new material, usually in lecture form. This material ought to be profound, something which they have not known before, and food upon which the discussion can become more than a mere argument. All too many of our character building institutions lose many of their possibilities by the overindulgence of this desire to discuss the "problems of life".

Two things need to be learned during this period. One is an intelligent attitude toward the whole store of past knowledge. School adjustment now becomes increasingly difficult, and instruction in study habits may now be as essential a part of character development as training in ethical principles themselves. Psychology and education have combined to discover by experimental methods the most economical ways of learning. They constitute mental coaching.

There are, of course, individual differences, but a mastery of these methods will improve anyone's efficiency in studying to an appreciable amount. A great many fine manuals have been published for this purpose.[6] There is no real reason why every adolescent boy and girl should not be happy and well adjusted to his educational requirements. Sometimes this is a matter of study habits; sometimes it is a matter of the choice of school. Differing temperaments and abilities require different types of training, and nothing could tend more to maladjustment than a regimented type of education which tries to force everyone into the same mold. Education, being required as it is by law well up into adolescence, and being one's hope of future advancement in one's vocation, requires an adjustment which will be happy and efficient.

The second principle which the adolescent needs to learn is a love of righteousness. This is not simply the statement of a platitude. He will now be getting intimately acquainted with the less idealistic phases of life. It will not be easy for him to keep his enthusiasm for righteousness in the face of the apparent success of unrighteousness. It requires concepts of religion and righteousness which are powerful, challenging and creative to hold his interest. If negative ethics continue to hold an adolescent boy or girl, this is likely to be an evidence of weak personality and mental maladjustment. Character building organizations which confine their teachings to negative ethics are not likely to find in their midst the highest quality of adolescent boy or girl.

Finally, sex education must now be a central factor in the youth's adjusting to life. The old fear motives for preserving virtue were harmful and unhealthy and, for the most part, are not believed today. As it has been pointed out, the discovery that sex is strength and that conservation of sexual energy is a source of power is a far stronger and more wholesome motive for moral integrity than fear.

[6] Kornhauser, A. W., *How to Study* (University of Chicago, 1937). Whipple, G. M., *How to Study Effectively* (Public School Publishing Co., 1927). These are two excellent volumes of this sort.

Faith in the Friendliness of the Universe

Insurmountable obstacles to success, on the one hand, and disillusionment from childhood idealism, on the other, are the two strongest forces which tend to destroy the adolescent faith in the friendliness of the universe. Physical deficiencies which bring a boy ridicule from his fellows and frustrate success with the opposite sex are not easily accepted as the will of a friendly God. At a time when social success seems of paramount importance, it is not strange that young people should resent the fate that has denied them those characteristics which make its achievement easy. The boy who is short of stature, or completely lacking in rhythm and coördination, or has other equally disconcerting physical characteristics, may become deeply depressed and feel certain that no Father-God could ever have been so cruel. And the girl who lacks most of the accepted features of physical attractiveness does not always find it easy to believe that the universe is friendly.

Then, when the adolescent becomes increasingly aware of the overwhelming amount of sin, disease, suffering, cruelty, tyranny, graft and injustice in the world, the disillusionment may often become a tremendous setback to his childhood faith in an omnipotent God who works His will in the world. As a father and son once looked down from the top of a mountain upon the awe-inspiring panorama that reached out before them, the father said, "Can you look at all this and not believe in a good God?" A few days later when the two were together again in the slum district of one of our large cities, the son turned to his father and said, "Can you look at all this and still believe in a good God?" It is not easy to maintain one's faith in a friendly universe in the face of such difficulties. Only the most superficial and thoughtless can fail to have his doubts. Yet this mental habit which consists in an indomitable faith that the universe is friendly is one of the basic essentials in mental hygiene. How shall we give it to the adolescent boy or girl?

In the first place every effort must be made to help him find a happy adjustment, and yet a realistic one, in the world he finds about him. Attention has been called several times to the over-ambition which so often brings him face to face with real insurmountable obstacles. If instead, his ambition has been geared to his capacities, and if he has been given a high vision for the tasks which he can perform, he is not so likely to bemoan the fate that did not endow him with an I.Q. of a hundred and eighty.

Then, in the next place, he can learn the secrets of popularity. Several investigations have been made, in every one of which the results have shown that a good disposition is far more important in gaining friendship than physical attractiveness. He or she who is physically attractive may well thank God for this added blessing. But it is well for young people to recognize that it is only by the mysterious laws of chance that they possess attractiveness while others do not. On the other hand, there is no endowment so modest that popularity cannot be gained. Furthermore, endowed blessings, even of this nature, carry with them their responsibilities. And not a few whom God has blessed with much natural beauty find themselves exceedingly unpopular, because of their inability to make the other, more important, social adjustments.

As for the problem of evil, the first step is to reveal to the youth the significance of evil in the human personality. Indeed, character, as such, presupposes the possibility for evil. Without it, we would be mere automatons without will, courage, loyalty, or any of those other qualities which command our deepest admiration. The question has often been asked a group of young people, "If you could press a button and by that means eliminate all of the sin and suffering and disease in the world, would you press the button?" At first glance it would seem to be a hardhearted individual indeed who would fail to press the button, for that seems to be the very essence of what we are all working for. But the question has been put to all kinds of young people. Some individuals were themselves the victims of disease, suffering, and injustice. But I have not met one young person who, after careful thought, would press the button. This does not mean that they want sin and suffering and disease in the world. It does mean, however, that if it is to be eliminated they want it to be as a result of their own efforts; they do not want it to be eliminated by the mere reflex action of an automaton.

A second step is to give the youth a picture of the progress which has been made by Christian civilization from the time of Christ until today. Yes, it is an inspiring picture in a total sense, despite wars and oppressions, and one which is likely to challenge a youth to dedicate his own life to its further progress.

Finally, he can come to recognize the achievements that are possible when men hold this indomitable faith and will not surrender it, however great the evidence against it. The whole progress of our modern science grew out of the indomitable faith that the universe is lawful, and it may truly be said that most of our social progress has grown out of the Christian faith that the universe is fatherly. This concept of meekness is one which will challenge and not repel the adolescent. This concept of religion is one which will inspire and not disgust him. Indeed, he will recognize in it a source of strength and not an institution of weakness.

One of the most important sources of faith is the home. It is necessary to lay at the doorstep of the home much of the discontent, delinquency, and failure among adolescents. This is the period when parents should disclaim the infallibility usually ascribed to them by their young children, and too often accepted by themselves as only a slight exaggeration. They need to be real human beings if they are to have the confidence and understanding with which to help the adolescent meet the many new problems which face him every day. Happy is the boy or girl whose father and mother are "regular". When parents reveal to their children their own adolescent difficulties and failures, they do much to inspire a similar confidence. Having received this confidence it is important that the parent accept it with understanding advice and guidance, and not with "holier-than-thou" negative ethics. In many instances, parents of adolescents encourage their children to call them by their first names. This often creates a most delightful means of becoming pals.

The problem of home, however, is not entirely solved by friendship with one's parents. At least two other qualities are equally important. The first one is pride. The boy or girl who cannot bring his or her friends into the home and be proud of it is indeed unfortunate. If the girl thinks that her father should not be found sitting in the living room in his shirtsleeves and bedroom slippers, then it is a very small price to pay for her regard to deny himself those comforts. If the children want a little better furniture in the living room than the parents can easily afford, they may well sacrifice a good many other things to add this attraction to the home. These things may seem rather small, but the size of the thing is not determined by objective means but by subjective means. These things are as important as the adolescent thinks they are. The other quality which he requires of his home is security. He may have plenty of self-confidence and independence, but he wants, not only during adolescence but for many years thereafter, the feeling that home is a rock of Gibraltar on whose strength he can depend whenever he needs it. It is not so much that he will ever ask for it, as it is the sense of security that comes from knowing that it is there. This does not mean that these qualities are unattainable to those in the lower levels of income. There are homes that have them in great abundance, whose monthly pay checks are small, and homes that lack them completely, with all that wealth can buy. When one sees the many mental ills and maladjustments so often characteristic of children from maladjusted homes, he recognizes how essential a good home is in the development of a faith in a Father-God.

Dominating Purpose

Now comes the necessary task of vocational choice. It would be highly desirable if every young person could make an intelligent vocational choice before graduation from high school. This should be a goal to be sought by every character-building institution, for purposiveness is the central factor in personality integration. As it is, probably not more than one-third of the young men and women who enter our colleges every fall as freshmen have a very definite idea of their vocational aims. And statistics indicate that not more than one-third of these eventually go into the vocation which they had chosen as freshmen. Indeed, an extremely large percentage of graduate seniors go into vocations entirely different from those they had expected to enter even at the end of their college years. There is no time beyond which one may say it is impossible to choose a vocation. One man decided to go into the ministry after his fiftieth birthday. He did so and was eminently successful in the twenty years that followed that decision. The fact remains, however, that vocational choice ought to be made during the high school age, if possible.

Vocational guidance is not to be confused with vocational choice. Vocational guidance is an effort to assist the adolescent in making his choice. It rarely gives advice so narrow that choice is no longer necessary. The niche fallacy, as it is called in psychology, is that there is one and only one vocation for every individual. We know now that this is not true. Most individuals could fit equally well in several vocations. It is well that this is so, for the value of choice in personality is large. The advances made by psychological measurements during the last two decades, however, make possible a quality of vocational guidance far beyond that which has been possible before. When these measurements become available to every high school boy and girl, it is probable that the number of misfits will be reduced by at least fifty percent. Probably more unhappiness comes from being in the wrong vocation than from any other single source. Psychological measurements, therefore, constitute a major contribution of science to human happiness.

Let the adolescent be challenged in the church to choose a vocation in the service of mankind. This does not mean that his choice be confined to a religious vocation or to social service occupations. There is no field of work in which service is not possible. But having learned what his abilities and aptitudes are, and with all the idealism that is characteristic of adolescence, he will probably choose more wisely than at any time in the future.

Vocational choice must not be made without recognizing the practical realities of life. It is foolish and absurd to tell a group of young men and young women that they are to give no thought to the financial side of their vocational choice. Even if they should believe it during this idealistic age, they will soon learn better. Yet, with full recognition of this practical side of the picture, it must never be permitted to become the primary factor in vocational choice. A boy who prepares himself in college for a field for which his interests and abilities fit him, and then takes a job in another field simply because it pays a larger salary, is being very unwise. However important income may be, it can never be as important as the joy and pleasure which come from a job for which one has the greatest enthusiasm. Men who love their jobs, whatever they may be, recognize that over and above the actual financial remuneration, they are receiving additional and immeasurable satisfaction values which money cannot buy.

Why choose a job in the service of mankind? Is this simply because of its ethical character? Could one be quite as happy in a thoroughly self-centered job of high achievement? The answer is clear. There can be no question but that achievement is always thrilling, and if one chooses a purely selfish job, and succeeds in it, he will gain a measure of satisfaction. But the fact is also clear that, because we are by nature social beings, it is far healthier and a much surer road to happiness to choose a vocation which serves one's fellow man.

FATHERLY LOVE

During this period, the central position of the parental drives is not so easily seen as at either earlier age levels or later. The activities of adolescents are usually acquired from the crowd with which they associate. Since all the members of the crowd are on the same level, and since falling in love has become the chief socializing factor, the power of the parental instinct seems for the moment to have been pushed into the background. Of course, these new drives, like all impulses in human nature, ought to be utilized to their fullest extent in the growth of personality. But the fact is the parental drive is still the best one with which to bring about the complete integration of personality. And, as we shall see in the discussion of the traits of fatherly love, it will be at the center of many of the social problems which adolescents encounter.

Being Sensitive to the Needs of Others

It is not easy to discuss these four traits of Christian love separately. As we approach maturity, the very fact of complete integration makes each simply a phase of the unified whole. The attitude or habit of mind which we are designating as being sensitive to the needs of others is of genuine value in the attainment of happiness by the adolescent. Quite apart from its ethical significance, self-centeredness is almost certain to result in unhappiness. When one looks with too great constancy at himself, his inferiorities become much too prominent. Social fears set in and compensations follow. For example, let us look again at the clique. Everyone recognizes its bad qualities, its intolerance for others and its cruelties to new members in the group. But it seems difficult to do anything about it. Why are cliques so exclusive? The answer is that the members of any group cling to that group for security, and fear of inferiority makes them maintain the group integrity and look with disfavor upon enlarging its membership. Question the members of such a clique. Ask them how easily they get along with strangers. Quite commonly the answer will be that they never know what to say to strangers. Teach them the art of meeting people and see how quickly the membership of the group or clique becomes more elastic. It is commonly supposed by many people that the ability to converse easily with strangers is a native gift, perhaps bolstered somewhat by wide experience. Actually such is not the case. Let anyone who has this difficulty try this scheme. Make a list of ten questions which you would like to know about people you meet—what their names are, where they come from, what their purpose is in coming to your town, how they like it, what their interests are, whom they know, etc. Keep this in mind. Then when you meet the next stranger, ask these questions. You will discover some very interesting things. In the first place you are almost certain to like him, for most people are very likable when we really know them. In the second place, you will find that the fear of not being able to make conversation will have entirely disappeared. In the third place, long before you have finished, you are likely to have made a good friend. This is the chief quality of conversation, being interested in the interests and needs and activities of others. For those who think of shyness as their besetting sin, this is one simple remedy which often produces good results.

Social conformity looms exceedingly large as one of the fundamentals of happiness during this period. Adolescents must dress alike, use the same slang, go to the same shows, and do all of the same things. In no period of life are fads and fashions so often changed and so universally adopted as during adolescence. Different groups often adopt different fads and fashions. It is often possible to recognize the undergraduates in some colleges simply by their style of dress and mode of walking and talking. These undergraduates are usually not very conscious of this imitation of each other. They do it because of this pressure of social conformity. Parents and teachers will do well to give due recognition to this unwritten law, and within the bounds of reason to obey it themselves.

Along with the inevitable disillusionment concerning the social evils of our civilization, should go the antidote of becoming equally familiar with the work of the various welfare agencies and other organizations which contribute so unselfishly to the happiness of the less fortunate. This is not an easy attitude to acquire. Adolescent social groups constituted of the upper middle and higher classes are very likely to be quite indifferent and even intolerant of the needs of the lower classes. It often happens that young people from poorer homes find themselves quite ill at ease and unconsciously snubbed when they attend social functions attended largely by these more fortunate young people. Yet, when one looks at the history of our class and race struggles, he is impressed with the fact that, in almost every instance, an important element in their cause is this same indifference and intolerance or even ignorance of each other. Going slumming out of curiosity is not the way to begin social work, and in all probability the appeal to young people of the upper class to become sensitive to the needs of the lower classes will not be accomplished in crowds. It must inevitably be a matter of personal work. If one young person can be brought into intimate contact with another from a different class or group, progress has been made. This needs to be continued in a wide variety of conditions until the youth has been brought into an intimate awareness of most of the problems that face his fellow man. It cannot be acquired through lectures, but only through experience. Again, then, it becomes obvious that it is only through the parental instinct that social coöperation can ever hope to be accomplished.

Forgiveness

The determination to give every man his chance at happiness and success is easy enough as an ideal, but very difficult in everyday practice. Watch the wallflowers at the next college dance and see, if you can, how few young men in that group seem determined to give every girl her chance at happiness and social success. Listen to the remarks which the young men make to each other about the visiting girls and vice versa, if you would discover how extremely cruel young people can be to one another. One young man in a certain college succeeded in making himself by all odds the most unpopular member of that student body. It is not likely that he sought this distinction, for later evidence revealed that it caused him only mental agony. Later, on one fateful day his mother came to see him. He was away when she arrived, and some of the other students entertained her while she waited. She proved to be a very charming woman, and to have high dreams and visions for her son. It was interesting to observe that after that the boy's popularity increased and he ceased to be just another student but became, rather, his mother's son, and everyone felt a parental responsibility for him. One could hardly find a more clear-cut illustration of the parental instinct in action than in this instance.

Again let it be emphasized that this cruelty is almost invariably a compensation for a sense of inferiority. When attention can be withdrawn from one individual and placed on another, this inferiority disappears. It often happens that young men or women with modest endowment in physical attractiveness give themselves so wholeheartedly to helping others find happiness that they achieve a popularity which is the envy of their more fortunately endowed fellows. A girl, not at all attractive, was finding life very miserable. There did not seem to be any way at all in which she could excel other girls. Finally, it was discovered that she had one trait not too common among adolescents, namely, dependability. Adolescents usually are interested in so many things that they cannot keep their minds on their obligations and, therefore, need a good deal of guidance in the performance of their contracted duties. This girl, however, could be depended upon to do anything required of her. She was given more and more tasks and from them gained a sense of achievement and the admiration of her friends. Her popularity increased and her personality became obviously more attractive and wholesome.

Theoretically, this is the easiest age of all in which to develop this trait. The idealism which comes along with sexual maturity makes it very easy to enlist the enthusiastic support of adolescents in any type of social welfare. To give the adolescent a realistic and enthusiastic view of our social institutions, and at the same time a zeal for social progress, is both the privilege and the duty of the character education program in any church.

Finally, the drama-type approach can be utilized to very good advantage in the achievement of this trait. A recognition of one's own strengths and weaknesses as well as the strengths and weaknesses of his fellows can bring about an easy recognition of the value of coöperation. To discover the importance of every part of our social structure is an important lesson in social growth. Projects should be devised for young people's groups which have in them tasks requiring the various abilities of the group's membership. Through them young people gain practice in this art of recognizing the importance of other people and discover that even for their own happiness it is important to see that others have their chance at happiness and success.

The pleasure that comes from seeing that others have happiness is discovered only by experience. Adolescents should be encouraged to be thoughtful of the less popular members of the group. This does not mean, however, that adolescents can be persuaded to choose the right friends by admonition. They regularly insist upon choosing their own friends. Guidance in the choice of friends for an adolescent has to be very wisely camouflaged if it is to be effective. Patience will usually bring the results desired by his elders. In the back of his mind is a real confidence in the wisdom of his parents. If they do not approve of his friends, sooner or later he is likely to discard them unless his parents stimulate the friendship by their antagonism. Furthermore, parents should keep it in mind that intersocial group experience in itself is fine social training. It is training in a democracy of a sort all too rare even in our American civilization. A most important point which parents must keep in mind in this matter of unwise friendships is to be sure that they do not accomplish their ends at the expense of the happiness of the friend. A child's friends should always be welcome in his home. They should go away feeling happy and glad to have been there. To hurt them by embarrassing experiences will do far more damage than any good which can conceivably be achieved by it.

Magnanimity

"The measure of a man is the size of the thing it takes to get his goat." Here is a concept which, once acquired, can do more to achieve magnanimity in the personality of the youth than almost any other method. Anger is unquestionably the most powerful enemy of peace in society and, along with fear, the most powerful in personality. It is best eliminated by changing one's attitudes so as to bring out a different response to the situations which once were reacted to with anger. The methods of controlling one's temper which were once so common in child training are seldom effective. To count ten before you strike is perhaps the most foolish of them all. Actually, when a situation arises to which the individual has learned to respond with anger, the response is immediate. It does not require reasoning and, as a matter of fact, reasoning is actually inhibited. It is an old trick to try to anger one's opponent in an argument so that he may not think so clearly.

Perhaps the best approach to the solution of the problem is to build up in the child an ideal of magnanimity. Our own anger always seems to be righteous indignation. It is quite easy to see, however, how petty this same indignation is in someone else. Truly great men are almost always characterized by their ability to control their tempers. The little man, who goes about with a chip on his shoulder, seldom commands very much respect in the eyes of those who know him. Once having seen this fact, the adolescent has learned the first lesson in the final development of this trait; namely, the desire for it. He cannot but admire this quality in Jesus which expressed itself so many times. Often his disciples were filled with anger when he himself showed no such tendency. And, even when he was being executed as a common criminal, he demonstrated the magnificence of his personality by showing that his thoughts were on those about him and not on himself.

Race and class discrimination and prejudice create factors of destruction in personality which are harmful both to the individual and to society. As has been pointed out, a part of it is due to the training the child has received at home at earlier age levels. It is astonishing, however, when we look at it, to discover how many factors in our educational system contribute to this end. In the public schools, sectioning of children by abilities into groups, A, B, and C, can become the source of a great deal of intergroup prejudice. It may be a practical necessity in order to utilize individual differences to the best advantage, but at least it does not need to be preached from the housetops, and it can be dealt with positively by changing the curriculum itself so that the lower groups feel that they are specializing in a different sort of work. Publicly branding children as stupid never does them any good. During the high school age, it is important that young men and women become aware of the level of their capacities, but this information should be thought of as personal and private and not something to be published on the bulletin board. Other factors which contribute to this same type of prejudice are discriminations against colored people, or Jewish people, or the foreign-born. Individual differences in race and nationality are facts. To ignore them is simply shutting one's eyes to reality. They have to be met and dealt with for what they are. But if it is recognized that each has a contribution to make to our social welfare, and if each admires the contribution of the other, a social structure can exist in which these prejudices and biases are not so destructive to personality as they now are. Economic discrimination is often stimulated by clothes, cars, and excessive allotments of spending money.

One of the most important sources of irritation during adolescence is the problem of parental authority. This is especially true with girls. It will be recalled that when young people express their interest in various problems girls usually put this one in first place. Boys are given a great deal more freedom and consequently the problem is a little less significant for them. There can be little question but that parents have all the unselfish intentions in the world in dealing with their children. They are primarily concerned for their welfare. They recognize how easy it is for young people in a moment of thoughtlessness to do something which will cause them much unhappiness. The young people themselves, however, have the most implicit confidence in their own self-reliance. The boy who drives his car at seventy miles an hour on a slippery road is only attempting to show off to his girl. He is quite sure of his ability to handle every possible situation. The girl who takes a drink or so in order that she may not be thought a poor sport is only doing what she thinks is necessary to gain social approval. In the one case, it is an appetite for achievement, and in the other for social approval. After all, these young people are mature and it is a part of their training as well as their right to have a very large measure of intelligent choice. On the other hand, the young people themselves are wrong in their estimations of the way to get achievement and social approval. The solution lies in exactly the same principle that we have been using throughout the book. Other forms of achievement and other forms of social approval must be found which do not involve these dangers nor require such strict parental authority. If young people can be given the concept that safety and self-control are evidences of maturity, they can learn to outgrow the more infantile concept of manliness, which consists in walking into mud puddles at seven and driving a car at exorbitant speeds at twenty-one. As for social approval, let them look for themselves at the individuals who are most popular and try to discover the qualities that give them popularity. This will be quite sufficient, for they will discover that recklessness is not one of the necessary roads to popularity. There has never been the remotest evidence in the studies that have been made which suggests that immoral behavior has any relationship whatsoever to popularity. Finally, parents must realize that in a very short while these young people are going out from their homes to form homes of their own, and that unless they have been taught the lessons necessary for taking care of themselves, they are not likely to be able to do this intelligently when the task is suddenly thrust upon them. That dangers beset the path of too much freedom for these young people, no one can deny, but far greater dangers result from over-protection. Many a boy or girl goes to college who, according to all reports, has led an exemplary life up to that time, and then proceeds to run wild. Often the colleges are blamed. That is seldom just. If young students come to college with the moral stamina which should have been gained from previous years of practice in self-reliance, they will leave college as fine and self-reliant as they entered it.

Christian Courage

There are two important phases in the final development of this trait. The first one has to do with leadership, the second with acquiring a philosophy of life built around the principle of vicarious sacrifice.

Genuine leadership now comes to the front and needs extensive training. Certainly one of the most important values which a young people's group in a church can contribute to its membership is training in leadership. The capacity for speaking in public can be acquired by the simple method of frequent practice. It is quite unfortunate, however, that most of our young people's groups do not have in them experts who can give advice in developing the quality of this capacity. Everyone who attends our various club meetings knows that a majority of men and women are capable and willing to stand in front of an audience and express their opinions. They know also that an astonishingly small percentage of them have the capacity to do this well. Every such organization ought to have a public speaking adviser whose task it is to help these young people not only acquire the courage to talk but to master the many principles which make for effective speaking. It is desirable that every young person, whatever his native endowment and intelligence and natural leadership ability, should learn to express himself in public. The fears that keep so many young men and women from learning this can be overcome better now than they ever can be again. Young people often think that when they are a little older it will be much easier. Actually, every adult knows that it becomes increasingly difficult.

It is not completely clear just what all the qualities of leadership are. There are a great many factors which enter into this ability. Natural leadership seems to some extent to be an inborn characteristic. It depends also on being able to excel in several things. If by leadership is meant the capacity to hold high office and dominate groups, then not everyone ought to be a leader. That is a special ability just as is art and musical performance. Training in *followership* may be quite as important as training in leadership. One of the most interesting studies which has been made on this subject [7] seems to indicate that the most important factor is mutual attractiveness between the leader and the members of his group. To dislike people is quite fatal to becoming a good leader. To be disliked by people is equally disastrous. But the ability to like people can be learned, as has been pointed out. Perhaps the willingness to contribute whatever one has to the welfare of the group as a whole is the best definition of leadership. Using this definition, everyone can have some leadership. If this contribution consists in undertaking positions of high responsibility, it is really no greater contribution than if the responsibilities are less conspicuous.

[7] Cole, L., *Psychology of Adolescence*, p. 116 (Farrar and Rinehart, Inc., New York, 1936).

One of the most important qualities to be developed by young people during this period is dependability. Everyone who has tried to find positions for young people knows that if, in his recommendation, he can comment with enthusiasm upon the dependability of the young person concerned, this will go further than almost any other single factor. Yet commonplace as this may seem, in one large group of young people less than one-tenth could be said to have this quality. A student who was doing some work for me some years ago, for which he was receiving government aid, spent many more hours on the job than the number for which he received government compensation. Everyone knows what a contrast this is to the attitude of a great many people who have received the same type of compensation. When he had graduated, a prospective employer wrote to me about him. When I described what he had done while with me he was immediately employed, for as the employer stated it, "That's the sort of man any employer wants." Someone has said, and this is an excellent philosophy for young people, "It is not very important to be paid as much as you are worth, but it is tremendously important to be worth as much as you are paid."

The other important phase of the development of this trait has to do with the principle of vicarious sacrifice. Why Jesus should have been crucified, or why any of the great men should have been persecuted, is not easy to see. But as one looks through the history of the growth of civilization it becomes obvious that little progress has been made except through the medium of vicarious sacrifice. A practical attitude to take toward social problems might be expressed, "Work for justice but do not expect it." However much logical objection might be brought against such a philosophy, and however unjust it may seem, the fact remains that if one is to be happy he must accept it. Discussing the Parable of the Prodigal Son, young people often resent the treatment of the elder brother. They insist that his contention is right, that he was not given a square deal. Yet everyone knows that that sort of thing happens every day and that the only person who suffered through the older brother's behavior was the older brother, himself.

A practical expression of this injustice has to do with getting appreciation for what one accomplishes. There can be no doubt in any man's mind that applause is sweet. The man who maintains that he does not like it is either deceiving himself or has a mental aberration. Every man likes it. But if it becomes one's main reward, and if one's energy and perseverance are entirely determined by how much applause he may get, then most certainly he will find his adjustment problems difficult. The opinion of others is always of value, but not necessarily always right. When one is easily swayed from his central purpose by such opinion, he is likely to become a pretty weak type of personality. From the point of view of happiness, if one worries about every criticism which he receives, he will spend most of his life worrying. It is good judgment to live and guide one's behavior according to the wishes of his fellow men as far as that is consistent with his purpose. But if he has done the best he can, and then gets criticism where he does not deserve it, it is far better to ignore it, or at most to evaluate it and then think no more about it. Trying to please everybody is the most hopeless task men ever invented. True Christian courage, then, consists in getting a vision of what one may expect to accomplish in life and dedicating his whole life to the achievement of that ambition regardless of what the consequences may be.

Another form of social injustice is gossip. Few forms of mental disease are as common or malicious as this one. Sometimes gossip becomes disastrous, but in most cases it is not worth the unhappiness and worry it causes. If the gossip is unfounded, which it almost always is, sooner or later the truth will come out and the effect of the gossip be dissipated. In any case, it is a great mistake in the search for happiness either to fight gossip or be swayed from one's duty by it.

Another aspect of this same trait was mentioned in connection with purpose. Very frequently, young people are brought up to have far too great a respect for money and too intense a fear of poverty. As has been pointed out, to deny the significance of such resources and the security that they carry with them is sheer impractical idealism. On the other hand, to make it central in one's thinking is equally dangerous to human happiness. In discussing the vocational problems of his son, one business man put it this way, "My son wants to be a business man and I believe he has the qualities to succeed. But I am trying to instill in him the idea that making money is not the chief evidence of success in business. I am telling him this, not because of some idealistic theory which I have acquired, but because as I look at my own life I find that the desire to make money and the fear of losing money have caused me more unhappiness than any other single factor." The things of which we are afraid and which, therefore, destroy courage are almost invariably associated with such values as wealth. Training in true courage consists in re-evaluating life and its experiences and putting the high estimates on those qualities which are certain, such as the capacity for achievement and contributing to social welfare. The principle of vicarious sacrifice is not some mystical, highly impractical principle; it is an indispensable principle by which genuine happiness and high courage can be gained and maintained.

The principle of vicarious sacrifice is certainly not foreign to human nature. There are many ways in which it expresses itself in every man's life, quite normally and wholesomely. When a young man falls in love he dreams of rescuing his beloved from some dangerous situation at the risk of his own life. This does not mean that he values his life less, but that he has found values which are greater. Many a football player risks life and limb in the less spectacular positions on the team. He knows that most of the glory will go to the ball carrier, but his interest is in the success of the team rather than in personal glory. Sacrifice will not be successfully inspired in many people by urging them to make it from a sense of duty. One does not sacrifice his own pleasures except when he sees more worthwhile achievements and greater values to be gained by it. We do things only to gain a sense of achievement, social approval, and the satisfaction of appetites. The principle of vicarious sacrifice is not an exception but an illustration of this fact.

Drama-type Education in the High School and College Age

We come now to the discussion of an actual program of character development which could be provided by a church for this age group. The same general principles which apply to drama-type education throughout the lower age levels need to be utilized in the development of this program. The formula of using the abilities of each individual to overcome his weaknesses or to inculcate needed traits applies here as before. The data on which this program has been built come from four distinct sources.

The first one is, of course, the psychological nature of the individual at this age level. As we have seen, the outstanding characteristic of mental life here, as distinguished from the earlier stages, is the capacity for what might be termed philosophical reasoning. The grasping of concepts of thought implied in educational, social, political, and religious theories can now for the first time be brought within the understanding of the individual. Adolescents like to discuss things and are highly idealistic. From the point of view of religion, then, it is easy to see that the chief aim ought to be the formation of a dynamic, forceful, Christian philosophy of life.

The second source of data comes from the interests of the adolescent. Because they are the things which attract him, these interests must be in the very center of any successful program. They represent individual differences; therefore one may anticipate that these differences will be of such a nature that a division into groups studying different problems will always be desirable. Just as in the lower age levels capacities were used for placing children in various rôles, so in this period interests form one of the chief sources for intelligent division. To be sure, test results on the profile also play an important part in this division, and an even more important part in the activity of each individual within his division. However, a close relationship will be found between the interests of the individual and his abilities.

The third source of data on which we construct our program consists of the problems and needs of this age group and individual members in it. In general, these problems correspond very closely to interests. However, there are many of them which the adolescent does not recognize in himself at all or which, if he does, he is not willing to admit. Indeed, there are many of them which are better not recognized too sharply. It is not particularly healthy mentally to call the attention of high school boys or girls to the fact that they are making a very bad social adjustment. A more wholesome plan is to give them places in the program in which they get training of this sort without recognizing its purpose to this end. These problems have already been enumerated so that they need not be elaborated here.

The last source of data is the social structure to which the adolescent is soon going to be required to adjust. He must now make a vocational choice. He must soon take his place in the development of a home. He has now come to the point in which the problem of education should be one in which he participates actively instead of on the basis of compulsory requirements. He is going to be a citizen and must understand the basic principles of good citizenship. He is going to be a member of his church and should begin to grasp the basic problems the churches face and prepare himself for taking his share of the responsibilities.

Here, then, is the basis upon which the following program has been built. Perhaps no section of the educational program of the Church has more to achieve in such a short space of time than during adolescence. To waste this time and interest without a specific purpose of accomplishment is a gross misappropriation of responsibility. The formation of a dynamic Christian philosophy which will mean something in the whole future life of the individual is no simple task when the time for it is as short as it is in most of our schools of religious education. Moreover, because of their mature intelligence, adolescents are able to distinguish easily between that which is solid and that which is superficial. They may attend and participate in a purely social program, as a form of recreation. They have greater respect for a worthwhile educational program, as a basic factor in their personality development. They may complain that it is too much like school, but if they recognize its worth, they will accept it.

Proposed Curriculum

A. The Christian Philosophy of Life

The basic course must be related to this title. Not infrequently, young people's groups discuss and argue about current events, various personal problems, and political issues, which may have a certain amount of value. The fact remains, however, that if our purpose is to give them a Christian philosophy of life, this must be done in a very definite and thorough fashion. It is false to suppose that they have acquired the fundamentals of Jesus' teaching in their earlier years and that by some mysterious capacity they are able to apply the Christian philosophy to these various problems. In the first place, their minds have not been mature enough to understand the Christian philosophy, even if it had been taught them. And in the second place, the simple committing to memory of sections of Scripture does not guarantee either understanding or application. The Christian philosophy is as complex and profound as that of any other theory of human life. It seems probable that one of the reasons for the decreasing influence of the Christian Church on society is that the great bulk of church members do not know and therefore cannot apply the fundamental principles of Christianity to the problems that face them. Common sense is not enough, and the notion that we inherit a conscience which tells us the difference between right and wrong is a fallacy. It is not true that if every man does what he thinks to be best, he will be a Christian. It is important, therefore, that the basic task of our work with adolescents be to give them the fundamental principles of Jesus' teachings. It would seem desirable that perhaps the first year of high school should be spent studying the life of Jesus as an orientation course, and that the other years be devoted to the grasping and application of the basic Christian principles. The main essentials of this Christian philosophy of life, which we emphasize above all others, are: first, the eight traits about which so much has already been said in this book, and secondly, the philosophy bound up in the Lord's Prayer, to be used as a blueprint for spiritual thinking. These should be applied, then, to as many different problems as possible.

It is assumed that every other course in this adolescent program will use these fundamental principles as their basic criteria for discussion.

B. Fields of Adjustment

The other courses in this senior curriculum have to do with the various types of adjustment which the adolescent is called upon to make. These fields of adjustment may be divided roughly into three groups: problems of personal adjustment, problems centering around the choice and preparation for a vocation, and social problems including citizenship, community responsibilities, home adjustments and preparation for church work. Around these fields of adjustment the following courses can be set up.

1. The Art of Living

The first of these courses has to do with all the personal problems in which the adolescent is interested. They vary from such questions as health and food to such problems as sex adjustment and emotional stability. The teachers for such a course as this must be very carefully chosen, first, for their fundamental knowledge of the Christian religion, second, for their competence to deal with these problems, and third, for their understanding and sympathy with adolescents themselves. Christian principles must be applied in the discussion of these problems quite as well as elsewhere. This is not a place for argument only, but discussion based on presented facts.

2. Choosing a Vocation

During the high school period, every boy and girl should, if possible, select the vocational field in which he proposes to spend his life. A course devoted to guidance in this task should include a careful study of all the possible fields of work, both as to their requirements in personality and training and as to their significance in a Christian social structure. The laboratory work of such a course would include tests and the study of the evidence gained in the personality profile for choosing one's vocation. Again, it is especially important that the teacher of such a course be constantly subjecting its problems and difficulties to the basic principles of the Christian philosophy of life.

3. Philosophy of Education

Previous to the high school age, education has been to the child one of the necessary requirements of his daily life. For the most part, he has taken it without much question and evaluated it in terms of likes and dislikes, success or failure. The time has come now, however, when he ought to see the basic principles underlying our various theories of education. This is not commonly done by high school students, but the fact is that they are asking many questions about the whys and wherefores of their high school courses. A fairly thorough understanding of the philosophical principles of education in general is needed as a foundation for answering these questions.[8] A personal interest in education, with a background of the Christian philosophy of life upon which to build, could do much toward making the school adjustment of our adolescent boys and girls happier and more purposeful. In our testing program, we have found a great many young people with mental endowments sufficient for superior academic work who rank reasonably low in their classes. Unquestionably the most important reason for this is a lack of vision concerning education and its methods. This course, like all others, would depend upon its leadership, but given the right leadership, it should be one of the most valuable in the entire curriculum. Then, too, such practical information as methods of study and reading efficiency is immensely helpful in the problem of adjustment. It is much easier to like to do things if we can do them well. Our enthusiasm for education will be enhanced if the acquiring of it is not too difficult.

4. Christian Citizenship

The widespread interest of young people's groups in the discussion of current events is ample evidence of the need for a course in Christian citizenship. To be sure, they take courses in civics and political science, both in high school and college. In the very nature of the case, however, these courses cannot include the basic principles of the Christian philosophy, and thus make it possible to distinguish between the Christian theory of political institutions and other theories. Such a course might well make use of the type of thing that is done in our model leagues and model assemblies, including debates and other similar activities. Local political problems as well as state, national and international ones, ought to be discussed. Let us be certain, however, that this course does not become a poor imitation of those given in school. There is no need for duplication. Let

[8] Douglass, Harl R., *Secondary Education for Youth in Modern America* (American Council on Education, Washington, D. C., 1937).

us concentrate on the Christian philosophy in its application to these problems.

5. The Work of the Church

When we look back upon the training that the great majority of our church leaders received, or rather did not receive, it is really remarkable that our churches are as efficient as they are. These high school boys and girls are very soon going to be taking their places as Sunday school teachers, officers in various church organizations, and finally as members of the official boards. How much more effective our church leadership will be if a good share of the time of these high school boys and girls is spent in actual training for church leadership. Such a course ought to give them a vision for the place of the church in society and especially in its potentialities as over and above its actualities. It ought to present for their discussion actual problems which church boards discuss. It should give them training in educational methods as well as the Christian philosophy of life, so that they can contribute in some genuine fashion to the teaching staff of our church schools. Finally it should give them an understanding of every aspect of the church life: its music, its various societies, and its far-reaching activities. Again, model church boards, model churches and many other types of laboratory work can be given in a course of this sort.

This is not an exhaustive list of the courses which can profitably be given in the senior departments of our church schools. These courses, however, do form the foundation for personality development, on the one hand, and for development of Christian leadership on the other. In all of them the Christian philosophy of life ought to be the central force, and in every one of them individual differences should be recognized, and the young people given training according to their own individual capacities and their own individual developmental needs.

Conclusion

It is evident that the limitations of this book have made necessary an inadequate discussion of these problems of adolescence. This does not mean that adolescence is any more important than any other stage in the development of personality, but it does mean that the increasing complexity of mental life, the coming of maturity and especially the need for developing a sound philosophy of life make any adequate discussion of adolescence necessarily very long.

The personality questionnaire which follows could be many times as long as it is. Only the most important aspects of the adolescent personality have been included. It is hoped, however, that it will be found adequate for gaining a more accurate recognition of the individual personalities with whom we come in contact as parents and teachers, and give purposiveness to our efforts in dealing with them.

QUESTIONNAIRE FOR ADOLESCENCE

In the square preceding each question write a number, 5, 4, 3, 2, or 1. After each question is a series of five possible answers to the question, numbered 5, 4, 3, 2, and 1, respectively. In the square use the number preceding the phrase which most nearly represents your answer.

In a few questions, some other information is desired. The nature of this and how to indicate the answer are included in the question involved.

Psychological Development

☐ 1. How much natural physical attractiveness has this young person?
5 Physically very attractive, 4 above average, 3 average, 2 modestly endowed in this respect, 1 physically very unattractive

☐ 2. What kind of food does he (she) prefer to eat?
5 Good wholesome food, 4 a reasonably healthy diet, 3 eats some rich and undigestible foods, 2 eats a great deal of unwholesome food, 1 eats almost nothing but rich unwholesome food

☐ 3. How subject is he (she) to skin infections such as pimples?

5 Has completely clear healthy skin, 4 has few skin infections, 3 some, 2 a great many, 1 has very bad skin

☐ 4. How interested is he (she) in athletic activities?

5 His (her) main interest, 4 a great deal of interest, 3 normal interest, 2 not much, 1 no interest at all

☐ 5. How mature is he (she) sexually from a physical point of view?

5 Completely mature, 4 somewhat mature for age, 3 maturing normally, 2 rather immature for age, 1 completely immature sexually

☐ 6. Has his (her) voice changed? (Girls' voices change as well as boys', although not so much.)

5 Has complete adult quality, 4 approaching adult status, 3 changing rapidly, 2 beginning to change, 1 has not changed at all

Trait I

☐ 7. How idealistic do you consider him (her) to be?

5 Has splendid ideals, 4 above average, 3 average, 2 does not seem to think much about ideals, 1 never thinks about ideals

☐ 8. How ambitious is he (she)? That is, does he (she) think and talk about the future and then do work toward that goal?

5 Very ambitious, 4 above average, 3 average, 2 does not have much ambition, 1 apparently has no ambition

☐ 9. Does he (she) daydream very much?

5 About normal, 4 never, 3 more than average, 2 a great deal, 1 almost continuously

☐ 10. Are his (her) daydreams stimulating or are they spent in imagining achievements which are impossible for him (her) in reality?

5 Very stimulating, 4 usually stimulating, 3 at least they are about things he (she) hopes to accomplish in the future, 2 dreams of achievements he (she) cannot make in reality, 1 his (her) daydreams are very unrealistic retreats from reality

☐ 11. What sort of vision does he (she) have for his (her) future vocation?
5 Stimulating and inspiring vision for it, 4 very enthusiastic about it, 3 looks forward to it, 2 rather indifferent to it, 1 has no respect for it at all except as a way to make money

☐ 12. What is his (her) conception of greatness?
5 A life successfully devoted to the service of men, 4 a job well done, 3 a job of outward importance, 2 winning fame and renown, 1 getting rich and having high social position

☐ 13. What sort of social vision does he (she) have? That is, as he (she) considers our present social chaos, what sort of notions does he (she) have about how to better them?
5 Rational and splendidly optimistic, 4 optimistic but not too practical, 3 very enthusiastic and idealistic but not at all real, 2 somewhat pessimistic and cynical, 1 has none

☐ 14. How much time does he (she) spend in careful thought?
5 A great deal, 4 more than average, 3 some, 2 a little, 1 almost none at all

15. How stimulating are the following activities to the quality and depth of his (her) imagination? Rate each separately.
5 Very stimulating, 4 stimulating, 3 of little value, 2 of no value, 1 he (she) does not even care for them

☐ Travel	☐ Clubs and hobbies
☐ Books and lectures	☐ Adventures in business

Trait II

☐ 16. What is his (her) concept of righteousness or being good?
5 Has challenging, positive and attractive ideas of goodness, 4 definitely positive, 3 somewhat negative, 2 entirely negative but socially desirable, 1 entirely negative, foolish and not to be sought after

☐ 17. What kind of moral principles govern his (her) behavior, regardless of his (her) professions and beliefs?
5 Splendidly wholesome ones, 4 realistic and healthy, 3 normal for age, 2 not completely moral, 1 definitely immoral

☐ 18. What is the quality of his (her) self-control from a moral point of view?

5 Gives the impression of having strong moral courage, 4 is rather idealistic but not very realistic, 3 his (her) morals are mostly negative and done only because they are right, 2 shows prudishness in unwholesome quantity, 1 is very prudish, even abnormal and neurotic.

☐ 19. What is the nature of the attitudes he (she) holds in regard to sex questions?

5 Indicate splendid moral integrity, 4 indicate moral courage without sufficient knowledge, 3 rather indifferent to these questions, 2 dreads them, 1 fears and refuses to discuss them

☐ 20. How complete and wholesome is his (her) sex education?

5 Very complete and wholesome, 4 wholesome but not complete, 3 somewhat inadequate, 2 inadequate and somewhat unwholesome, 1 has none except that picked up from undesirable sources

☐ 21. How much interest does he (she) have in religion?

5 Very much, 4 more than average, 3 some, 2 not much, 1 none at all

22. How much interest does he (she) have in the following?

5 Very much, 4 more than average, 3 some, 2 not much, 1 none at all

☐ Bible classes
☐ Religious discussion groups
☐ Theological problems
☐ Philosophical problems
☐ Social and political problems
☐ Problems of adjustment
☐ Educational problems
☐ Just arguing

☐ 23. How much genuine understanding does he (she) have of the teachings of Jesus?

5 Very thorough and profound, 4 more than average, 3 some but not very thorough, 2 entirely superficial and inadequate, 1 none at all

☐ 24. How well adjusted is he (she) to his (her) educational work?

5 Perfectly adjusted, 4 satisfactorily adjusted, 3

rather indifferent to school work, 2 somewhat bored and unadjusted, 1 antagonistic and badly maladjusted

25. How efficient are his (her) study habits, especially the ones listed below?

5 Very efficient, 4 fair, 3 average, 2 poor, 1 exceedingly inefficient

- ☐ Concentration
- ☐ Work schedule
- ☐ Notebooks
- ☐ Organization of material
- ☐ Taking notes
- ☐ Reading speed
- ☐ Reading comprehension
- ☐ Relating materials of different courses to each other

Trait III

☐ 26. Is he (she) in general optimistic or pessimistic toward life?

5 Has an intelligent optimism, 4 rather unrealistic optimism, 3 does not think much about it, 2 tends to be rather pessimistic, 1 very pessimistic and cynical

27. What is his (her) attitude toward his (her) own natural endowments?

5 Enthusiastic and confident, 4 satisfied, 3 does not think much about them, 2 rather inclined to feel inferior, 1 feels very unhappy and inferior about them

☐ Intelligence ☐ Strength and athletic ability
☐ Special aptitudes ☐ Physical attractiveness

☐ 28. What is his (her) concept of God?

5 Thinks of Him as friendly and powerful, 4 powerful but rather impersonal, 3 powerful but very impersonal, 2 cruel and tyrannical, 1 believes there is none

☐ 29. What is his (her) attitude toward the problem of evil? That is, what does he (she) think of the sin, suffering, disease, physical handicaps, and social injustices in the world?

5 Believes that behind it is a challenge to learn the spiritual laws of a friendly universe, 4 does not understand it but accepts it with faith in a good God, 3 does

not think much about it, 2 thinks it disproves idea of Father-God, 1 entirely pessimistic and bitter

☐ 30. How much of a sense of disillusionment does he (she) have in regard to the idealistic concepts he (she) acquired as a child?

5 His (her) ideals have matured through the years, leaving no sense of disillusionment at all, 4 very little sense of disillusionment, 3 has accepted necessary changes in childhood ideas without much worry, 2 has a fairly strong bitter sense of disillusionment, 1 is still as naïvely idealistic as a child

☐ 31. What is his (her) reaction to popularity? That is, is he (she) willing to sacrifice his (her) principles to gain it or does he (she) always have the courage of his (her) convictions?

5 Enjoys popularity but always has the courage of his (her) convictions, 4 very seldom sacrifices a principle for popularity, 3 usually conforms to the ideals of the crowd and does what they do, 2 very easily influenced by those about him (her), 1 frequently does things of immoral nature in an effort to gain popularity

☐ 32. What is his (her) attitude toward his (her) home and parents?

5 Enthusiastic and confident, 4 holds them in high regard, 3 considers them about average, 2 has little regard for or interest in them, 1 dislikes them and wishes to get away from them

☐ 33. What is his (her) attitude toward religion and church?

5 An active participation and wholesome attitude, 4 fairly active participation, 3 rather indifferent to it, 2 completely indifferent, 1 holds it in contempt

☐ 34. What is his (her) concept of prayer?

5 A wholesome source of strength, 4 useful in meditation, 3 accepts it rather mechanically, 2 has a somewhat superstitious Santa Claus notion of it, 1 has no interest in it at all

Trait IV

☐ 35. How definitely has he (she) chosen his (her) vocation?

5 Knows exactly what he (she) wants to do, and bends every effort in preparing for it, 4 is fairly sure of what

he (she) wants to do, 3 has chosen a vocation but not entirely sure of it, 2 very doubtful of what vocation he (she) will enter, 1 has not even thought of a vocation which appeals to him (her)

☐ 36. How well informed is he (she) about the various vocations?

5 Has thoroughly investigated the nature of all of the important ones, 4 knows quite a lot about the important ones, 3 has about average information, 2 does not know much about most of them, 1 has little or no vocational information

37. What is his (her) concept of the nature and value of each of the following vocations?

5 Very interesting and worthwhile, 4 reasonably so, 3 an acceptable vocation, 2 good way to make a living, but not interesting, 1 very undesirable from all points of view

☐ Business
☐ Ministry
☐ Medicine
☐ High school teaching
☐ Engineering
☐ Work as mechanic
☐ Commercial travelling
☐ Railroad work
☐ Aviation
☐ Stenography
☐ Religious work
☐ Writing
☐ Forms of fine art
☐ Army and navy
☐ Clerical work
☐ Law
☐ College teaching
☐ Grade school teaching
☐ Research work
☐ Work as grocery clerk
☐ Work as store salesman
☐ Garage work
☐ Nursing
☐ Housekeeping
☐ Carpentry
☐ Painting and papering
☐ Musical vocations
☐ Gardening

☐ 38. How well does he (she) know the nature and extent of his (her) aptitudes and abilities?

5 Has obtained results of psychological tests, 4 has turned to other sources, such as opinions of friends, 3 has his (her) own ideas backed up by experience, 2 has very little notion of his (her) abilities, 1 has taken no thought about them at all

☐ 39. How much professional vocational guidance has he (she) secured?

5 A great deal, 4 some, 3 a little, 2 very little, 1 none

☐ 40. How rational a vocational choice has he (she) made?

5 It fits his (her) abilities and opportunities splendidly, 4 somewhat over-idealistic, 3 a normal sensible choice, 2 based entirely on financial returns, 1 completely out of line with both his (her) abilities and opportunities

☐ 41. How dependable is he (she) in carrying out the tasks assigned to him (her)?

5 Completely dependable, 4 above average, 3 average, 2 not very dependable, 1 completely unreliable

42. How talented is he (she) in the following aptitudes?

5 Very talented, 4 above average, 3 some ability, 2 very little ability, 1 almost no ability

☐ Imagination ☐ Art
☐ Music ☐ Mechanical aptitude

43. In the following special aptitudes does he (she) have many opportunities of expression, either by hobbies, school courses, or vocation?

5 Constant opportunity, 4 frequent opportunities, 3 some opportunities, 2 not many opportunities, 1 no opportunities

☐ Imagination ☐ Art
☐ Music ☐ Mechanical aptitude

44. How much interest does he (she) have in the following special aptitudes?

5 Very great interest, 4 above average, 3 some interest, 2 a little interest, 1 almost no interest

☐ Imagination ☐ Art
☐ Music ☐ Mechanical aptitude

Trait V

☐ 45. How much interest and sensitiveness does he (she) show to the wishes and activities of those about him (her)?

5 Very much alive to the wishes of those about him (her), 4 shows considerable interest in others, 3 shows some such interest, 2 is not much concerned with what others think, 1 entirely self-centered

46. How popular is he (she) with young people his (her) own age? Rate each sex separately.

    5 Very popular, 4 above average, 3 average, 2 rather unpopular, 1 very unpopular

    ☐ Members of the same sex
    ☐ Members of the opposite sex

☐ 47. How generally affectionate is he (she) by nature?

    5 Very affectionate, 4 above average, 3 average, 2 not very affectionate, 1 very unaffectionate

☐ 48. How often does he (she) fall in love?

    5 Very frequently, 4 fairly often, 3 rarely, 2 only once, 1 never

☐ 49. How intolerant and closely bound is the clique of which he (she) is a member?

    5 Very loosely bound, with frequent changes and new admissions, 4 not too difficult for new members to gain admission, 3 fairly large clique, but difficult to join, 2 small clique which stays entirely by itself, 1 stays alone, does not belong to any clique or crowd

☐ 50. How much given is he (she) to meeting strangers and making them feel at home in the group?

    5 A splendid mixer, makes everyone feel at home, 4 above average, 3 greets strangers but feels ill at ease about finding conversation, 2 avoids meeting strangers whenever possible, 1 very shy and avoids crowds as much as possible

51. How much does he (she) conform to the habits and customs of the group of which he (she) is a member?

    5 Conforms wholesomely, without being a slave to the group, 4 usually conforms, 3 conforms too rigidly, 2 rather likes to be different in an obvious fashion, 1 rigid conformity because of fear to differ

    ☐ In dress ☐ Morals
    ☐ Slang ☐ Amusements and games

☐ 52. How much knowledge and sympathy has he (she) with the conditions and needs of classes and groups less fortunate than himself (herself)?

    5 Has very great interest in them, 4 some interest, 3 a little interest, 2 little or no interest, 1 does not even know anything about their conditions and needs

Trait VI

☐ 53. How keen is his (her) sense of fair play?
5 Tries to see that everyone has a chance at winning, 4 never breaks a rule, but is not an especially good loser, 3 never breaks a rule but refuses to play a game he (she) cannot win, 2 will cheat from time to time to win, 1 wants to win at any cost, with no thought of anyone else

☐ 54. How good a team player is he (she)?
5 Willing to submerge his (her) own personality entirely for team success, 4 a good team player, 3 a good team player if he (she) gets some glory, 2 rather a grandstand player, 1 refuses to play on the team except for his (her) own glory

☐ 55. What is his (her) attitude toward wallflowers or unpopular members of the group?
5 Goes out of his (her) way to see that they have a good time, 4 fairly thoughtful of them, 3 tends to be indifferent to them, 2 avoids them carefully, 1 often very unkind and rude to them

☐ 56. How large a part does jealousy play in his (her) life?
5 None at all, 4 not much, 3 some, 2 a considerable amount, 1 very large

☐ 57. How often does he (she) tend to blame others for his (her) own failings?
5 Never, 4 rarely, 3 sometimes, 2 often, 1 constantly

☐ 58. How fully and actively does he (she) recognize the value of social coöperation?
5 Coöperates completely in any capacity, 4 usually cooperates well, 3 willing to do his (her) share, 2 cooperates only if his (her) task is a prominent one, 1 never coöperates at all

☐ 59. How much class and race prejudice does he (she) have?
5 None at all, 4 very little, 3 some, 2 more than average, 1 a great deal

☐ 60. How actively does he (she) participate in social welfare?
5 Very actively, 4 considerably, 3 some, 2 a little, 1 not at all

☐ 61. What is his (her) attitude toward younger children?
5 Willing to spend time helping them with their games and other activities, 4 helps them to some extent, 3 helps them occasionally, 2 quite indifferent to them, 1 teases them or bullies them

Trait VII

☐ 62. How often does he (she) experience anger?
5 Never, 4 occasionally, 3 sometimes, 2 often, 1 very often

☐ 63. How intense are his (her) outbursts of temper usually?
5 Very light, 4 not very intense, 3 average, 2 rather violent, 1 very severe

☐ 64. How long do his (her) outbursts of temper last?
5 Over very quickly, 4 do not last long, 3 average, 2 last quite a while, 1 last a very long time

65. How likely is he (she) to be aroused to anger by the following types of causes?
5 Never, 4 rarely, 3 sometimes, 2 frequently, 1 almost always

☐ Frustration of his (her) wishes
☐ Being delayed in doing something
☐ Real or imagined injustice to himself (herself)
☐ Injustice to his (her) friends
☐ The principle of the thing
☐ Standing up for his (her) rights
☐ Criticism by others

☐ 66. How well does he (she) adjust to parental authority?
5 Splendid spirit of comradeship, 4 respects and obeys parental authority, 3 obeys parents' authority with considerable grumbling, 2 disobeys parental authority whenever he (she) can get away with it, 1 very disobedient and antagonistic

☐ 67. How wisely does he (she) use the freedom from authority given him by his (her) parents?
5 Very wisely and dependably, 4 usually very well, 3 about average, 2 often shows himself (herself) incapable of using his (her) freedom wisely, 1 no self-control or wisdom at all in his (her) freedom from authority

☐ 68. How responsible is he (she) in such matters as automobile driving, drinking, sex morals and the like?
5 Very responsible and stable, 4 usually responsible, 3 average, 2 fairly irresponsible, 1 totally irresponsible

☐ 69. How completely does he (she) respect property rights?
5 Completely, 4 usually, 3 more often than not, 2 fairly selfish, 1 takes whatever he (she) wants that he (she) can get

Trait VIII

☐ 70. How much natural leadership ability has he (she)?
5 A natural born leader, 4 above average, 3 some, 2 not much, 1 none at all

☐ 71. How much opportunity has he (she) had for holding such offices as president, captain, and the like?
5 Very often, 4 frequently, 3 sometimes, 2 rarely, 1 never

☐ 72. How much opportunity has he (she) had for holding such subordinate offices as secretary, treasurer, and the like?
5 Very often, 4 frequently, 3 sometimes, 2 rarely, 1 never

☐ 73. How much opportunity does he (she) have for public speaking?
5 Very often, 4 frequently, 3 sometimes, 2 rarely, 1 never

☐ 74. How much training has he (she) had in public speaking?
5 A great deal, 4 some, 3 very little, 2 none, 1 has been discouraged from public speaking

☐ 75. How much does he (she) dream of sacrificing himself (herself) for someone or something he (she) loves?
5 Constantly, 4 often, 3 sometimes, 2 rarely, 1 never does

☐ 76. How good a follower is he (she)?
5 Gives splendid support to the leader, 4 a good follower, 3 prefers to lead but will follow to some extent, 2 rarely follows, prefers to lead, 1 will not join a group he (she) cannot dominate

☐ 77. What is his (her) attitude toward money rewards for his (her) services?

5 Determined to be worth more than paid, 4 wants to be worth his (her) salary, 3 does only as much as he (she) is paid for, 2 only interested in salary, 1 the highest salary for the least work is his (her) ideal

☐ 78. Is he (she) capable of liking people and serving them even if they are sometimes unjust to him (her)?

5 Very much so, 4 usually, 3 sometimes, 2 rarely, 1 very revengeful

☐ 79. How much physical courage has he (she)?

5 Very courageous, 4 courageous, 3 average, 2 somewhat timid, 1 very fearful

☐ 80. How sensitive is he (she) to public opinion?

5 Always has the courage of his (her) convictions, 4 very little fear of public opinion, 3 some fear of what others think, 2 rather afraid to do what he (she) believes to be right in the face of public opinion, 1 very fearful of public opinion

☐ 81. How dependent is he (she) on applause and appreciation for satisfaction in his (her) work?

5 Likes praise but does not consider it of major importance, 4 does not consider it very important, 3 about equally important with the job well done, 2 considers it the important reward, 1 cannot work without it

☐ 82. How dependable is he (she) as a friend in need?

5 Always, 4 usually, 3 often, 2 sometimes, 1 never

☐ 83. How completely does he (she) carry out the dictates of his (her) conscience when it costs something in effort or sacrifice?

5 Always does, 4 usually does, 3 sometimes, 2 rarely, 1 never does

XIII

The Mature Personality

GRADUATION IS STILL BEING USED to describe the end of a college career. The basic implication is that learning goes on through the rest of life, or at least it should. One of the important characteristics of the transition from the preschool age to the elementary school age is that incidental learning ceases to predominate and intentional learning takes its place. All too often, when people's formal education is completed, there is a retrogression back to the preschool type of incidental learning. Of course, experience is a great teacher, but to rely upon it as the only source of wisdom is a sad mistake. Personality, too, can continue to develop long after maturity is reached. To say that temperament is largely formed by three and character by seven may represent, in a rather loose way, a description of what does happen in most cases, but it certainly does not describe potentialities. To be sure, there are steps which need to be taken at every age level from birth to maturity, and one of the principal emphases of this book has been that the only right time to take them is when they occur. Yet, however splendid our efforts may be and however well-developed the personality is when it enters maturity, none can doubt that there are many things yet to achieve in the attainment of the stature of personality of which Jesus dreamed.

In some ways, this is the most difficult of all the chapters of the book to write. It would be easy enough to fill the pages with platitudes and admonitions. If inspiring enough, these might even lead to good intentions on the part of the reader. But everyone is familiar with the goal, the road to which is paved with good intentions. But this chapter will be of no great value unless practical methods are given whereby men and women actually can go about developing their personalities. Principles will be laid down for accomplishing this, and a few illustrations of each will be suggested. With every effort, then, to avoid the trite, and every intention of presenting useful and practical methods of growth, let us turn to the adult personality.

Physical Development

The first way in which we begin to get old has to do with our physical development. A professional athlete is thought of as having reached old age at forty, and school girl complexions are not very common beyond this same age level. Physical prowess usually reaches its peak in the twenties. Full growth, maximum strength and coördination are probably attained in the very early twenties. But experience and good coaching serve to increase the effective physical level of accomplishment well up into the late twenties and even the early thirties. Very few, however, succeed by any means in extending this peak of efficiency beyond the thirty-five mark. After that, the decline in one's physical efficiency is faster than any possible increase that good coaching can contribute.

The senses, especially vision and hearing, grow steadily less acute and less adaptable from adolescence on. Presbyopia, which means literally "old sightedness", is a good illustration of this fact. Hold before your eyes some object with small decorations such as those usually found on the eraser end of a pencil. Focus upon these decorations and bring the pencil toward your eyes until you can no longer keep these small objects in clear focus. At just the nearest point at which you can keep them in focus, measure the distance to your eyes. Assuming that your vision is normal, your age can be estimated by a knowledge of this distance. This distance grows larger and larger, until eventually it is necessary to use bifocal lenses so that we have one adjustment for distance vision and one adjustment for reading.

Susceptibility to most diseases grows after the peak of our physical efficiency is past. Indeed, some diseases probably lie dormant in our make-up from childhood, but cannot become active until our physical fitness has decreased so far that it can no longer inhibit their power. However much care we give to our bodies, deterioration through the greater part of maturity is inevitable.

One who builds his life's work and happiness on personal physical prowess must of necessity find the greater portion of his life on the declining side. Physical fitness and vigor are worthy goals to be sought, but they are hardly the most adequate ones about which to live a happy life. The fact remains that strong character and wholesome personality are more easily acquired when one has good health and physical fitness. To acquire and maintain them as far as possible is as much a part of one's spiritual obligations as any other. Physical decline is not pleasant to experience, and every man or woman who has been blessed with good health in early life feels something sad and irrevocable at the gradually accumulating evidences of old age. One does not like to put away his football uniform for the last time, nor does an aging baseball player enjoy seeing a youngster replace him on the diamond. But these are facts of life which must be accepted, and over against them are many others of a more optimistic variety. Some of the greatest achievements in the history of civilization have been accomplished by invalids. Beethoven wrote most of his greatest symphonies after being afflicted with the disease which eventually brought about his death. If Steinmetz had depended upon physical perfection to accomplish his life's work, he would hardly have achieved so high a place in the electrical world. Even old age with all its infirmities is unable to defeat the triumphant personality. When one visits the great art galleries of Europe, he is impressed by the large number of paintings of old men and women from every walk of life. It seems highly probable that these men and women had found the secret of living a useful life, even against the handicaps of age, to make them able to challenge the interest of the artist.

Mental Development

Intelligence matures between fourteen and eighteen years of age, but wisdom may increase until ninety. The capacity for learning is never completely lost and decreases only a little in old age. Old dogs can learn new tricks, at least if they want to. Many investigations have been made to measure accurately the mental decline that comes with age. Learning ability is highest, not during early childhood, but between twenty and thirty. It is not uncommon to hear some adult say even of a pre-school child, "If my mind were only as plastic as his." But experimental evidence is quite abundant to show that learning ability is higher at fifty than it is at fifteen, and greater at seventy than at ten.[1]

Adolescents can think as rapidly but certainly not as profoundly as adults whose intellectual habits create in them the material for profundity. Those whose professions require of them continuous and systematic study through the years will bear witness that however keen and alert the minds of adolescents are, their own greater experience as adults makes them able to learn more rapidly than can their younger friends. Most college professors find young people in their classes whom they know to be more intelligent than they. They do not expect, however, that these young people will surpass them in their fields of study for many years. If parents expect to retain the respect of their children, it is necessary that they take advantage of this ability for increasing in wisdom through the years. Sunday school teachers who come before adolescent groups, obviously no better informed on the subjects with which they are dealing than those before them, are not likely to command the respect of their pupils. Growth in wisdom is possible however long one lives. Growth in wisdom is necessary if one is to maintain the respect of youth.

[1] Thorndike, E. L., et al., *Adult Learning* (Macmillan, 1928).

Special Aptitudes

Unquestionably, precisely the same thing may be said about the special aptitudes as has been said about physical and mental development. How early they reach their maturity and begin to decline is still a problem for future research. Yet great achievements in music and art and invention continue far into old age. A great deal of emphasis is placed on youth and it is common to pay special attention to those achievements which seem unusual because of youthfulness. The fact is, however, that the added wisdom of maturity brings about a majority of the great achievements in middle life and later. The wise young man is the one who picks for himself a task which requires those capacities which he will have in greater abundance as the years pass by. A little while ago I was talking to a professor who had already passed the age of fifty. His achievements have brought him recognition and honor of a very high order from the other members of his profession. And yet, as I talked to him, it was obvious that he thought of these years as simply preparatory and of the really worthwhile achievements as still to come. One of the great contributions that psychology has made to human happiness is in destroying the old notion that learning is necessarily confined to childhood and growth to youth.

Social and Emotional Maturity

Every phase of personality depends partly upon heredity and partly upon training and experience. This is true of our social and emotional life just as it is true of our physical make-up. The relative importance of these two factors, however, differs widely. Heredity is far more important in our physical make-up, but it plays the smaller rôle in our social and emotional maturity. It is possible to achieve a well-trained body by twenty-one and to equip the mind for its maximum output by thirty. But the quality of personality that grows out of the highest social and emotional maturity is probably not reached earlier than fifty. The most cultured graduate of our best finishing schools can never approach the graciousness of her mother, if the latter has continued to grow socially through the years. The most stable and wholesome college graduate must of necessity appear immature and shallow beside his father, if the latter has continued to grow in depth and power. Growth, then, is most characteristic of childhood and youth, but in its most important phases it is still possible however long one lives.

Outward display of physical bravado usually decreases with age. One does not commonly find a man of fifty driving his car at eighty miles an hour. This is not because he has less courage than his undergraduate son, but because he has greater maturity. He has forms of achievement that make fast driving seem infantile by comparison. His fears are quite as numerous as ever, but they are aroused by situations of which the youth is not even aware. If his religion has become anything more than a description of some of his Sunday habits, fear is likely to play a smaller and smaller part in the determination of his behavior.

During maturity, the last common excuse for temper tantrums appears. The excuse is bound up in the phrase "the principle of the thing". This, of course, is another form of wounded vanity and is always an indication of shallowness in character. Being offended, not because of the obvious facts, but purely because of the principle of the thing, is a common form of compensation for an inferiority complex. When we take stock of the pettiness that is found in most of our social institutions, which in one way or another relates to this simple phrase, we recognize how much is still possible in the development of human personality. Again, if religion in its true nature has become an integral part of personality, those things that dwarf human character tend to disappear.

Violent expressions of fear, anger, hate, suspicion and lust are all forms of emotional immaturity. The strong personality will rarely exhibit them. At the present stage of mental measurements, it is, of course, impossible to measure the strength of the total personality, and even more difficult to determine how great its strength could conceivably become. Efforts have been made to estimate the potentialities of personality and our present status in the attainment of them. It seems safe to assume that, on the whole, we have not attained more than fifty percent of our possible personality strength. Of course, there have been rare instances in which men have achieved remarkable quality of character. When we consider native endowments, however, there are thousands of others who have all the innate capacities of these men who have achieved greatness. What reason is there to suppose that we may not eventually find methods of achieving the same greatness for these other thousands of men and women?

Experimental Faith

One of the principles on which the theory of character development is based, as set forth in this book, is that the highest type of personality and character cannot be attained without religion. The thoughtful reader will probably have discovered many elements which contribute to that belief. A great many books on psychology have been written which describe the nature of fear and suggest useful methods by which it can be overcome. How to get rid of fear of water, fear of snakes, fear of strangers, fear of failure, fear of death, fear of insanity, and the like, constitutes the body of a great deal of psychological literature. The fact remains that more people are cured of hysteria every year at Catholic shrines than by the efforts of all the psychiatrists in history. That psychology, with its use of the scientific method, can contribute information of inestimable value in the intelligent use of personality forces no one can deny. But it is not probable that a way of eliminating fear from the human personality will be found except through a powerful type of religious faith. That does not mean that this faith should be mere superstition to be used ignorantly. Great miracles have been accomplished by faith through all the ages. Many greater ones will be accomplished by faith when science has contributed its element of understanding. It seems likely that this contribution will make our use of this great spiritual force as efficient as science has made our use of the natural forces. But the natural sciences have achieved nothing except by the use of the natural forces. They do not deny their existence, nor do they create anything new. Neither will the science of psychology achieve its miracles by denying the forces of personality which have wrought such great things in mankind through all the ages. However much rethinking needs to be done about our religious concepts, only the sheerest folly can warrant our attempt to deny the universal forces that are in them. Let us, then, seek to discover what kind of faith characterizes the mature personality and envision, if we can, the effect of it upon the individual and upon the society of which he is a part.

Vision

An objective estimate of the amount of greatness most of us actually attain falls so far short of the dreams of our childhood that it is only natural that we should attempt to make it seem larger than it is. We explain away all our shortcomings and try to convince ourselves as well as others that our achievements are of a high order. Having the mental habit of always looking for greater achievements is one of the fundamental qualities of true religion. It is a very difficult habit to acquire. We grow into set ways of thinking and acting. Our institutions appear to us as in their final form, and new things are difficult to initiate because of this inertia which so characterizes most adult minds. For example, consider a character education program in any church, of the type which we have been describing. It involves much greater expenditure of time and effort and money than we customarily expect to give. It will not be surprising if some churches hold up their hands in surrender and say that it cannot be done. A conservative estimate indicates that the minimum expenditure for a church would be ten dollars per child per year. A church with a Sunday school membership of five hundred, if asked to add five thousand dollars a year to its budget, might gasp at the enormity of the task. And yet the congregation would not expect the public schools to contribute their share to the growing personalities of their children for less than many times that figure. Jesus was not an impractical dreamer. He did not challenge men to do things which were impossible, but he did challenge them to look with care to discover what things were possible. Probably, the development of Christian character is the most important task which faces the Church today. But one thing is certain, it will not be accomplished except in those churches where the men and women have a vision for their task characterized by this trait of being poor in spirit. This is a habit of mind which ought to be acquired in early childhood and developed throughout the years approaching maturity, but it can be achieved in adulthood. The most practical method of acquiring this habit of mind is the same one which was suggested for earlier age levels. Its simplest form consists in acting on our daydreams. The trouble is that too often we allow our daydreams to end in a sigh. Let us do something about each one of them. If our daydreams and our good intentions always carry over into action, the strength and usefulness of our personalities will increase.

Love of Righteousness and Truth

One of the by-products of the scientific method is the salutary effect that it has upon the minds of those using it. The scientific attitude has been responsible for a great many remarkable discoveries in the field of natural law. But it has also been of immense value to those who have acquired it as a habit of thinking. This objective attitude is not natural to the human mind in the sense that we inherit it. It must be acquired. It is interesting to observe historically that the scientific method was not discovered for many centuries after the dawn of modern civilization. Furthermore, it is not easily taught. Thousands of students in high school and college study science in one or more forms every year, and probably not one percent of them acquire any considerable understanding of the scientific method. At times, even our greatest scientists are prone to forget their training in this method, in fields of activity outside the one in which they do their research. In order to teach a person the scientific method, so that he would apply it everywhere, it would have to be done in much the same way that traits are developed in young children. He would have to be taught to apply it in one situation after another until almost all the possible situations he might meet had been included. Because such a process is, for all practical purposes, impossible for the great majority of mankind we must look elsewhere for a method.

For this purpose we turn to a part of religion from which an enormous amount of good has come in the past, and which constitutes a natural basis for acquiring all that is valuable in the objective attitude. This phase of religion is prayer. Obviously not all prayer is either intelligent or objective. But prayer has played too prominent a part in the lives of men to imagine that its adulterations constitute its true nature. When prayer is regarded as spiritual problem-solving, in which the conscious purpose of the one praying is to know the will of God, prayer becomes objective. Prayer is comprehensible to all men and it can be taught as a habit from early childhood. If its quality is made to grow consistently with the development of the mind, it will constitute a thoroughgoing objective attitude in the mature personality. The will of God can be defined as truth and goodness, so that the aim of prayer is to determine, with respect to every problem which arises, what solution is true and good. Whether it be a scientist who is seeking truth in the laboratory, or a voter who is endeavoring to know what is right to do with his ballot, or men and women in their homes trying to solve intelligently all the problems that arise there, the true prayer attitude will make a remarkable difference in the whole aspect of human thinking. Jesus gave the Lord's Prayer as a blueprint for such spiritual thinking.

It includes in its brief sentences all of the major concepts of Christianity, and, if applied to our problems intelligently, will solve them more adequately. Here, then, is a habit of mind which needs to be learned by everybody, and which, through the medium of an existing religious power, can be learned. Those scientists who are sceptical about the value of religion in human life may well consider this fact. The objective attitude is necessary and important, but except through the medium of religion it is impossible to give it to mankind as a whole. This is another evidence in defense of the hypothesis that religion is necessary for the highest possible development of human personality.

It is obvious that this one point is not an exhaustive discussion of the development of this trait in the adult personality. It represents one important way in which the mature personality can continue to grow.

Faith in the Friendliness of the Universe

Man's greatest enemy is probably fear. It has been discussed in most of its aspects in the course of this book. The great problem is how to overcome it. Most books on the subject are difficult, complex, and unconvincing. They certainly cannot be applied to all mankind everywhere. Just as prayer is the only hope for universal thoughtfulness, so faith is the only hope for universal courage. An indomitable faith that the universe is friendly is necessary to an intelligent optimism. The problem of evil is always with us. Injustices are a constant experience. It is not easy when one looks at our world affairs today to believe that the will of a good God is working in them. Nor is the future much brighter to the thoughtful man. Taken at face value, fear is a natural response to our existing conditions. When faced with this same problem, Jesus insisted upon his faith in a Father-God. There certainly were times when he was tempted almost to the breaking point, but he never lost his faith in the Father-God.

Whatever may be the other evidences for or against the

existence of such a universal friendly spirit, the fact is that a faith in such a spirit is an indispensable element in strong personality. From the pragmatic point of view, this itself is evidence of its truthfulness. There is no better evidence for the existence of atoms. No one has ever seen an atom and the only reason physicists believe in them is because if they assume the existence of atoms, their experiments are predictable. This is precisely the same kind of evidence for belief in the friendliness of the universe.

Granting that the world will be a lot happier and more wholesome if such an indomitable faith can be held by all men, increased meaning needs to be added to this concept of fatherliness, making it more rational and more intelligent. The power of the Church is in direct proportion to the knowledge of the Bible possessed by its adult membership. It is impossible to teach what one does not know. When one listens to the average parents answer the religious questions of their children, it becomes painfully obvious how poorly informed our church people are nowadays about the faith that they profess. Superficial knowledge is easily detected by one's students, whatever their age or relationship to the teacher. Faith in the friendliness of the universe is possible only when one knows its basis and all its implications. Simply to say that one has faith in a fatherly God is not a much more adequate statement of Christian faith than to say that all that goes up must come down is an adequate description of the laws of gravitation. Here, then, is another habit of mind which can be acquired by all men of whatever intellectual endowment and which can continue to grow in depth and profundity however long one studies it. If its contribution consists in the elimination of fear from the world, it will have contributed beyond measure to human happiness.

Dominating Purpose

The desire for achievement is as intense in human nature as any other appetite. It constitutes in the normal individual the greatest source of happiness. It is quite impossible to have the strongest personality of which one is capable unless he can make some contribution which gives him a sense of achievement. One's vocation should be the center of his activity. Unfortunate indeed is the man whose vocation is only a means to an end, a form of activity which he dislikes and only does to get resources for more interesting forms of activity. Not everyone has or perhaps can have the good fortune to be in a vocation which is exactly what he would like. Sometimes fate and the lack of opportunity force a man to spend his life doing one thing when he would much rather be doing something else.

Again, two habits of mind, both an integral part of the religious personality, can contribute to the happiness and value of such people. The first one has to do with meekness, the trait we have just described. An intelligent and practical belief in divine providence is indispensable to happiness and has been shown to be of practical value. Nothing is more irritating than to hear people who have wasted their native endowments and have come into consequent misfortune say, "Thy will be done." But when one has secured the best possible training for himself and left nothing undone to live life as he hoped to live it, then if it does not turn out as he expected, he may well adopt Jesus' own statement and believe that it is the will of God. It would be unfortunate indeed if this should leave the impression that a belief in divine providence is a sort of superstitious, irrational way to delude ourselves into accepting an unhappy lot. But if one does believe in it, and if he begins seeking ways to contribute to human happiness in whatever field he finds himself, it will not be long before his job will begin to assume aspects of importance. His whole personality will grow and broaden as a result. Whatever may be its philosophical defense, it is good sense to throw one's whole heart and soul into whatever work he is doing, as if it were the most important work in the world. He will be happier, more contented and of a healthier frame of mind. Once again a religious force is found to be essential to the greatest human happiness. And again it is true that it is applicable both to the humblest and the most gifted of men.

Finally, it is important to believe in our power to achieve. Far too often do we imagine that what we think or do is so small as to be unimportant. But the fact is that the layman is usually quite as important as the leader in the success of any venture. One's task, then, need not be large but it can be important. It is to be hoped that this will not form another good rationalization for the "much ado about nothing" policy of so many people.

Every person going into a church or into any other social institution ought to dedicate an appreciable portion of his time to it. If every church member, as a part of his responsibility, would give five years of intensive service to it, the accomplishments of our churches would be infinitely greater. It is equally true of citizenship or membership in any other social institution. It is obvious that church school teaching of the type described in this book is no simple task. It requires training and long, patient endeavor. But if a large proportion of our church membership makes adequate preparation and then gives four years of service, the teaching problem of our church schools will be solved. Church school work needs to be quite as efficient, and perhaps even more so, than the teaching in our public schools. There is nothing inconsistent in paying our Sunday school teachers, and it may well be that this is the only adequate solution to the problem.

A dominating purpose in the service of mankind must be a growing and a changing one. Few people carry throughout their lives the visions that challenged their minds in youth. Furthermore, their concepts of service must grow and broaden according to the opportunities and needs of their social environment. But the mental habit of being purposive is one which is serviceable to personality throughout life.

Fatherly Love

The other great enemy of human personality is anger. From earliest childhood we are told how important it is to learn to control our tempers. Various methods have been described in this and other books of a psychological nature giving all of the effective methods available to bring about this end. Probably nowhere in the civilized world today do men seek to be angry. The control of one's temper is everywhere recognized as a virtue. But, despite this fact, the abundance of anger in the world is everywhere obvious. Suspicion and hatred, rage and violence, tyranny and revolution, strikes and wars, all are for the most part outbursts of temper. Of course, we do not call them temper tantrums; we call them expressions of righteous indignation. But righteous indignation is quite as effective in producing indigestion, constipation, and decreased capacity for abstract reasoning as a temper tantrum. Psychologically, there is no difference between the two. If human personality is to reach its maximum efficiency, anger must be pretty largely eliminated from human experience, whatever its causes. Psychological methods for reducing anger are effective only within a narrow range, unless backed up by forces of larger calibre than psychology usually employs. The alternative to righteous indignation is neither a blind tolerance nor a weak surrender type of reaction which permits injustice in the world without protest. Just as faith is the only universal and powerful answer to the problem of fear, so love in the religious sense is the only answer to the problem of anger. Let us turn, then, to the four traits of fatherly love.

Being Sensitive to the Needs of Others

Of all the Christian ideals, this one has come closest to being learned and made a part of our social structure. When we observe the tremendous power it has exerted in society, we have evidence both of the power of religion and of the fact that human nature can be changed. When we consider such movements as the Red Cross, community chest, family welfare organizations, hospitals, free schools, public libraries, educational scholarships, and relief agencies, we cannot but be amazed at what they mean, for they emphasize eloquently how sensitive men are, at least to the physical needs of other men. This has not always been true, nor is it true everywhere in the world even today. It has been a contribution of Christianity to civilization.

This trait, built as it is on the natural sympathy which is a part of human nature, is one of the easiest to develop and keep alive. It is one of the most human things about us and, at the same time, one of the most divine. We are strongest, not weakest, when we let it work its best in us. The difficulty with our present status of the Good Samaritan ideal is that up to the present time we have confined it almost entirely to man's physical welfare. The efforts that have been made to deal with his more spiritual side are by no means so far-reaching. They are not entirely lacking, to be sure. Playgrounds, boys' clubs, Y.W.C.A. and Y.M.C.A. organizations, the various missions and the Salvation Army, as well as our churches, are all contributing to that end. But we do not recognize spiritual lacks as constituting a crisis in the same way we do the physical. Many sermons have been preached about this and much has been written with the purpose of bringing it about, but thus far the effectiveness of these efforts is not large. How shall we stimulate men and women generally, including ourselves, to grow in this trait more fully than we have up to the present time?

The answer again is to be found in an attitude of mind based on the parental drive. As long as the limit of our duty to our fellow man is thought of in terms of brotherly love, we shall probably not improve upon our present status. But as soon as we think of our obligations as being like those of parents to children, our sense of social responsibility will grow tremendously. We covet for our own children a great deal more than merely food, clothing, and freedom from disease. This should become our characteristic attitude toward all mankind. It should be clear that this habit of mind is based on an instinctive drive in human nature, which is not confined to the relationship between parents and their own children, but which from earliest childhood can be stimulated in any individual toward any other in need.

Forgiveness

Enough has been said so that it should be clear to everyone that mercy and forgiveness are not negative characteristics. They refer rather to the quality of regeneration. When they are thought of as a habit of mind, it is well to define them in terms of the original description of this trait: that is, the determination to give every man his chance at happiness and success. It is obvious that this is a far different point of view from the one usually applied to mercy. Thus, for example, when a child is in need of punishment and pleads for "mercy", it may be the most unmerciful thing the parent can do to withhold the punishment. On the other hand, when parents help their children by every means available to find their ideal vocations in life, they are practicing real mercy and forgiveness, because in so doing they are accomplishing all they can to give those children their chance at happiness and success. Men who endow scholarships and fellowships or laboratories and libraries are likewise practicing this trait, for they bring about this same result. The challenge to rebuild our social structure to make it possible for every individual to find his chance at happiness and success is quite as Christian as it is American.

It is obvious to every parent that he cannot treat all his children alike. One needs punishment, another becomes sullen with it; one is inspired by encouragement, and another is made conceited and lazy. Every teacher recognizes how different are the effects of high and low grades on different students. High grades are stimulating to some, to others they are a signal for lessened activity. Low grades to some are an indication of the need for increased effort, and to others the time for complete surrender. The implication of this is, of course, that in our efforts to deal with men in wholesale we cannot deal with them alike. Furthermore, it is not just to do so.

How this ideal, which is more personal and far more parental in its nature, is to be worked out in practice is not easy to see. But the principle behind it is almost certainly a prerequisite to finding a solution to our present social chaos. It may well be that the drama-type approach which we have been emphasizing throughout this book is applicable here, giving to each according to his needs and demanding from each according to his abilities.

Magnanimity

Whenever political leaders or social reformers or propagandists endeavor to arouse in us anger, hate and suspicion, they destroy personality whether their cause is good or evil. We shall not eliminate propaganda from our civilization, however, as long as it is effective. Newspaper jingoists do not write lurid headlines unless they produce results in the readers. Those who try to incite us to race and class prejudice do so only because men and women are sensitive to the type of stimulation they set forth. Anger is not a rational reaction, nor can it be controlled simply by the will to do so. All of the things which produce in us anger in adult life are things to which we were taught to respond with anger in childhood. We cannot teach children race prejudice and national bigotry at ten and expect magnanimity to be one of their major virtues at forty.

Much has been said already about practical methods for getting rid of anger reactions. Each of us ought to make an inventory of the situations which make him angry. It is possible that many of us do not even realize that these anger reactions are habits. We think of each situation as a thing in itself. But if one keeps a diary of his righteous indignations, he will discover that they are nothing more than habits. Just as the child of three is regularly angry when his teddy bear is taken away from him, so the man of forty becomes angry because of the "principle of the thing". The only way to cure anger is to transform these same situations so that they bring out responses other than anger. As a rule, this is more easily said than done. One example is to replace the ideal of the "principle of the thing" with the objective attitude. The "principle of the thing" type of reaction is to resent the action whether good or bad. The objective attitude method is to see what the results achieved are and to judge them in terms of their objective value. This is a changed point of view which is a habit of mind that can be acquired.

Christian Courage

"Happy are ye, when men shall revile you, and persecute you, and shall say all manner of evil against you falsely, for my sake. Rejoice, and be exceeding glad: for great is your reward in heaven: for so persecuted they the prophets which were before you."[2] The principle of vicarious sacrifice has been at the base of almost all the progress of the history of civilization, but very few of us set out to seek sacrifice. Most of us endeavor to live life as painlessly as possible. Has this trait of Christian courage, then, any practical significance in the development of our own personalities?

In the first place, as we look more carefully at Jesus' statement of this trait, it is true. The leaders who have made progress have, with few exceptions, had to do so in the face of persecution, but they have usually been happy. Their happiness did not come because of the persecution, but because of the sense of achievement which made them willing to carry on even in the face of persecution. All of us want to have courage, and the effect of courage upon personality is a reciprocal process. Courage increases the power of our personality, and this, in turn, increases the level of our courage. The weakness of churches, as well as of the people in them, is that they are not challenged to achievements which seem impossible.

[2] Matthew 5:11.

Again it is to the parental urge that we must turn for the motivation on which to build this trait. Parents regularly sacrifice for their children and give almost no thought to the fact at all. Young people sometimes decide to forego their education because they feel their parents cannot afford it. What they fail to realize is that if this additional education would increase their opportunity for happiness and success, their parents are willing and anxious to make the necessary sacrifices. Consider, then, the needs in your community which you have the capacity to meet. Envision for yourself a task which does seem impossible and you will have made important strides toward the development of this trait, which is an essential one, both to strong personality and human progress.

Conclusion

That this is far from being an exhaustive discussion of adult personality will be obvious to all who read it. Probably, the element of the drama-type principle is the one which needs most to be emphasized; namely, that each find his own method of development in terms of his own abilities and needs and opportunities.

One could eulogize on the values to civilization of Christian personalities, but these eulogies would have little practical value here. That Jesus believed such personalities would have remarkable power is obvious from his teaching. His own life and those of the other great characters in history demonstrate to what heights human personality can reach. How far the rest of us can go remains for the future to reveal. It is at least a thrilling possibility that Jesus was right. It is to be hoped that many adults reading these pages will find in them some practical methods for undertaking such growth.

XIV

Social Integration

HOWEVER MANY SOCIAL TENDENCIES we inherit, getting along with people is not one of them. It is very true that we cannot live without one another; but it is equally true that it is very difficult to live with one another. The difference is that the first is impossible, the second can be achieved. Rugged individualism has its real as well as its sentimental values; but if it means the suppression of the weak by the strong, the poor by the rich, the less intelligent by the more intelligent, it is only a matter of time until an explosion occurs and social institutions are destroyed. If rugged individualism means all for one and one for all, then it is an ideal much to be coveted by our modern world. But it has to be learned. It does not come instinctively, nor can it be put on and taken off like a suit of clothes. From earliest childhood we must learn to live with one another.

In our educational institutions, secular or religious, little organized and intelligently planned effort is made to help us learn to live together. We are urged to do so, but we are not shown how. A football team gets such training for its specialized purpose. But the football coach does not get this result by exhortations about coöperation; he gets it by showing each man how he can contribute to the unified and integrated end result. Furthermore, the spirit of teamwork is not acquired overnight. Every coach knows that some very fine players are almost useless to a team because they cannot learn the methods of coöperation. Teamwork must be built up, step by step, from childhood, if it is to be achieved at all. The same principles which apply to building a winning football team are just as essential to society as a whole.

Social integration is a fine art. It is not to be had simply by wishing for it. The boy who approaches his algebra examination without having learned the subject as he went along is not helped either by repentance or wholehearted wishing. Getting along together is no more a matter of good will than is algebra. It requires the will, but quite as much the methods. With all our social strife, both individual and national, and our criticism of one another, the fact is that there are very few individuals and probably not a single nation which does not desire peace and social coöperation. The trouble is that we do not know how. It is an art that we have never learned.

Secular education has all but ignored the problem. In general, its curricular materials are based on a principle which approaches regimentation. Classes are taught as if their members were all alike. They are given the same assignments and marked by the same standards. To be sure, there are electives in the upper levels, and classes are sometimes divided on the basis of intellectual capacity. But this is division, not integration. It does have the value that it recognizes individual differences. Progressive education utilizes, to the extreme, differing individual capacities. Children are urged to progress in the various academic fields as rapidly as they are able and no more rapidly. This has the practical difficulty of requiring enormous teaching staffs, and it adds to division and social adjustment difficulties.

But these two methods of education are not the only possible alternatives. We can get a clue for a third from the drama. The drama is a unit and an integrated whole, with each character playing his own rôle according to his fitness for it. Drama-type education is built on this principle. It implies the use of curricular units in which each individual receives the training he needs in a rôle best fitted to his own personality. Such curricular units provide splendid training in social integration. In the nursery, this social integration must consist of all the members of the group working toward a common goal. They are not likely to experience or show much evidence of coöperation. The coöperation has to to be worked out by those who build the unit. In the kindergarten a much larger element of conscious coöperation can be brought about. This progresses from age to age until the highly abstract principles which underlie our most complex social institutions are learned by the growing personality.

It may occur to some that this makes standardization of curricular materials impossible. Actually that is not true. Almost as complete standardization is possible with this method as by the traditional method of regimentation. This is due to the way in which individuals differ. That is, they differ always in the same way. Whether we choose such factors as height and weight or intelligence and artistic ability, the extent and nature of individual differences are always the same from group to group; excepting, of course, such factors of selection as may enter into the formation of any particular group. This will be clear to those who have been teaching for several years. The same types of children are found in each new class. There is the shy child, the aggressive child, the cheerful child, the solitary child, and so on. When each class goes on and another takes its place, the same types are there. This rather obvious and simple illustration is only one result of a consistence in individual differences which is so regular that it can be stated by a mathematical formula. Of course, in practical experience, groups differ slightly from each other, but curricular materials based on this principle would fit them far better than the older forms which assumed that all members of the group are average. In our laboratory, we have tested many hundreds of children, and we have never yet found one child who tested average in all his tests or came anywhere near doing so. So long as we aim our education at the average child, we can be perfectly sure that it will fit none. When this method which we designate as drama-type education is used, it will very closely conform to the structure of groups as they actually are.

Preparing Curricular Units for Character Education

If the aim of religious education is the development of character, it is clear that the curriculum is a means to an end and not an end in itself. This has not always been true.

For generations, it was assumed that the aim of religious education was to learn the Bible, church doctrine, and ethical codes. It was expected that these would have beneficial results in character. Unfortunately, many researches have shown that this expectation was not well-founded. But at least the job of religious education under such a system was much easier. A teacher needed only to acquire sufficient knowledge about these materials and she was prepared to teach a Sunday school class. Even that would not be so simple today, inasmuch as parents are not nearly so coöperative in insisting on attendance or study on the part of their children. The assignment of study material from the church school is almost unheard of nowadays. Indeed, it is more the custom for children, with moral support from their parents, to insist that the church school work should not be too much like the day school, that Sunday be much more a day of rest. That is partly the fault of religious education. Its visible merits have not always been so great as to be immediately obvious to parents or children.

The use of curricular materials for the purpose of character development involves two parts. The first has to do with the preparation and teaching of the materials themselves. While the purpose of religious education is character development, this will not be accomplished unless the Biblical and other religious materials used for the purpose are learned in themselves. There are few means of teaching traits so well as through the great moral lessons of the Bible. Let us see what characteristics must pertain to our lesson material.

In the first place it must be new. Do not teach the child anything he already knows. Far too much Bible teaching is trite, over-pious, and platitudinous. No child enjoys this and few respect it. Certainly, material of this sort is not of such a quality that our children will literally hunger and thirst for it. This is not entirely the fault of the children. It is quite as much or more the fault of the material. There is so much that is little known, interesting, and valuable in the Bible without teaching the obvious and the trite.

In the second place it must be respectable. In this case I am using the term *respectable* literally. That is, it must be capable of commanding respect in our pupils. It is not easy to teach the Parable of the Good Samaritan to a crowd of early teen-age boys and make them like it. They detest sham and superficiality at a very early age. With all their pretended complaints at not wanting church school to be like day school, they recognize poor quality when they see it. In a recent graduation exercise in a church school, one girl of eleven said, "The trouble with these diplomas is you cannot help but get one." Any unearned rewards serve only to stimulate disrespect and not to interest normal children.

In the third place, it must be interesting. And the word *interesting* is not synonymous with the word *entertaining*. Among college students, "snap courses" are not always either the most interesting or respected. Interest comes from work rather than the reverse. Give material which requires effort on the part of the pupils, and the interest will be far greater than if interest is sought through the medium of a few stories and foolish activities.

Finally, lessons must be repeated until they are learned. A professor once said to his class, "One book read ten times will teach you ten times as much as ten books read one time." This discerning statement has much of value in it. In how many classes have you seen a teacher in one class hour cover all of the eight Beatitudes, with the salt of the earth and the light of the world thrown in for good measure. Repetition does not involve using the same material over and over again. It means rather approaching the material from many different points of view and considering all of its possible implications.

When our lesson materials are new, respectable, interesting, and thoroughly taught we shall have a far better chance of achieving the difficult task of character education through them. This will be more obvious when the illustrative curricular unit is presented.

But there is a second part to this task of preparing curricular units, and that is the application of the material to the central purpose at hand, character development. Let us see what the steps are in this process.

In the first place, it is important to decide just what character trait we are trying to form in the lesson at hand. Consider each of the eight traits. Which one can best be taught by this material? Study this trait by using the chart so that its nature and its developmental growth are clearly in mind. Then study with care the age level with which you are dealing, with especial emphasis on the steps which should be taken during this age level in the development of this particular trait. Then, consider just how the lesson material can be used to advantage for this purpose.

Secondly, with all the available information at hand about each child, think through what is to be accomplished with each member of the class in the development of this trait and how this is to be brought about. This needs to be done with a clear comprehension of his interests, character traits and his abilities and aptitudes. This can be done thoroughly only if one has at hand a complete and accurate personality profile of each member of the group.

Finally, take all this material prepared in this way for each member of the class and organize it into a unified and integrated curricular unit. An activity program provides the best means of bringing to a climax the ultimate goal of such a unit. Activity projects are of the greatest value, unless they are trivial and incapable of challenging either the interest or abilities of the children involved.

For a long time to come, the number of such units which have been prepared and standardized will be very small indeed. It is earnestly hoped that such materials will be prepared as rapidly as possible. In the meantime, we would very much like to know of any efforts of this sort being made. This drama-type method can be demonstrated most easily by the description of a specific curricular unit which has been prepared by its use.

An Illustrative Curricular Unit

Let us consider how the Parable of the Good Samaritan could be applied to a class of twelve-year-old boys, to develop in them attitudes contributing to the growth of the trait to which we have given the name, "Forgiveness". Because these eight traits are integral parts of a concept of the total personality, it is inevitable that others of them will be involved in any such unit.

The first step consists in an understanding of the parable itself.

Then an expert in the Law got up to test him and said,
"Master, what must I do to make sure of eternal life?"
Jesus said to him,
"What does the Law say? How does it read?"
He answered,
"'You must love the Lord your God with your whole heart, your whole soul, your whole strength, and your whole mind,' and 'your neighbor as you do yourself.'"
Jesus said to him,
"You are right. Do that, and you will live."
But he, wishing to justify his question, said,
"And who is my neighbor?"
Jesus replied,
"A man was on his way down from Jerusalem to Jericho, when he fell into the hands of robbers, and they stripped him and beat him and went off leaving him half dead. Now a priest happened to be going that way, and when he saw him, he went by on the other side of the road. And a Levite also came to the place, and when he saw him, he went by on the other side. But a Samaritan who was traveling that way came upon him, and when he saw him he pitied him, and he went up to him and dressed his wounds with oil and wine and bound them up. And he put him on his own mule and brought him to an inn and took care of him. The next day he took out a dollar and gave it to the innkeeper and said, 'Take care of him, and whatever more you spend I will refund to you on my way back.' Which of these three do you think proved himself a neighbor to the man who fell into the robbers' hands?"
He said,
"The man who took pity on him."

Jesus said to him,
"Go and do so yourself!"[1]

It will be observed that this is the Goodspeed translation of the parable. However much enthusiasm we may have for the older versions of the Bible, certainly to no age so much as to this one is it important to express ourselves succinctly. A translation of this sort contributes a great deal to making the Biblical material understandable, interesting and capable of commanding the respect of twelve-year-old boys.

A complete exposition of the parable is neither necessary nor desirable for our purposes. When we consider the age level with which we are dealing, adventure is the key word. At least on the boys' side of the picture, we may assume that no curricular material can successfully be used which does not appeal to an adventure motive; nor can any trait be taught which does not appeal to their spirit of adventure. Let us observe, then, a few of the significant points which are emphasized in the Parable of the Good Samaritan which are new, interesting, respectable, and adventurous. If we are contented with saying a few platitudinous things about the desirability of being kind to people in trouble, we are not likely to challenge either the interest or the respect of boys at this age. However, there are important lessons to be derived from the Parable of the Good Samaritan, far more profound and thrilling than this very obvious one. Furthermore, to a vast majority of our class they will be quite new; for not many adults, much less children, have ever made that deep a study of this parable. Without suggesting that this is an exhaustive exposition, these points need to be emphasized. In the first place, the Samaritan dared to do a thing which neither the leaders of the people, the priests, nor the professionally religious people, the Levites, would do. Just why the priest and the Levite passed by on the other side is not told us in the Bible story; but it is safe to as-

[1] J. M. P. Smith and Edgar J. Goodspeed, *The Bible, An American Translation* (1928). Reprinted by permission of the University of Chicago Press.

sume that at least one of the reasons was that they themselves might have fallen among thieves and been stripped of their raiment and beaten. Only the Samaritan had the courage to help this man in need, even when his own life was endangered in the process. Not many twelve-year-old boys will fail to respond to the courage of the Samaritan as they do to the courage of a man who risks his life to save someone from drowning or from a burning house. This is even more remarkable when so prominent a figure as a priest could not summon up the courage to do what the Samaritan did.

But this is not all. Most certainly the man who fell among thieves was a Jew, and the Jews had the greatest contempt for the Samaritans. Jesus' disciples were completely surprised at him when he condescended to talk to a Samaritan woman. It is not probable that the Samaritans failed to react to this insulting contempt with a deep hatred on their part. It is extremely likely that if the Samaritan had fallen among thieves the Jew would have passed by on the other side, as did the priest and the Levite. Yet here was a man who not only had the courage to brave danger, but he had the bigness of heart to help a man who was his enemy. This was even more remarkable when this enemy's own leaders did not dare to do so.

There are undoubtedly many other lessons involved in the Parable of the Good Samaritan, but these two will serve as a basis for our curricular unit with twelve-year-old boys.

Now let us consider the character trait which we are trying to develop with the use of this lesson material; namely, forgiveness. When we consider the word, forgiveness, as it is usually thought of, it does not seem very adventurous, however desirable it may be. Ask the average twelve-year-old boy to define forgiveness. How does he define it? Here are a few actual answers: "If somebody does something wrong, you try to forget it as if they had never done it"; "When they've done something wrong, you tell them that you excuse them"; "You say it's all right, let it pass this time"; "If somebody does something to you, forget about what they did"; "If somebody does something bad, you give them another chance"; "Be friends again"; "You're not angry with them any more"; "To overlook what somebody did to you." These are common definitions typical of most people of high school and even college age, and for that matter, of a vast majority of adults. If this is the full meaning of forgiveness, we may as well not try to teach it to twelve-year-old boys. In the first place, they already know it, and in the second place, it certainly is not a very thrilling thing to tell them. However, if we look at the full description of this trait, we find that it has a far deeper connotation than that suggested by these definitions.[2] Jesus defined it as mercy, and in this illustration he pointed out the necessity of showing mercy to strangers as well as to friends, and enemies as well as to those whom we love. The definition given on the chart may be a good one to use, especially at this age level, "Determined to see that every man gets his chance at happiness and success." This is sportsmanship in the best sense of that word. If we can get over to these boys this concept of forgiveness, and along with it an enthusiasm for it, we shall have achieved a real victory in the development of their characters.

Our next task is to study the profile of each boy with whom we are dealing, and see just what we can best contribute to his life by this process. Let us look at a typical class of eight boys.

Sam C—— is a rather easy-going, good-natured, very highly endowed, well-liked boy. He is a fair athlete, a good student, and the sort of boy whom everyone admires and thinks of as a very real red-blooded boy. What can we do for him? If we are thinking in terms of morbid traits to be cured, the answer is we can do nothing; for he does not have any such traits. But if we are challenged to see what can be done with such a splendid endowment, there is much. How can we make this boy a still happier, bigger, more useful personality? Like most boys of his age and type, he is not

[2] Consult the ninth column of the chart in the back of the book.

actively cruel to younger or unpopular boys. But on the other hand, he does not have much respect for them, especially for the sissies, and in general, tends to leave them alone. But these unpopular boys, who lack the native endowment and training that he has, are the very ones who need his help most. If we can give him an enthusiasm for befriending them, for helping each of them to find forms of achievement and social popularity, we shall have taught him a lesson in this larger concept of forgiveness which will truly make of him a finer personality.

Edward H—— is a somewhat conceited but extremely well-endowed boy. He is a good athlete, fine student, very high in musical and mechanical ability, is popular, comes from a reasonably wealthy family and has all of the characteristics necessary for high achievement. He has led his class in school almost from the beginning. His pride in his school work leads him to gloat over those less successful and to be highly impatient with those boys whose modest intellectual abilities make school achievement extremely difficult. If we can instill in this boy an enthusiasm for using his own talents to help, instead of despising those less fortunate, again this trait can contribute much to the splendid personality of which he is capable.

King L—— is also a popular boy. He is not nearly so athletic as the other two, but he has achieved a measure of success as a pitcher in baseball and devotes most of his energy and ambition to it. He has been successful enough to gain the respect of his fellows by means of it. His school work is reasonably good and his intellectual endowment is moderately high. A study of his special aptitudes shows him to have unusual artistic talent. For this ability he has the greatest disdain. He considers art the activity of a sissy and would not admit or use his ability in this respect for any reason at all. But because of his social capacities, which lead him to a high level of popularity, he could by the strength of his personality make art popular among the boys in his school. Furthermore, for those boys who have art ability, but not much natural endowment for social achievement, he could create a field of achievement which would give them standing among their fellows and make them much happier than they now are. If we could get over to this boy a desire for achievement of this sort, our efforts would be well repaid.

Stephen Q—— is the best athlete in the group; tall, well built, well coördinated—his whole life is dedicated to that end. His intelligence is above average and he keeps his school grades well above the median of his class. He, too, is well endowed with both musical and artistic ability. He is not quite so contemptuous of them as King, but he certainly does not regard them as anything better than a hobby and looks to athletics for "a man's job". He is quite intolerant of non-athletic boys and his derision of sissies causes a great deal of pain and unhappiness to many of his fellows who fall in that category. It should be quite obvious now what our job is for him. He can join King in making art and music popular; and if he learns to recognize them as sources of achievement of quite as great value as athletics, he will add to the happiness of a great many boys, to whom his contribution now is unhappiness.

Norman S—— is not too good an athlete. By far his best ability is music. He loves it and devotes a great deal of time to it. But he has a defense mechanism for his lack of athletic ability which takes the form of a chip on his shoulder. He is sure that he is not popular for this reason, and has a strong tendency to withdraw from other boys, with the excuse that he needs to devote more time to his music. He feels somewhat persecuted and his sense of his unpopularity makes him interpret everything that others do as being to his disadvantage. For him, we need to find a type of forgiveness which will make him able to admire the athletic ability of his fellows, even if they do not in return admire his musical ability. If he tries, he will find ways in which he can return to them good for evil, and become big enough not to let them make him angry. Probably no boy in the class has the capacity for so much growth in this trait as he has. Anyone at all acquainted with mental hygiene will rec ognize what an important contribution can be made to his personality and mental health if this change in his thinking can be brought about.

Kenneth S—— is the shortest boy in the group. He is certainly the most touchy and pugnacious. While he is not too highly endowed athletically, he devotes all of his time and energy to athletics. He is constantly plaguing and teasing his friends in and out of the school room. Poking, kicking and otherwise tormenting those about him is his major activity. There can be little doubt that the motive for this activity is a compensation for his small stature and deficiency in athletic ability. His aptitudes are not outstanding in any respect. However, in both art and music he could do well enough to get considerable pleasure. He is certainly not qualified to be a leader in any specialized activity, but if he were challenged to become an energetic follower his contribution to his social group would be one of real importance. There is hardly a single feature of his personality so little endowed but that he could play an important rôle with credit and value. Let him take pride in being able to do many things well, even if he is master of none, and learn to offer his assistance with enthusiasm to those qualified to lead in whatever activities are set forth. Few boys could acquire such all-round ability as he. If we can bring this about, we shall have laid in him the foundation for being that type of man to whom we so often refer as the very "salt of the earth". Another boy whom I have known in the past carried this so far that he worked hard at a skilled laboring job for many years to send his more brilliant brother through school, college, and graduate school. That was forgiveness of a high order. The gain on his part was probably quite as great as that of his brother.

Sheldon U—— is the best musician of the group. His endowment in this respect approaches genius level. He should, beyond all doubt, become a professional musician and with the right opportunities should reach high levels in that field. At the same time, he is the most introverted boy in the group. He tends to be indifferent to the others and he is not especially well liked. He thinks most other boys are rather silly and worthless. He expresses a deep desire to learn something of the finer things in life. In church school, he wants to study the Bible much more thoroughly than is usual among youths of his age. As a result, he is rather non-coöperative and disinterested in most of the activities of his class. He needs to learn to admire all of the various types of achievement which account for the differences among his fellows. He is the most intelligent of the group and this contributes to his intolerance. If he can learn to apply his abilities to the best interests of the group as a whole, as well as to recognize the contribution which others can make to the total achievement of the group, his adjustment will be a much happier one and his personality a great deal more wholesome.

Kim W—— is the least endowed of the group. Both intellectually and physically, his abilities are very modest. He is quite aware of this fact and has a bad inferiority complex. He is certain that there is nothing he can do of real value, and equally certain that the rest of his fellows look down on him. As a matter of fact, while his athletic ability is not outstanding, with concentrated effort he could achieve a measure of success in it, especially in a secondary rôle. His reading ability is very poor, but if that is corrected, he will manage to pass his academic requirements successfully, at least through the high school level. He is better than average in both artistic and mechanical ability. At present his social capacities are very low, and emotionally he is quite immature. Like Kenneth S——, he needs to learn to take pleasure in being a good follower. He can be quite popular if he becomes coöperative and throws all of his abilities into helping other individuals. At present he is quite sensitive to insults. If he can learn to be more tolerant of them and also to return good for evil, they will grow fewer in their number and his personality will grow apace.

Here, then, are the eight boys with whom we are dealing, and the task to be achieved with each one. We are now prepared to develop a curricular unit which will tend to bring about these changes in their personalities. It would require a great deal of space to describe in detail all of the materials which can be drawn upon to bring this about. However, it will be recalled that one of our tasks is to measure progress. We need to give these boys an examination before we start to see where we are in the beginning of our teaching, and the same examination at the end to see how much progress we have made. When the examination itself is set forth, the wealth of material on which we can draw and most of the methods for character development will be obvious. After the following examination is read, observe how completely it measures all of these things which we have talked about and, at the same time, shows the method by which we go about dealing with them.

Intermediate Age Examination
FOR
The Study of the Parable of the Good Samaritan

1. What is your idea of the kind of life each of these men lived? Write a number in each square to indicate your answer. Write the number preceding the answer you consider most correct.

   5 Full of adventure, 4 exciting, 3 interesting, 2 normal, 1 dull, 0 do not know

☐ Napoleon	☐ Mozart	☐ Sir Walter Scott
☐ Washington	☐ Wycliffe	☐ Michael Faraday
☐ Augustine	☐ Jesus	☐ Jeremiah
☐ Leonardo da Vinci	☐ Huss	☐ Raphael
	☐ Paul	☐ Beethoven
☐ John Wesley	☐ Copernicus	☐ Kagawa
☐ Wagner		

2. How interesting do you consider each of the following vocations? Write a number in each square to indicate your answer for that vocation.

   5 Highly adventurous, 4 thrilling, 3 exciting, 2 normal, 1 very dull, 0 do not know

☐ Ministry	☐ Diplomatic service	☐ Banking
☐ Professional baseball		☐ Law
	☐ Exploring	☐ Medicine
☐ Missionary service	☐ Farming	☐ Politics

☐ Music
☐ Art
☐ Electrical engineering
☐ Civil engineering
☐ Railroad engineering
☐ Shoemaking
☐ Work as janitor
☐ Work as chauffeur
☐ Aviation

3. What do you know about the story of the Good Samaritan? Was the Samaritan ☐ a Jew, ☐ a gentile, ☐ a Roman, ☐ a tax collector, ☐ a doctor? Make a check in the square preceding the answer you consider correct.

4. What was his relation to the man who fell among thieves? ☐ Stranger, ☐ friend, ☐ neighbor, ☐ enemy, ☐ acquaintance

5. What attitude would the man who fell among thieves probably have taken toward the Samaritan if they had met before this event? ☐ Greeted him cordially, ☐ barely spoken to him, ☐ struck him, ☐ ignored him, ☐ insulted him

6. Why did the priest and the Levite pass by on the other side? ☐ Afraid of being robbed, ☐ too much trouble, ☐ did not know him, ☐ in too much of a hurry, ☐ afraid it would cost too much

7. What was a Levite? ☐ A priest, ☐ a tax collector, ☐ a lawyer, ☐ a doctor, ☐ a janitor

8. Why did the Samaritan stop? ☐ Because the man lived next door to him, ☐ because he was a doctor, ☐ because the man did not like him, ☐ because the man was in trouble, ☐ because he was not afraid of thieves

9. Who then are one's neighbors? ☐ Those living close at hand, ☐ those in our own country, ☐ our enemies, ☐ those who despise us, ☐ everybody in the world

10. What does it mean to love one's neighbor? ☐ Speak to him, ☐ give him presents, ☐ help him when he is in trouble, ☐ pay his hotel bill, ☐ help him even if he would not help you

11. For which of these things would you forgive a person? Check the ones you would forgive.
    ☐ 1. If he struck you without meaning to do so.
    ☐ 2. If he stole from you something you liked very much.
    ☐ 3. If he said mean things about you or your family.
    ☐ 4. If he was a bully.
    ☐ 5. If he was a foreigner and said insulting things about America.

☐ 6. If he cheated in a game.
☐ 7. If he was a sissy.

12. What does it mean to forgive a person? Check the answer or answers you consider correct.
☐ 1. Forget what he did and let it pass.
☐ 2. Be friends with him again.
☐ 3. Do something good for him.
☐ 4. Help him become happier and better.
☐ 5. Help him even if everybody else dislikes him.
☐ 6. Help him even if he dislikes you.

13. Was what the Good Samaritan did—check which—
☐ Very brave, ☐ unusually good, ☐ generous,
☐ just decent, ☐ foolish? Why?

14. Is forgiving people—check correct answer—
☐ Highly adventurous, ☐ thrilling, ☐ decent, ☐ dull,
☐ rather "sissy"? Why?

15. Which of these men led the most forgiving lives? Check which.

☐ Napoleon	☐ Edison
☐ Washington	☐ Pasteur
☐ Luther	☐ Wesley

Why?

16. Check all of these vocations which provide lots of opportunity for forgiveness and state your reasons briefly.

Name of Vocation	Reasons
☐ Ministry	
☐ Professional baseball	
☐ Missionary service	
☐ Diplomatic service	
☐ Exploring	
☐ Farming	
☐ Banking	
☐ Law	
☐ Medicine	
☐ Politics	
☐ Music	
☐ Art	
☐ Electrical engineering	
☐ Civil engineering	
☐ Railroad engineering	
☐ Shoemaking	

- ☐ Work as janitor
- ☐ Work as chauffeur
- ☐ Aviation

Everyone who reads carefully the various questions of this examination will see clearly both the purpose and materials to be used during the class instruction for this curricular unit. With respect to Question 1, it seems probable that, in the beginning, most boys of the intermediate age will think of Napoleon and Washington as being the ones in the list whose lives were full of adventure. It will be observed that the list includes religious characters, musicians, artists, writers and scientists. It is the task of the teacher to show, first, the lives of these men with special emphasis on their high quality of adventure and, second, to bring out those phases of their lives in which they show the courage and the spirit of the Good Samaritan. This does not need to be pointed out overtly; in fact, it should not be.

Question 2 attempts to do the same thing on the vocational side that Question 1 did on the biographical side. It is not likely that, in the beginning, boys of twelve will consider most of these vocations as highly adventurous. Exploring, aviation and professional baseball probably will be, but certainly being an artist or a musician or a farmer is not likely to be. Again, it is the task of the teacher to make all of these vocations seem highly adventurous and, at the same time, capable of contributing to the happiness of men. It will be observed that every type of vocation is here, from the humblest to the most complex, and those emphasizing each of the aptitudes.

Questions 3 through 10 are designed to discover how much the class originally knew about the Parable of the Good Samaritan and will, of course, reveal how much has been learned when the project is finished. A study of the questions will show that they are designed to bring out the adventurous and the admirable qualities of the Samaritan.

Questions 11 through 16 are designed to measure attitudes as they exist in the members of the class in the beginning, and provide, at the same time, means of discovering at the end what changes have been wrought. It is not likely that, having made a study of this proposed examination, any teacher will feel the need of further guidance as to where he shall get his materials or how he shall go about teaching them. It should be obvious that an abundance of thrilling and interesting materials can be found to cover as long a period of time as seems desirable. When one considers the personality changes that we are endeavoring to make, it would be profitable to spend a whole year with this one parable.

The Activity Program

Character education, however, does not consist alone in oral instruction on the part of the teacher. It is a well-known fact that we learn best when we learn by doing. Indeed, there is evidence that would seem to indicate that we hardly learn at all unless instruction is accompanied by practice. Furthermore, in a class of this sort, a great many fine lessons can be taught by providing projects in which the various members of the class with their varying abilities can participate. If, in connection with this curricular unit on the Parable of the Good Samaritan, a general project can be planned utilizing all of the abilities of these boys to the achievement of a common end, even more important lessons can be learned in the art of social integration. The principle of drama-type education is applied in the preparation of the lesson material, but its best application can be found in the activity programs.

Unfortunately, a vast majority of the activity programs which have been utilized in our church schools in the past have been trivial and quite incapable of commanding the respect of those participating in them. As was true of the lesson material itself, this activity must be respectable; that is, capable of commanding the respect of those engaged in it. For example, a kindergarten child, when asked what he did in church school, replied with enthusiasm, "Oh, we cut and paste and draw and everything!" Whereas an intermediate boy or girl answering the same question, says with great contempt, "All we do is draw and cut out and paste." The difference is that cutting and pasting is a respectable activity for a kindergarten child, but not for an intermediate. Let us see what sort of activity program could be planned for this curricular unit with which we have been dealing.

A pageant might well be the end result of such a unit. Perhaps *pageant* is not the correct name for it; it can perhaps be described as a demonstration showing the significance of the Parable of the Good Samaritan in all its fullness in the world today. This final pageant might well contain a play, or at least an oral presentation of the findings. It should contain pictures that will bring out modern conditions involving this parable. It might well include biographical sketches of some of the men they have studied, or models showing the adventurous sides of some of the vocations. It ought to be accompanied by music chosen or composed to carry with it the emotional tone desired. Perhaps if we look again at the individual boys to see what each can contribute, the reader can see how their contributions can be integrated into a single unit. As a matter of fact, units of this sort should be extremely flexible, following partly the interests and enthusiasms of the boys themselves. Sam C—— is the best writer in the group. He should be put in charge of manuscript preparation for whatever purpose it may be needed. He might well be helped by Norman S—— and Sheldon U——, who also test high in language ability. Edward H—— is one of the outstanding musicians. Assisted by the same two boys, Norman S—— and Sheldon U——, he might be made responsible for the musical side of this pageant, the study of the biographies of great musicians, and the choice of musical materials for the pageant. It is not impossible that one or more of these boys could actually compose some materials to be used. Stephen Q—— is the outstanding artist of the group. Assisted by King L—— and Kim W——, it would be his task to select pictures and to prepare such scenery as might be needed for the presentation. Kim W—— is the most mechanically minded and, with the assistance of Edward H—— and Stephen Q——, would have charge of building, making models and the study of the biography of the scientists and builders involved. These last two groups, the artistic and the mechanical, might well coöperate in camera work, making pictures in the slum districts and the danger spots of our cities. It is possible that they might secure the help of newspaper photographers in getting some real and rather adventurous experiences in this field. Such photographs enlarged and with proper titles would make a real contribution to the pageant. The mechanics might also build models to demonstrate some of the things which they have discovered. King L—— has the most outstanding social ability. It might well be his job to make a study of our social institutions. Assisted by Kenneth S——, they might make a fairly complete survey of the Community Chest activities in their own city, a study of the hospitals and all of the service institutions. The results of their findings could be turned over to some of the other committees for presentation. Norman S—— has the most brilliant imagination. Helped by Edward H—— and Sheldon U——, and coöperating with the writing committee headed by Sam C——, they might well provide the plot for the pageant. Sheldon U—— is the most brilliant. Assisted by Sam C—— and Edward H——, it would be his job to do the more difficult types of research, seeking for materials in the libraries, especially materials difficult to find. In the course of the study, they might well present some debates to bring out various aspects of the problems being studied. Kenneth S—— might be made chairman of what could be called the athletic committee, not so much with the job of doing things athletic as making a study of the place of athletics in our social life. Assisted by Kim W—— and Stephen Q——, they might study our playgrounds, our school gymnasiums, and our school athletic programs with the purpose of discovering how they contribute to human happiness.

A survey of this material will show that each of the eight boys has a responsible and important and challenging job to accomplish. Furthermore, each of the eight is on at least one other committee, five of them are on three of the committees, and one on four. Such an organization requires a great deal of coöperation and should bring out both the necessity of coöperation and the whole spirit of the drama-type approach. Organizing all this into one huge project, a pageant of music, art, costumes, pictures and models, biographical sketches and the like, could be made an enterprise about which any twelve-year-old boy might be keenly enthusiastic. The development of the whole, of course, ought to be very flexible, guided intelligently by the teacher, but being done as much by the boys themselves as is possible at their age level.

Conclusion

Here, then, is the method of the drama-type approach. Through it we can hope to achieve a high measure of social integration. The illustration which has been given is based on only one class group. It is to be hoped that this material will be found useful for any other group of boys of the same age, as there will be boys in almost any other groups like the ones we have described. The problem of types in psychology is a difficult one, and most psychologists are inclined to believe that types as such do not exist, maintaining that, in whatever variable we choose there is a continuous gradation from one extreme to the other with no dividing lines at any point. The fact remains that, in actual practice, we do recognize types. Whatever may be the theoretical status of the problem, then, we may assume the existence of types at almost every age level and look forward to the construction of standardized, drama-type curricular units based on these types.

XV

Happy Are They

THE RATHER OVERWHELMING character development program set forth in this book is only a logical outgrowth of the teachings of Jesus, on the one hand, and the scientific method, on the other. Before a recent series of lectures in which this material was to be presented,[1] one of the leaders asked this question: "Is this vision of religious education going to help us in our practical church school problems and as parents in dealing with our children, or is it going to discourage us because of its impossibilities?" Letters often come to us of which the burden is, "This is all very well for the large financially strong church, aided by the well-equipped laboratory, but what about the small church and the poor church without these resources?" The reader, now having examined this program from beginning to end, can formulate his own answer to these questions. There are no impossibilities involved. It is true, however, as was pointed out in the very beginning, that it is not a simple approach, and it is the conviction of the author that character education will never be simple. Character is complex. Human personality is mystifying in its many intricacies. Over-simplified systems are doomed to failure before they begin.

It may be well to summarize the prerequisites for success in such an endeavor as this. In the first place, it requires trained teachers. They must be trained in method and background. They must be well-prepared for the specific problems that are constantly confronting them, and they must be thoroughly equipped in the knowledge of and favor with youth. Whether it is necessary to pay our church school

[1] Most of the materials of this book have been presented in lecture series in the Trinity Methodist Church of Schenectady, New York, and the Westminster Presbyterian Church of Albany, New York.

teachers in order to get this quality is an open question. It is the conviction of the author that it is. On the other hand, there are many hundreds of splendid volunteer teachers whose efficiency is measured not only in terms of their devotion and sacrifice, but in the more practical terms of their capacity and training. There can be little doubt in anyone's mind that it requires no less ability to teach in character education than in secular education. We cannot expect to require less of our church school teachers than we do of our public school teachers. Our young people going to college should include in their college courses a training in psychology, education, and religion. Undoubtedly, their value to the church when they return will be inestimable. Whatever the methods employed, there can be no question but that success in character education can be hoped for only if this requirement of trained teachers is met.

The second prerequisite is parental coöperation. Character education has been and always must be achieved fundamentally in the home. The Hartshorne and May researches furnished abundant evidence of how much more influential the home is in the formation of character than any other institution. The modern tendency of parents to delegate their responsibilities to other agencies will never be successful. Parents, too, must be well-trained. To be sure, many of the child-training books of the past have been so filled with negative admonitions that they have done more harm than good. Psychology is coming to recognize this sin and the more positive tone of the newer books is noticeable. Parents, then, must expect to spend a considerable amount of time, not only studying their children, but in gaining for themselves the useful information that comes out of our psychological laboratories and research projects. Common sense may be sufficient to make us come in out of the rain, but it certainly has its limitations in character training. In our own project we expect of parents that they coöperate with the testing program, both in bringing their children to the laboratory and in coming themselves for the subsequent interview. This has been the most successful part of our program so far and the most fruitful. Their enthusiasm for it has been largely responsible for the continued success of the program in the church. We expect of parents that they make it possible for their children to maintain as consistent attendance at the sessions of the church school as in the day school. We expect them to read at least two books a year, one in religion and one in the field of psychology.[2] Various lectures and discussion groups are held in the course of the year primarily for the benefit of the parents. Regular attendance at all of these is expected of them. Finally, the parents are kept informed of the various steps that are being made in the church school for character development and how they may coöperate in the conduct of this effort. More and more they are given specific duties to perform which make our character development program a seven-day-a-week process.

In addition to these, many dependable workers are essential to carrying out the administrative complexities of such a project. With all that careful organization and planning can do, a great many detail jobs still remain; they are as necessary to the success of the work as the more conspicuous tasks. These positions require perseverance and tact as well as ability and training. Secretarial work, statistical work, as well as administrative and committee jobs, demand staff members whose devotion to them insures their being well done.

Finally, generous financial backing is a necessary part of the total task. The tuition for most of our first class colleges at present is in the neighborhood of four hundred dollars a year. It does not occur to most parents that they cannot afford this. They believe that it has values for their children, and when this is true they are willing to make whatever sacrifices are necessary to gain those values. When character education produces definite results, parents will

[2] The two which we recommended during the past year were Fosdick, H. E., *A Guide to Understanding the Bible* (Harper and Brothers, 1938), and Strang, R. M., *An Introduction to Child Study,* Revised Edition (The Macmillan Company, 1938).

pay whatever it costs. The college boy is in class approximately fifteen hours per week. A character development program of the sort described in this book presupposes at least a two hour a week church school. A proportionate reasonable tuition would, therefore, be around fifty dollars per year per child. Fortunately, it need not cost that much, or even half that much. But this fact alone shows that the costs involved are not exorbitant when measured in terms of other educational fees. Even financially, then, such a program as this is not impossible. It is easily within the reach of every church with enough vision to attempt it.

Undoubtedly there are many other prerequisites that ought to be mentioned, but these are the most important and, if they are available, the others can easily be found. To be sure, character education programs of this sort have not been tried in the past, but no one in our modern world can imagine that this means that they are impossible to accomplish in the future.

At the end of this chapter will be found a short bibliography of some of the more important books on psychology which will be of value to parents and teachers in this work. The church school library should certainly include all of these. It is not an exhaustive list, nor does it pretend even to be the best that could be prepared. It pretends only to be a good one.

Conclusion

The inevitable question which always arises when new ideas in child guidance are presented is this, "How did our parents and grandparents ever get along without all these new-fangled ideas?" The emotional implication of the question is that our parents and grandparents did remarkable jobs as evidenced by our own personalities. Of course, the true answer is that they did not. We have not succeeded in achieving even fifty percent of the potential power of human personality. Personalities of the calibre of our greatest men and women ought to be the rule, not the exception, in our society. We are only beginning the real task of character development and the prospects for the future are bright.

A prominent theologian in a recent article says that the time has come to discard religious education because it has been found to be of no value. His alternative is a return to theological discussion. The work of theology is of inestimable value in man's effort to understand the nature and will of God, but to suppose that it can do the task of character development is as absurd as to suppose that we can buy it at the grocery store. The fact is that religious education did not have the real possibilities of success until scientific psychology had made available the principles of child development and the methods of mental measurement. What its achievements will be in the next generation can only be guessed, but certainly we need not be surprised if religion and science together produce new miracles, when in the past each of them wrought them separately.

"Can human nature be changed?" Men and women look and act about as they did three or four thousand years ago. The proportion of great men does not seem to be much larger now than it was in ancient Athens. Nineteen hundred years of Christian history have certainly fallen far short of realizing the vision Jesus had for human personality. What reason have we to suppose that we can expect such miracles now? However, five thousand years of history saw far less change in our use of natural law than the last hundred. When the scientific method began to be applied to natural phenomena, our ability to do great things with them increased enormously. Is human nature any less obedient to the laws of God than nature itself? Is it just a dream that we may make as great changes in the stature of personality in the next fifty years as we have in the natural sciences during the last? It is the hypothesis of this book that we shall do just that. If the book provides not simply some of the inspiration but some of the practical methods by which it can be achieved, it will have served its purpose.

BIBLIOGRAPHY

Baldwin, B. T., Psychology of the Preschool Child. D. Appleton-Century Co., Inc., New York, 1925.

Blatz, W. E., and Bott, H., Parents and The Preschool Child. William Morrow and Co., Inc., New York, 1929.

Brooks, Fowler D., Child Psychology. Houghton Mifflin Co., Boston, 1937.

Cole, Luella, Psychology of Adolescence. Farrar and Rinehart, Inc., New York, 1936.

Faegre, M. L., and Anderson, J. E., Child Care and Training, Fourth Edition. University of Minnesota Press, 1937.

Fenton, Jessie C., A Practical Psychology of Babyhood. Houghton Mifflin Co., Boston, 1925.

Goodenough, F. L., Developmental Psychology. D. Appleton-Century Co., Inc., New York, 1934.

Goodenough, F. L., and Anderson, J. E., Your Child Year by Year. Parents' Magazine, New York, 1937.

Inskeep, A. L., Child Adjustment in Relation to Growth and Development. D. Appleton-Century Co., Inc., New York, 1930.

Kirkpatrick, E. A., Mental Hygiene for Effective Living. D. Appleton-Century Co., Inc., New York, 1934.

Link, H. C., The Rediscovery of Man. The Macmillan Company, New York, 1938.

Morgan, J. J. B., Child Psychology. Farrar and Rinehart, Inc., New York, 1934.

Patri, Angelo, The Questioning Child. D. Appleton-Century Co., Inc., New York, 1931.

Richmond, W. V., Personality: Its Development and Hygiene. Farrar and Rinehart, Inc., New York, 1937.

Ruch, F. L., Psychology and Life. Scott, Foresman and Co., New York, 1937.

Shaffer, Laurance E., THE PSYCHOLOGY OF ADJUSTMENT. Houghton Mifflin Co., Boston, 1936.

Stoddard, G. D., and Wellman, B. L., CHILD PSYCHOLOGY. The Macmillan Company, New York, 1934.

Strang, R. M., AN INTRODUCTION TO CHILD STUDY, Revised Edition. The Macmillan Company, New York, 1938.

Terman, L. M., and Lima, M., CHILDREN'S READING: A GUIDE FOR PARENTS AND TEACHERS. D. Appleton and Co., New York, 1926.

Thom, D. A., EVERYDAY PROBLEMS OF THE EVERYDAY CHILD. D. Appleton and Co., New York, 1926.

Thom, D. A., NORMAL YOUTH AND ITS EVERYDAY PROBLEMS. D. Appleton-Century Co., Inc., New York, 1932.

Wagoner, L. C., THE DEVELOPMENT OF LEARNING IN YOUNG CHILDREN. McGraw-Hill Book Co., Inc., New York, 1933.

INDEX